GODS ON EARTH

A VIVID RETELLING OF MAHABHARATA

by Krishna Dharma

ISBN: 9798703805459

This book was previously published as Mahabharata: The Condensed Version of the World's Greatest Epic.

CONTENTS

Contents

INTRODUCTION

Mahabharata, a part of the ancient Vedas of India, is a story quite unlike any other. There are few books which have survived for as long as this five thousand year old epic. Its enduring popularity is itself testimony to the profound wisdom held within its pages. It includes the Bhagavad-gita—a masterpiece of spiritual knowledge revered by millions worldwide—and is the narration of the historical events which surrounded the speaking of that illuminating text.

Mahabharata therefore deals with the activities of Krishna, who spoke the Bhagavad-gita and is described by the Vedas as the supreme person or God. This gives it a unique quality. Although from the external point of view it is an exciting tale of conflict and intrigue among kings, demons, gods and sages, there is a deeper mysticism which pervades the work. It is intended to bring us closer to an understanding of the divine, and awaken a transcendental pleasure surpassing all other happiness. It can be read many times without becoming stale. Indeed, one will feel increasingly uplifted by connecting with its profound spiritual messages.

As well as its mystical dimension and its gripping narrative, Mahabharata also presents a fascinating insight into life in the ancient world, where virtue and self knowledge were paramount. It has been called a 'cultural encyclopedia of India', but its scope is even broader than that, embracing as it does universal truths common to all men. The range of subjects covered in Mahabharata is too numerous to mention, but in one famous verse of the original it is said that whatever is not found in Mahabharata will be impossible to find anywhere else. It is by far the most popular book in India and has been told and retold by bards and poets throughout the ages in so many forms.

Anyway, I shall leave it to you to discover for yourself the wonderful treasure house that is the Mahabharata. This is only an abridged version, the original text is some 100,000 verses of Sanskrit poetry, but

I hope it will stimulate your interest to go on to read more complete texts. I should mention here that I have also written a longer dramatisation which runs to around nine hundred pages. Before leaving you though, I must give all credit to Srila Vyasadeva, the immortal sage and author of this work, still residing somewhere in the high Himalayas. May he bless us all that we can penetrate the deepest meaning of Mahabharata.

Krishna Dharma

January 2021

Acknowledgments

Thanks are due to my daughters Radhika and Janaki Anderson for designing the cover, with the assistance of Gaura-lila Gladwell, who provided the artwork. Thanks also to Janaki for doing the layout. Finally, my deepest thanks are due to my spiritual teacher Srila Prabhupada, without whose guidance I would never have been able to comprehend Mahabharata's profound spiritual themes. I therefore dedicate this book to him.

CHAPTER ONE

FIVE GODLY BOYS

Spring had arrived in the mountains. The atmosphere was delightfully fresh. Pandu strolled through a field of fragrant flowers, admiring the celestial scenery. Cuckoos sang in the nearby *champaka* trees, and black bees hummed as they swarmed around the bright yellow blossoms. Pandu's young wife Madri walked ahead of him, her long silk robe flowing in the gentle breeze. She sang softly to herself as she stooped to gather flowers. As Pandu approached, she turned and smiled at him. The warm sun shone from behind her. Pandu could see the silhouette of her graceful form through her billowing dress. She was indeed beautiful. The bright sunlight shone through her golden hair, framing her perfect features. Pandu's heart stirred. Seven years had passed since he last embraced her. An irresistible urge overpowered him. Dropping the sack of wild vegetables he had gathered, he moved toward his wife.

Madri at once understood his feelings. Seeing him seized by desire, the princess was fearful. "My lord, remember the sage's words!" She spoke urgently, but Pandu seemed not to hear. She put up her hands to stop him, shaking her head. "king! Stop! O great hero control your mind. A deadly danger now threatens you."

Pandu was oblivious to her warnings. Her attempts to make him desist only stoked his desire. Taking hold of her outsretched arms he pulled them around his body and took her in a firm embrace. Madri struggled desperately, trying to free herself. Entirely overcome by passion, Pandu laughed. He dropped to the soft grass, dragging Madri down with him. With the queen clasped in his powerful arms he rolled over. Pinning her to the ground he sought her lips with his own.

Suddenly Pandu began to writhe. "My chest! I cannot breathe!"

He gasped and his limbs froze. As his horrifed wife looked on he fell from her body. With a stifled cry he breathed a final choking breath and his lifeless form went limp.

Madri cried out and scrambled toward him, great sobs wracking her frame. It was too late. The *rishi's* curse had come to pass. Pandu was gone. The queen fell on his body and wept uncontrollably. She lamented piteously, addressing her dead husband. "O unconquerable one, how were you conquered by lust? Alas, I blame myself. Why did I go alone with you to these woods? How was I so foolish? My lord, my protector, my love! How can I live without you? I shall surely follow the path you have taken."

Her cries rose up and were carried on the breeze. They echoed through the woods. Not far away, in Pandu's forest ashram, his other wife Kunti was preparing a fire to cook their evening meal. Madri's wails reached her and she stood still, trying to ascertain where they were coming from. Madri's two young sons, Nakula and Sahadeva, were with her and they too heard the cries. "What is it, mother Kunti?" they asked. "Who is that?"

"I am not sure, but I will go and see. Where are your brothers?"

"They are just coming from the river," Nakula replied.

"Then you two boys should stay here and wait for them. Tell them to follow me when they get here."

Kunti made her way into the woods, quickly going toward the direction of the cries. It sounded like Madri. What could have happened? Was it Kindama's curse? Kunti's heart began to sink.

As she came out of the woods into the field her fears were confirmed. Her face fell in horror as she saw the fallen Pandu, his head cradled in Madri's lap. For some moments—seconds that felt like hours—she stood staring, her mouth agape. Then, her legs feeling leaden, she ran toward them. She slumped to the ground by Pandu's side. When she realised he was dead Kunti wailed in uncontrolled sorrow. She looked with streaming eyes at the anguished Madri. "O sister! What happened?"

Kunti's voice was accusatory. How had Madri allowed the king to become allured? She knew well about the curse. "Dear Madri, I was ever careful in our lord's presence. I would hardly even smile at him. He was always grave and self-controlled, remembering Kindama's words. How did he lose his composure in your presence?"

Kunti's words came between sobs. Her head fell on Pandu's chest. Where had he gone? How could she live without him?

Madri buried her face in her hands, weeping silently. It was already unbearable that she had caused Pandu's death. Kunti's words only exacerbated her pain. She took a deep breath and tried to compose herself. "Noble Kunti, dear sister, with tears in my eyes I tried to stop the king, but I was helpless."

Seeing Madri's piteous expression, Kunti felt compassion. She spoke more softly. "You are surely more fortunate than me, for you saw our lord's face light up with joy as he approached you."

Kunti winced at this deeply painful thought. She fought back her envy as Madri shook her head and replied, "I am utterly undone. It seemed the king was intent on making the *rishi's* curse come true. There was nothing I could do."

Kunti felt her anger subside. Madri was surely being truthful. Somehow this tragedy must be the Lord's will. What now was her duty? She looked at the face of her husband, serene in death. The virtuous monarch had certainly gone to the higher worlds. Could she follow and serve him there? Doubtlessly Madri would also wish for that. Yet someone would have to look after the boys. Kunti took hold of Madri's hand. "Sister, I am the senior wife. It is therefore my right to go with our lord to the region of the dead. Do not prevent me. Rise up and rear our children. I shall enter the fire with our husband."

Madri looked up pleadingly. "See how I am still clasping our lord and have not allowed him to go. Let me follow him. He came to me with the desire for intercourse. That desire is not yet satiated. Should I not therefore go to Yamaraja's kingdom to gratify him?"

Madri saw that Kunti had stiffened slightly. It seemed her natural womanly jealousy was being aroused. Madri reached out to hold Kunti's hand and said, "Revered sister, how could I raise the children as well as you? Unlike you, I will not be able to see them all with an equal eye. Please stay and serve the king by looking after his sons. Grant me leave to enter the fire and go where he has gone."

Kunti looked at Madri, fallen again onto Pandu's body. It would be hard for her to carry on living with the memory of this moment. Guilt would consume her. And she was right about the boys. One of Pandu's wives had to remain in order to take care of his sons, and Kunti, with the greater number of sons herself, knew that it was more her duty than Madri's. It would be better to let Madri go.

Kunti rose to her feet and said softly, "Let it be as you wish, dear sister."

Getting up slowly, she walked back toward her cottage. The boys would have to be told.

* * *

Not long after Kunti had left the cottage, her three sons returned. They saw the twins, Nakula and Sahadeva, sitting alone. The eldest of the brothers, Yudhisthira, asked them, "Where is mother Kunti? We heard cries. Was it her?"

The twins shook their heads. Nakula replied, "No. Mother Kunti also heard the cries and has gone into the woods. She said you should follow her."

Yudhisthira looked at his two brothers, Bhima and Arjuna. "Come on! Let's go quickly. Mother may need us."

He raced off into the woods, followed by all four of his brothers. The cries had stopped and he was not sure which way to go, but he chose the path leading to the fields. That was the way father usually went to collect vegetables for their meals. Yudhisthira had a feeling that the cries were something to do with him. As he ran, he saw his mother ahead, stumbling toward them, her head in her hands. Obviously, something terrible had happened.

As Kunti approached the brothers they could see the tearstreaks on her face. Seeing her sons, she tried to smile. With the five boys gathered round her, she said, "Dear sons, our only shelter now is the Lord. Father is no more. He has gone to the abode of your ancestors."

The boys looked at her in shock. None of them could speak. Kunti wept softly. Finally, Yudhisthira said, "How did it happen? Surely no one could have killed Father. Was it an accident?"

Yudhisthira knew his father to be a powerful warrior. He also knew that they were living in a place where practically everyone was an ascetic, devoted to meditation and the practice of religion. Who could have harmed his father?

Struggling to contain her grief, Kunti replied, "Your father has fallen victim to a rishi's curse. He is lying on the other side of this wood. Madri is with him."

The boys ran past their mother and burst out of the woods. Seeing their father lying dead and Madri next to him they cried out. They dropped to the ground, wailing and rolling about in grief. Madri, feeling more peaceful knowing that she would soon follow her husband, spoke gently to the twins, who had run to her side. "My dear sons, the ways of the Lord are mysterious. You must now serve your mother Kunti with love. She will take care of you. I must follow your father into the next world."

The twins stared at their mother. They did not know what to say. This was only their eighth summer and they could hardly comprehend what was happening. The situation was completely overwhelming. They ran to Kunti and she held them to her bosom, her tears falling on their heads. Their three brothers continued to vent their grief with loud wails. Hearing the cries, a number of rishis came into the field. Seeing the dead king they went over to him and immediately began performing his last rites. As they rythmically chanted the holy mantras the boys felt soothed and they stood up with folded palms. The distraught Kunti stood by their side, watching as the rishis led Madri away from Pandu. They lifted his body onto a bier and began carrying it out of the woods toward the river, followed by the weeping Madri.

Supported by her two eldest sons, Kunti walked behind Madri. Some of the rishis led the younger boys back to the ashram as Pandu's body was taken to the riverbank. It was garlanded with forest flowers and daubed with the sacred Ganges clay. A large pyre was built by the water's edge and the body was placed upon it. With the rishis constantly reciting Vedic mantras, Yudhisthira set fire to the sandalwood pyre. As the flames rose up Madri suddenly threw herself onto the body, crying out, "My lord!"

Kunti cried terribly. Her sons stood by with tears streaming down their faces. As the flames subsided the rishis spoke wisdom from the

Vedas, describing the eternality of the soul. Pacified by the sages' words, Kunti and the boys slowly returned to their ashram. It seemed empty and lonely. They looked at each other in silence, realising that they could not stay there any longer without Pandu.

As they sat in sorrow a leader of the rishis came into the cottage and spoke to Kunti. "Now that your protector has gone you must return to your family in Hastinapura. In due time Yudhisthira must assume the throne, assisted by his mighty brothers."

The boys knew their father had been the king in Hastinapura, the great capital of the world and seat of the powerful Kuru dynasty. He had told them he came to the forest as a result of a rishi's curse, but they did not know the full details. It must have been a truly terrible imprecation. What had he done to deserve it? They looked querulously at their mother.

Devastated by the sudden loss of her husband and co-wife, Kunti found it difficult to speak. "I will try to explain as we travel to the city," she said, wiping her face with the end of her sari. "Your father and I had been meaning to tell you."

The sage said they should leave at once. He and the other rishis would accompany them to the city. Kunti agreed and she began gathering her few belongings together, telling the boys to do the same. Within a short time, they were ready to go.

A long line of rishis set out for Hastinapura, with Kunti and her sons in their midst. They were accompanied by many Siddhas and Charanas, celestial beings who also dwelt on the mountain where they lived.

As they walked Kunti tried to gather her senses. She had to tell her sons about the curse—and especially about their births. Bringing the boys around her, she said, "Once when your father was hunting in the forest, he accidently slew a rishi called Kindama who had assumed the form of a deer. To free him from the reaction of that sin the rishi uttered a curse. Your father had shot Kindama when he was just about to beget a child on his wife. The sage therefore told the king that if he ever tried to beget children he would immediately die. Your father then decided to live a life of asceticism."

Kunti explained that Pandu, unable to beget children, had sought some other way of continuing his line. "I told him of a boon I had received from another rishi when I was a girl. That sage, named

Durvasa, had been pleased by my service. He blessed me that I would be able to summon any god I desired. Thus, your father had me call various great deities. Firstly, Dharma, the god of religion."

She looked across at her eldest son, who was listening intently. "Dear Yudhisthira, that powerful god is your seminal father."

Kunti said that Bhima was the son of Vayu, god of the winds. Arjuna was the son of Indra, the king of the gods, and the twins were born of the twin Ashvini gods, the celestial physicians. "In this way were you three eldest boys born of myself, and the twins of Madri, who had begged me that she be allowed to use the mantra. A heavenly voice was heard at each of your births, prophesying great things for all of you. Yudhisthira will be the lord of the earth, Bhima the most powerful man, Arjuna the greatest among archers, and the twins possessed of celestial beauty and energy."

The boys looked at each other. They had never guessed the truth. Sons of the gods! Their father had often told them a great destiny awaited them, that one day they would return to Hastinapura to become rulers. But he had never explained how they had been born.

Kunti smiled a little through her grief. "Your ancestors have long ruled the earth, keeping it firmly on the path of religion. That duty will surely fall to you boys in due course."

In what seemed only a short while, they saw the city ahead of them. They were walking on a broad, paved road that had great archways over it, carved with numerous representations of the gods. Cultivated fields lay on either side of the road, filled with neat rows of vegetables and patches of golden wheat. Everywhere farmers worked the land, tilling the ground with teams of black oxen. They looked in wonder at the procession of celestials and rishis, saluting them as they walked by, and the sages offered them blessings.

By late afternoon the procession reached the city gates, which were set in the huge granite wall that surrounded the entire city. Messengers went quickly to inform the king, and soon a large crowd of citizens came out of the city. They were astonished to see the many rishis and other celestial beings, which resembled an assembly of the gods.

When the greetings were complete, a leading rishi told the king what had happened. "Steadily adhering to the path of virtue, Pandu has ascended to heaven along with his chaste wife Madri. Here are his five sons, born of the gods."

The rishi named each of the deities who had fathered the five boys. After instructing the king to take care of their welfare and studies, he rejoined the other rishis. Then, before the eyes of the amazed citizens, all the sages and celestials disappeared from the spot.

One of the leading Kurus came up to Kunti and greeted her with folded palms. The boys looked at him in awe. He seemed like a god. Tall and powerfully built, he was dressed in white robes bordered in gold, and had long white hair and a white beard. He smiled at the five boys and Kunti introduced him. "This is your grandfather Bhishma." The boys bowed low in respect. Bhishma then led Kunti and her sons into the city, arranging their accomodation in the royal palace.

The last rites ceremony was performed for Pandu and Madri. All the leading Kurus along with thousands of citizens entered the Ganges and made offerings for the departed souls. A twelve day period of mourning then followed for the whole city, concluding with a great feast. Large amounts of wealth were given in charity to the brahmins and everyone in the city was fed sumptuously by the king. Life then returned to normal and Pandu's sons took their place in the royal family.

CHAPTER TWO

SEEDS OF CONFLICT

When they were settled in Hastinapura, Kunti told her sons the Kurus' history. She explained how Pandu, after he was cursed, had handed over the rule of the kingdom to his elder brother Dhritarastra, who had been unable to assume the throne before Pandu as he was born blind. When Pandu left it fell to Dhritarastra to take his place. He was assisted by Bhishma, and by another brother of Pandu named Vidura, the prime minister. Vidura had been born of a maidservant and could not therefore become the king himself.

The boys were curious to know why Bhishma, as the seniormost Kuru, was not the ruler. Kunti told them his history.

"Long ago Hastinapura was ruled by king Shantanu, who fell in love with the Goddess Ganga when he saw her one day by the riverside. They married, and their son, whom she raised and educated among the gods, was named Bhishma."

Kunti described how Shantanu had later become infatuated by another maiden, this time the daughter of a fisherman who set a condition for her marriage to Shantanu. The fisherman insisted that his daughter's son be next in line for the throne. Shantanu could not agree as he had already installed the highly qualified Bhishma as prince regent. He tried to forget the girl, but when Bhishma learned of his father's disappointment he approached the fisherman. He promised that he would never become king, but still the man would not agree, fearful that Bhishma's sons would demand the throne. Bhishma realised there was only one way to settle the matter. "I will never marry," he declared. The fisherman then relented and gave his daughter.

Kunti concluded her story, "Thus Shantanu married the fisherman's daughter, Satyavati. Her son was your grandfather, who unfortunately died before having any children. At that time the Kurus became anxious their dynasty would end. They asked the great sage Vyasadeva if he could help. In accord with scripture, Vyasadeva then fathered three sons on your grandfather's two wives; Dhritarastra, Vidura and your father."

As the months passed, Pandu's sons, who were known as the Pandavas, became increasingly dear to the Kuru elders. The five brothers exhibited every good quality. Humble and submissive to their elders, they were pious and ever truthful. As they grew to maturity, the Kuru elders saw that they would be worthy successors to the throne. The Kurus were delighted with the godly boys.

However, not everyone in the city liked the Pandavas. Thanks to a blessing from Vyasadeva, Dhritarastra had one hundred sons. These princes, known as the Kauravas, seethed with envy on seeing the popularity of Pandu's sons. The eldest of them, Duryodhana, could hardly tolerate their presence. Until they arrived, he had fully expected to inherit the throne. That was now far from certain. He and his brothers had never displayed the same virtue as the Pandavas. There had been widespread concern about Duryodhana becoming king, as his birth had been accompanied by many fearful omens. It was clear to everyone that Yudhisthira would be a much better choice.

Duryodhana became insufferable to everyone around him. He stormed around his palace, venting his spleen at hapless servants and smashing furniture. He sat brooding for long periods. Why was everyone so enamoured of the Pandavas? What did they have that he lacked? How was their claim to the throne greater than his own? It was his father who was the king. The fact that Dhritarastra had taken the throne by default was irrelevant. He would have had first claim had he not been blind.

Duryodhana's mortification at losing his status in the Kuru house was compounded by the way Bhima treated him and his brothers. The second eldest Pandava had no time for the arrogant Kauravas. He found the haughty Duryodhana especially nauseating. A rivalry quickly developed between the two princes. From Bhima's side it was mainly boyish and a source of fun, but for Duryodhana it grew increasingly earnest. He found Bhima's antics intolerable. The son of Vayu possessed incomparable physical strength. He would laughingly challenge all hundred Kauravas together to a wrestling contest. When they came at him, he would toss them about like so many pieces of straw. He delighted in practical jokes and would frequently embarrass his weaker cousins.

One day, after Bhima had shaken him out of a huge fruit tree he had climbed, Duryodhana felt he could take no more. It was time to act. He took the next eldest Kaurava, Dushasana, aside and said, "This Bhima is a constant thorn in our sides. We cannot better him at anything. Even at eating he consumes as much as twenty of us together. I tell you, brother, it is driving me to madness. Something must be done, and indeed I have a plan."

Duryodhana had been consulting with his uncle Shakuni, whom he found a sympathetic confidante. Shakuni bore a grudge against the Kurus. He felt deeply offended by Bhishma, who had gone to the kingdom of Gandhara asking for his sister Gandhari as a bride for Dhritarastra. Her father had agreed, even though Dhritarastra was blind, considering an alliance with the mighty Kuru house desirable under any circumstance. Shakuni was angered. Why had his beautiful and qualified sister, who had received a boon from Shiva that she would have a hundred sons, not been given to Pandu, the incumbent Kuru king? Shakuni went with Gandhari to Hastinapura and began looking for ways to get back at Bhishma. He soon found his chance in Duryodhana. The young Kaurava quickly accepted his scheming uncle as a mentor. Shakuni had given the prince an idea how to deal with the Pandavas, whom he knew were dear to Bhishma.

The corners of Duryodhana's mouth lifted in a slight smile. "Listen Dushasana, tomorrow we shall go to the river with the Pandavas. Once there we can enjoy a feast with our dear cousins. I shall personally arrange for some special dishes for the ever hungry Bhima."

Looking about furtively, Duryodhana showed his brother a stem from the deadly poisonous *datura* plant. "I hear this makes a delicious preparation when cooked with various spices. I am sure Bhima will eat a potful. He will surely not survive and with the powerful Bhima gone what can the other Pandavas do? My claim to the throne will be safe."

Dushasana smiled. He had also been suffering at Bhima's hands, and he only wanted to do whatever was pleasing to Duryodhana.

Laughing together, the two princes rejoined their brothers and began walking along the wooded path back to the palace. They watched Bhima bounding ahead and laughed even more.

The next morning Duryodhana suggested that the princes go to the river for some water sports. It was a hot day and they all agreed. They mounted their gleaming gold chariots and set off with loud cheers, sending up clouds of dust as they raced away. Reaching the river, they jumped down from their cars and entered the pleasure-house which the king had built for them, an elegant seven storey mansion constructed of white marble. Rows of colourful flags flew from its high roof. Inside were dozens of well-appointed rooms offering every kind of luxury. Royal musicians and dancers entertained the princes, and one hundred armed bodyguards stood ready to protect them.

Duryodhana led the way through the mansion and out into the central gardens. "Come, my brothers, let us take our lunch together and then go for some fun in the river."

The prince knew that Bhima would not easily succumb to the poison. It would likely be some time before it took effect. He wanted to administer it as soon as possible and he brought the princes to the large lawn where the food was waiting. Sitting places had been arranged for all of them, with gold plates and cups laid out on low tables.

Suspecting nothing, the Pandavas looked around the beautiful garden, with its large lake filled with lotuses and surrounded by soft grass. The sweet scent of blossoms spread everywhere, and the sound of nearby waterfalls resembled tinkling crystals.

Servants showed the boys to their seats and began to serve the food. The expertly prepared dishes were delicious and the boys ate hungrily. Duryodhana went to the kitchen where a trusted servant had placed the poisoned food meant for Bhima. He personally fetched it out and, with a pretense of affection, served Bhima with his own hand. The Kaurava prince smiled in glee as the guileless Bhima wolfed down the deadly dishes. Duryodhana piled Bhima's plate with many cakes and pies, and poured him sweet drinks, everything indetectably laced with poison.

After the meal was over and the boys had rested for a while, they went out of the mansion to sport in the river. They raced down the forest path to the grassy riverbank. Throwing off their silken robes they dived into the clear waters. They wrestled and tossed each other about, laughing and splashing around. Bhima, not yet affected by the poison, was his usual energetic self. He lifted and hurled the Kaurava princes way out into the river. Thrashing his well-muscled arms, he created great waves that threw the princes off their feet.

As the sun made its way toward the western horizon the boys began to tire. "Let's head back to the city," said Duryodhana.

They dressed and gradually began to make their way back. Bhima at last began to feel the effects of the poison. His head swam and his eyes felt unbearably heavy. Falling behind the others he lay on the riverbank and fell into a deep coma.

The Kauravas were following behind. When Duryodhana saw Bhima laying down he pulled Dushasana aside and said, "Now is our chance."

The two Kauravas waited till their other brothers had gone ahead and then fetched a long length of hemp they had concealed nearby. They knew that Bhima could possibly survive even the huge amount of poison they had managed to feed him. As a back-up plan, they intended to throw him into the river. Looking around furtively to ensure they were alone, they crept up to Bhima. After tightly binding him with the rope they rolled him into the river. As the unconscious prince sank beneath the waters, they turned and got back onto their chariot, praising each other for a job well done.

By the gods' will, Bhima was carried by underwater currents, which swept him along a mystical watery path. It led to the abode of the celestial serpents known as the Nagas, through which the Ganges also flows. Seeing a human mysteriously arrived among them, the angry Nagas at once bit him all over. Their venom acted as an antidote to the poison administered by Duryodhana. Bhima slowly came to his senses and looked around him. He was lying on a strange riverbank, surrounded by large hissing serpents, their fangs bared. Bhima flexed his muscles and burst open his cords. Leaping to his feet, he picked up the snakes with both hands and dashed them to the ground. Some he pressed into the earth with his feet and others he threw to a distance.

When dozens had been rendered unconscious by Bhima the others fled. They went to their king, Vasuki, and fearfully said, "A very powerful human has come into our midst. We could not overcome him. He is by the river."

Vasuki knew that no ordinary human could come there. He had to be either a rishi or a god. The Naga king assumed a human form and rose from his jewelled throne. He went toward the river, accompanied by another chief Naga named Arka. Many years before Arka had lived in human society. He was Kunti's ancestor and by his celestial vision he recognised Bhima as his great grandson. He introduced himself to the Pandava and embraced him warmly.

Vasuki felt pleased to see the pious Kuru prince. Realising that the gods must have brought him there for some purpose, he asked Arka, "What good can we do for this boy?"

Arka looked at the strapping youth and smiled. "I think this prince would benefit most from drinking our *rasa.*

Vasuki agreed at once. "Yes, bring him to the palace and let the *rasa* be fetched."

The Nagas' ambrosial beverage was distilled from many heavenly herbs. It conferred upon the drinker celestial power. The Nagas watched in amazement as Bhima sat and quaffed eight pots one after another. After finishing the drink Bhima again felt drowsy. Vasuki showed him to a bed in his palace and he lay down. For eight days he remained in a deep sleep as his body digested the *rasa.* On the ninth day he awoke, feeling almost unlimitedly powerful. Arka said to him, "You now have the strength of ten thousand elephants. None will be able to defeat you in battle. Come now and eat something. I shall then return you to the surface. Your family are anxious for you."

The Nagas offered Bhima celestial dishes, dressed him in fine silks and golden ornaments, then returned him to the river. Telling him to close his eyes, Arka entered the water with him and within moments Bhima found himself standing alone on the Ganges bank near to the mansion. He immediately began to sprint back to Hastinapura.

In the city Kunti sat sighing with worry. Where was Bhima? His brothers had been surprised to see that he was not in the city when they returned. After failing to find him anywhere near the river, they assumed he had gone on ahead.

Kunti suspected some evil doing. She knew of Duryodhana's disposition toward her sons. Revealing her mind to Vidura, she said, "I fear the Kaurava prince may have killed my son."

Vidura shook his head. "That can never be, dear queen. The all-knowing rishi Vyasadeva has prophesied that your sons will live long. The gods also have predicted a great future for Bhima. Those words cannot prove wrong."

But remembering the malefic omens seen at Duryodhana's birth, Vidura nevertheless warned Kunti to be on her guard. "The Kaurava prince might try anything, even against you."

During the eight days of Bhima's absence Kunti and her other sons were in complete anxiety. Surely Bhima had met with some calamity. Then, soon after sunrise on the ninth day they saw him running along the road toward the palace, his white silks billowing in the breeze. He went straight to his overjoyed mother and respectfully touched her feet. His brothers embraced him with tears in their eyes, eagerly asking him where he had been.

Bhima understood what had happened. When he had seen his cords he immediately suspected Duryodhana, and his fears had been confirmed by Vasuki, who could see everything with his clairvoyance. Bhima told his family about his visit to the celestial world of the Nagas. They all thanked God for his safe return. It seemed that by divine arrangement Bhima had been fortunate, despite Duryodhana's efforts to dispose of him.

Yudhisthira was shocked to learn of Duryodhana's antagonism. He considered the situation carefully and discussed it with his mother and brothers. He concluded it would be best to remain silent. If the Kuru elders were informed, there would be open hostility between the two sets of brothers. With their father Pandu dead their position was weak. Dhritarastra was now the king and he doted on his own sons. He would be unlikely to go against them in order to protect his nephews.

Vidura was the one person they trusted, and Kunti confided in him. He confirmed Yudhisthira's decision. The brothers therefore said nothing about the incident, but from that day they were vigilant, always expecting some other treachery from Duryodhana.

* * *

Through their godly behaviour, the Pandavas became great favourites of Bhishma and Vidura. Bhishma was especially fond of them, acting just like their father. The brothers also became dear to their martial arts teacher, Kripa, the son of a rishi named Sharadvan who taught his son every martial skill.

The Kurus were pleased with Kripa's teachings. Their sons were becoming adept at all forms of weaponry. Still, Bhishma realised that for their education to receive its finishing touches they needed another teacher. There were hundreds of pupils in Kripa's school—kings from many countries had sent their sons to take advantage of the talented brahmin. It was difficult for him to spend time teaching the princes the finer points of the science of arms. Bhishma therefore began wondering where he could find someone who was Kripa's equal, and who could concentrate on honing the boys' martial skills to perfection. He had been searching for some time, but without success.

One day some of the boys ran to him. After bowing at his feet, they said excitedly, "O grandfather, we have been sent to you by an unusual brahmin we met outside the city. He said you would know of him."

The boys told Bhishma how they had been playing ball in the woods. Their ball had dropped down a deep unused well. They were standing around the well wondering what to do when the brahmin approached them. Laughing, he said, "Just see the great Kuru princes, baffled by the loss of their ball. Where is your prowess in arms?"

The dark-complexioned brahmin told the blushing boys that he would retrieve their ball in exchange for a meal. He took a ring from his finger and threw it in the well, saying, "I shall show you how to bring out even that ring."

Yudhisthira replied, "Esteemed sir, if you can recover the ball and the ring then be assured you will find a permanent livelihood in Hastinapura."

With a smile the brahmin took up a handful of long grass. He chanted mantras and threw a blade into the well, piercing the ball. The other blades of grass were all thrown after the first in quick succession. Sticking together they formed a long chain, which the brahmin pulled out to recover the ball. Then, taking a bow from one of the princes, he concentrated for a moment and shot an arrow into the well. By the power of a mystical incantation intoned by the brahmin it came straight out again with the ring on its point.

The princes crowded round the brahmin, clamouring to be taught the skills he had displayed. He told them to go to Bhishma and relate what they had seen. The Kuru chief would know who he was. If Bhishma was agreeable, then the brahmin said he would come to Hastinapura.

Hearing this tale Bhishma's eyes lit up. This brahmin was surely Drona, a disciple of his own martial guru Parasurama. Drona's fame had spread far and wide. He was the son of Bharadvaja, a great rishi who had practiced asceticism for thousands of years. What better instructor could there be for the princes? Bhishma went in person to see him, immediately offering him the post of royal teacher. Drona accepted and went to Hastinapura with Bhishma.

On Bhishma's request, Drona told the curious princes about himself. Although a brahmin, Drona was inclined to the military arts. He explained how he had learned all the secrets of weaponry from Agnivesha, a powerful brahmin who was dwelling in his father's ashram. He had received further training from Parasurama, who was said to be an empowered incarnation of the Supreme.

"However, despite all my learning I am poverty stricken, with hardly the means to maintain my family," said Drona. "I came here in search of students who might afford me a little charity in return for my lessons."

Bhishma smiled. "Your search is over, brahmin. We shall give you everything you need. The Kurus are at your command. Whatever wealth we possess is also yours. Teach our sons your matchless skills. It is our good fortune that you have arrived here."

Drona then took up residence in Hastinapura. He had his wife and son brought to the city to live with him. Opening a school, he accepted both the Kauravas and Pandavas as his students. kings from many surrounding countries also sent their sons to take training from him, sending great offerings of wealth along with their boys.

Under Drona's tutelage the princes' martial skills became highly developed. He had them practicing daily from dawn till dusk. Among all the boys Arjuna excelled. He quickly mastered the use of all weapons and became particularly adept at archery. His ability, speed and perseverance were unmatched. Seeing his humble and respectful attitude, Drona felt increasing affection for Arjuna, and he carefully taught him every skill he knew. "None on earth shall equal you in combat," he told Arjuna.

Ever more determined in his studies Arjuna would spend time refining his skills long after the other princes had left the school. Even late at night he would stand with his bow, shooting at invisible targets. With his eyes closed he could lift and string his great bow, fire an arrow and strike the target all in a matter of seconds.

Bhima and Duryodhana, deadly rivals, both became unmatched in mace fighting, and they too would spend long hours at practice, each trying to outdo the other. Among the other princes, Yudhisthira was the finest spearman and the twins developed incomparable skills in swordsmanship.

CHAPTER THREE

A TRIAL OF ARMS

The time came when Drona considered that the Kuru princes had completed their education. All of them were proficient in the martial arts, capable of fighting from chariots, horseback or on foot. They could wield any weapon and knew the secrets of the mystical missiles presided over by the gods. Drona was confident they could take their place as protectors of the people and stand against any antagonist.

Drona therefore went to Dhritarastra and said, "O king, your sons' training is complete. If you permit, they can display their prowess. I shall arrange an exhibition."

Thanking Drona, the king replied, "Let it be so. I envy those who will be able to witness my sons' skills. Make preparations. O best of brahmins, I shall attend the display with Vidura. He will be my eyes."

Drona selected a suitable site near the city and had a great stadium constructed. It could hold hundreds of thousands of people and its tiered seats seemed to rise to the sky. Rows of golden thrones encrusted with gems were built on the royal platform. From the high walls flew tall flags that fluttered in the breeze.

The stadium was sanctified by brahmins who performed ceremonies to satisfy the gods. Then on a day marked by favourable stars, the citizens of Hastinapura entered the vast building. When it was full the king came in followed by all his ministers. The royal ladies accompanied them, dressed in fine robes, their heads covered by silk veils. As they went up to the royal dais, the senior Kurus with their wives resembled so many gods and goddesses ascending the celestial Mount Meru.

The stadium buzzed with excitement, sounding like the roar of the ocean. Trumpets were blown and drums beaten, and the blast of conches resounded everywhere. Drona then made his entrance along with his son Ashvatthama. Dressed in white robes, with a white garland around his neck, he resembled the rising full moon. The people loudly cheered him, and he raised his hands to silence them.

When the stadium was quiet, the princes entered with Yudhisthira at their head. They strode in like so many lions, clad in brilliant armour and equipped with all kinds of weapons. At Drona's command they began to display their skills, one by one. Mounting tall chargers, they sped about the arena wielding their weapons. Arrows flew in all directions, striking both moving and stationary targets. Some citizens ducked in fear, while others sat fearless, wide-eyed in wonder. Shouts of 'Well done! First class!' resounded throughout the stadium.

On Drona's order Bhima and Duryodhana came together for a mock mace battle. They squared up to each other with fury in their eyes. At Drona's shout they clashed like two enraged bulls, their heavy iron maces smashing together with showers of sparks. Thrusting and parrying, they appeared like expert dancers on a stage.

As the crowd gasped, Vidura described the scene to Dhritarastra. Kunti also did the same for Gandhari, who, when she had learned of her husband's blindness had decided to always wear a blindfold over her eyes in order not to exceed him in any way.

Everyone became absorbed in the contest, which was becoming more than an exhibition. The crowds' loyalties were divided, with some shouting for Bhima and others for Duryodhana. Drona saw that the fight was becoming too earnest. He told his son to step between them. Ashvatthama quickly went forward and managed to separate the roaring princes, who stood back glaring at one another.

Drona then announced that Arjuna would display his talents. "This son of Indra is the finest of all warriors and best protector of the Kurus. Watch now and be dazzled by his skills."

The people all cheered loudly. Dhritarastra asked Vidura about the reason for the uproar. When Vidura told him he replied, "Blessed am I to have such boys as Kunti's sons in my care. They are like so many blazing sacrificial fires."

However, the blind king secretly felt resentment. Why had the people not cheered Duryodhana in the same way? Was he inferior to Arjuna? Dhritarastra writhed in his seat. If only he could see for himself what was happening.

As the crowd quietened, Arjuna began to display his mastery over the celestial weapons. With the Agneya weapon, presided over by the fire-god Agni, he produced blazing fire which he extinguished with the Varunastra, controlled by the god of the waters. Then the wind-god's weapon was invoked, and a great wind rushed through the stadium, which Arjuna checked by means of the Parvatya weapon, which caused a hill to appear in the arena. He demonstrated a number of other mystical weapons before the astonished gaze of the people, then began to display his skill with the bow. Drona had a mechanical boar run swiftly across the arena and Arjuna released five arrows straight into its mouth, as if they were a single shaft. He then shot twenty arrows into the hollow of a cow's horn that swung around a pole on a rope. After this Arjuna showed his skill and dexterity with the sword and the mace.

The crowd cheered and waved their garments. Arjuna bowed and returned to Drona's side. The exhibition was drawing to a close and the musicians began to play gentle music, calming the crowd. Suddenly they heard a man bellowing at the stadium gates, sounding like an infuriated elephant. All heads turned in that direction and they saw a tall, golden figure striding into the arena. He forcefully slapped his arms, creating a noise like the splitting of rocks. He wore a brilliant coat-of-mail which seemed to be a part of his body, and fire-coloured earrings swung back and forth as he walked straight toward Drona.

The people stared silently at this new arrival. He looked like a moving hill and shone like the sun. His heavy steps seemed to shake the earth. Reaching Drona, he offered a half bow, not showing much respect. He did the same to Kripa, then spoke to Drona in a booming voice. "I am Karna. If you permit, O brahmin, I shall display skills which exceed even those of Arjuna. Prepare to be amazed."

Hearing this bold proclamation, the crowd rose up as if they were one person. They cheered and shouted encouragment to the unknown warrior. Arjuna turned a deep red. He clasped his bow and glowered at Karna.

Drona waved a hand. "Very well, show us your skills then."

The broad-chested youth stepped into the center of the arena and began his demonstration. Matching every feat shown by Arjuna, he frequently threw him disdainful glances. The crowd roared their approval. When he had finished Duryodhana went over and embraced him warmly. Here was someone who could match Arjuna. For too long the proud Pandava had been the main attraction. Perhaps that would now change.

In a loud voice Duryodhana said, "Welcome is your appearance here, O hero. You have shown wonderful skills. What can the Kurus do for your pleasure in return?"

Duryodhana smiled at the smouldering Arjuna. Seeing their obvious enmity, Karna replied, "O king, your friendship is all I desire. Grant me just one request. I desire single combat with Arjuna"

Arjuna stiffened. This interloper needed to be taught a lesson. The Pandava looked at Drona, seeking his permission to fight. Maybe he would get an immediate chance to curb Karna's arrogance.

Drona nodded and Arjuna turned to face Karna. Duryodhana again embraced Karna and urged him to step forward for combat. As the two men closed slowly on each other, the sky grew overcast. Flashes of lightning were seen, and a great rainbow appeared overhead. "Indra's bow!" exclaimed Bhima, realising that Arjuna's father was looking down on him. At the same time brilliant shafts of sunlight shone through the clouds onto Karna, gleaming on his golden armour.

As she witnessed the scene in the arena Kunti was horrified. She suddenly fainted and fell to the floor of the royal dais. Vidura jumped up in alarm and sprinkled her face with water. She came round and he asked her what was wrong. Kunti sighed. How could she tell him the truth—the secret she had carefully kept for so many years? "It was just the heat," she replied, taking her seat again. Looking down on the arena she struggled to conceal her anxiety.

Just as the duel was about to commence, Kripa stepped forward and spoke. He knew all the rules of combat and, in accord with custom, he asked Karna to announce himself and his lineage. Duels were only to be fought between equals.

Karna looked embarrassed. He said nothing. It seemed he was not from any royal line. Realising this and seeing Karna's discomfort, Duryodhana said, "Birth is not the only factor which determines nobility. Power and heroism are also to be considered. However, if it is a problem for Arjuna then I shall here and now confer a kingdom upon Karna."

Duryodhana immediately arranged an installation ceremony for Karna. As everyone looked on in bemusement, he had water fetched and sprinkled it over Karna's head, saying, "You shall be the king of Anga." Brahmins performed the rituals and when they were complete the people cheered as Karna stood up, his head still wet and his body covered with rice grains thrown during the ritual. He was deeply moved by Duryodhana's gesture of friendship. In a choked voice he said, "O king, I can never repay you."

Duryodhana placed an arm round his shoulder. "I only desire your friendship."

Karna turned to face Arjuna again. The crowd murmured with excitement. Surely now the fight would go ahead. Suddenly another man ran into the arena. He was elderly and supported himself on a staff. He went up to Karna, who at once bowed at his feet. "This is my father, Adiratha," Karna explained to Duryodhana. "He adopted me as a small child."

Adiratha had been in the crowd and when he saw his son crowned as a king, unable to contain his excitement, he came into the arena to congratulate him. By his name and dress he was plainly a charioteer and seeing this Bhima laughed out loud. "How does this charioteer's son deserve death at Arjuna's hands?" he jeered. "Indeed, he should never be made a king, any more than a dog should be given the sacrificial offerings meant for the gods."

Karna blushed deeply. Duryodhana leapt up and exclaimed, "Bhima, you have no right to speak in this way. Karna's birth may be mysterious, but then so is yours and your brothers. How can this man be low born? We have all seen his power. See his natural armour; how he shines like the blazing sun. I take him to be the best of heroes and warriors."

Duryodhana looked around, his eyes flashing. "If anyone wishes to take issue with my words then let him step forward and bend his bow in combat."

Roused by Duryodhana's heroic speech, the crowd cheered. They looked on expecting a fight of some sort to soon start. But the sun had reached the horizon. Drona called a close to the day's proceedings. The dispute would have to be settled another day. Duryodhana took Karna's hand and led him out of the arena. Drona also went out, followed by the Pandavas. Gradually the citizens dispersed, talking excitedly together.

Kunti watched as Karna left with Duryodhana. There was no doubt that he was the child she had long ago abandoned. She remembered that painful day only too well. Having just received Durvasa's boon, she had lain on her bed idly wondering if it would really work. Seeing the sun shining into her room she began chanting the mantra the sage had given her. To her astonishment the blazing form of the sun-god, Surya, suddenly appeared within the sun disc. He was brilliantly handsome, and she felt her mind being attracted to him. The next moment he was standing before her. His deep voice had filled the room. "What shall I do for you, O gentle maiden?"

Kunti's mouth fell open in surprise. "I do not desire anything," she replied in a shaky voice. "I was merely testing the mantra. Please forgive me. O great god, you may return to your abode."

But the sun-god had said that he could not leave without giving her something. "You have desired me, therefore let me bestow upon you a celestial child."

Kunti had been shocked. How could she, as a maiden, accept a man's embrace? Surya had smiled. He reassured her. Even though conceiving a child by him she would retain her virginity. And so it had come to pass. Unknown to anyone in the palace except her most trusted servants, Kunti gave birth to a boy. She recalled how she had marvelled at his natural bodily armour and glowing earrings—the very ornaments she had seen on Karna as he marched into the arena. She remembered also the day she had let the child go, too scared to tell her elders what had happened. Praying to the sun-god to protect the boy, she had placed him in a basket and pushed him out into the swiftly flowing Ganges current. The memory of that moment was still vivid in her mind—watching with tear-filled eyes as the basket bobbed away and finally disappeared in the distance. Adhiratha must have later found him and adopted him. Kunti looked over at the tall young man leaving the arena with Duryodhana. It seemed their destinies were interwoven. Her heart felt tremulous. Without doubt Duryodhana would feed Karna's obvious envy of her other sons. Torn by conflicting emotions and praying for strength, she stood up and led Gandhari out of the arena.

CHAPTER FOUR

THE BLIND KING

The day came for the princes to leave Drona's school. It was time for them to give him *dakshina*, the traditional fee a teacher asked of his students. Drona wanted only one thing. "Bring me as a captive, king Drupada of Panchala."

The princes knew why Drona had made this request. He had told them how he and Drupada had once been friends, living together in Rishi Agnivesha's ashram. Drupada had promised Drona that when he inherited his father's kingdom, he would give him half. When many years later that time came, and the penniless Drona had reminded his old friend of the promise, he had been insulted. "What use are past friendships," Drupada had laughingly asked. "Only equals can be friends. You are now a poor mendicant, and I a great king. Do not try to revive a long dead relationship."

Offering him only a little charity, Drupada had sent Drona on his way. Offended and unhappy that the king had broken his word, Drona left. Since then he had acquired an unrivalled skill at arms, but he had no desire to wreak vengeance on Drupada by killing him. It would be better to simply curb his pride and oblige him to keep his promise. The best way to do that would be by having him accept defeat at the hands of the princes, Drona's students.

Duryodhana clasped hold of his bow. "Master, consider it done. You will soon see that arrogant king brought here tightly bound."

Mounting his chariot, he sped away toward Drupada's capital, Kampilya, followed by his brothers. They rushed into the city with weapons raised, bellowing their war cries. The Pandavas waited outside with Drona. They did not expect the Kauravas' impetuous attack to succeed against the powerful Drupada. "Let us make our assault after theirs is repulsed," Arjuna suggested.

Discovering that his city was under attack, Drupada at once mounted his war-chariot and sped toward his aggressors. An army quickly assembled, and they met the Kauravas on the city streets. Drupada assailed them with countless arrows, twirling in his chariot like a dancer on a stage. His soldiers engaged all the hundred princes from every side. Kampilya's citizens also joined the fray, coming out of their houses to fight the Kauravas with clubs and sticks.

Fiercely attacked by thousands of soldiers and citizens, the Kauravas found themselves being driven back. As Drupada's arrows began finding their mark, the princes, howling in pain, turned to flee. They bolted back out of the city with the Panchalas in hot pursuit.

The Pandavas laughed. Arjuna said to Yudhisthira, "These brash princes are all talk. It is time for us to tackle Drupada. Allow me and the others to fight while you remain here with Drona."

Yudhisthira gave his permission and his brothers offered their obeisance to Drona, then turned to face the Panchalas. Expecting another attack, Drupada had arranged a row of great war elephants in front of the city wall. Bhima bounded toward them whirling his mace. He was followed by Arjuna on his chariot, flanked by the twins. Arjuna released arrows in such large numbers that they appeared like swarms of black bees descending on the Panchalas. Bhima reached the elephants and began to smite them with tremendous blows from his mace. The huge beasts screamed and toppled over. Bhima resembled a tornado as he careered into ranks of the Panchalas. He drove them back as a herdsman drives cattle.

Bursting into the city, the four brothers encountered Drupada surrounded by his troops. Arjuna shouted his battle cry and immediately shot volleys of arrows at those forces. Shafts left his bow in a straight line and shot in all directions as he fearlessly entered among the enemy.

The Panchalas fought back with furious energy. Arrows, darts, spears and clubs flew at the Pandavas. The brothers expertly parried the attack, striking down the missiles with their own weapons. Arjuna became enraged. He fought with redoubled energy. No one could detect any interval between his taking up his arrows and firing them. They flew from his bow without cessation. At the same time Bhima rushed about with his mace whirling. The two brothers were unapproachable and the Panchala soldiers fled in terror.

Only Drupada stood his ground to face them. He stood on a great golden chariot drawn by four horses. Praising the Pandavas' prowess, he raised his bow and let go a number of razor-headed arrows. They struck Arjuna forcefully and glanced off his armour. Other shafts sped toward Bhima, who struck them down with his mace. In seconds Arjuna responded with fifty arrows that broke apart Drupada's bow, smashed his flagstaff and slew his steeds. Another wave of arrows sent the Panchala king reeling.

Arjuna threw down his bow and took up a gleaming sword. Leaping down from his chariot he raced over to the stunned Drupada. He jumped up and seized the king, holding the sword to his throat. The four brothers then withdrew from the city and presented the captive king to Drona.

Drona smiled. "So, great monarch, it seems your kingdom and riches are now mine."

Drupada stood with his head bowed. He could not make any reply. Drona put an arm round his shoulder. "Do not fear. I am a brahmin and am bound by duty to always forgive. Indeed, I still feel affection for you and would like our friendship to continue. How though can unequals be friends? I shall therefore give you back half of the Panchala kingdom."

Drupada breathed heavily through clenched teeth. Drawing on all his patience he managed a smile and replied, "Dear Drona, you are truly a noble soul. Let us again be friends, as you wish, each ruling a half of the Panchalas."

After brahmins had performed the ceremonies to install Drona as the ruler of the northern Panchalas, Drona ordered Drupada's release. Left with only the southern half of his kingdom, the king went away seething with anger and humiliation. His dishonour had to be avenged. But how? Who could face Drona in battle? Even his students were invincible, it seemed. The king slowly returned to his palace.

* * *

The situation in Hastinapura remained tense for the Pandavas. They were constantly on their guard, expecting Duryodhana to attempt further treachery at any time. The Kaurava prince was always arrogant and given to licentious behavior. He and his brothers took pleasure in wine and women and they laughed at the Pandavas, who strictly adhered to virtuous principles. Dhritarastra was kind toward his nephews, but he over-indulged his own sons, allowing them their excesses and not checking their antagonism toward the Pandavas.

An emissary from nearby Mathura arrived one day to visit Dhritarastra. Mathura was the capital of the Yadus and Vrishnis, who were friendly with the Kurus. They had a family link through Kunti, who had been born in the Vrishni line. Her brother Vasudeva had a son called Krishna, who was said by the rishis to be the Supreme, descended to earth in human form. Hearing of the tension that his aunt Kunti and her young sons were experiencing in Hastinapura, Krishna sent his counsellor Akrura to the city to assess the situation.

After the Kurus had formally received Akrura in friendship, he visited Kunti. She was overjoyed to see him and began asking about her family members. Kunti was especially interested to hear about Krishna whom she knew was God. In her anxiety for her sons she was continuously praying to him for protection. "Is my nephew Krishna thinking of me and my sons?" she asked Akrura. "Does he know how I am suffering here amidst so many enemies, like a deer among wolves?"

Kunti was sure that Krishna was aware of everything. Nothing could be outside of his knowledge. Akrura's arrival in Hastinapura was proof enough that Krishna was thinking of her. She was simply revealing her feelings to Akrura.

Akrura gently reassured her. Krishna often spoke about her. He had heard of Duryodhana's antagonism and would surely come to see her before long, after he had taken care of pressing business in Mathura.

Kunti had heard how Krishna had recently killed a vicious king named Kamsa, who had somehow come to rule Mathura. Kamsa had repeatedly tried to have Krishna and his brother Balarama killed. The two boys had been raised in a small village called Vrindavan. Hearing a prophecy that Krishna would be the cause of his death, Kamsa sent numerous great demons to destroy him, but all of them were slain by Krishna and Balarama. Finally, the divine boys had gone to Mathura and killed Kamsa himself.

Akrura comforted the weeping Kunti. "Your sons are expansions of the gods. Besides that, they are the Lord's devotees and thus always under his protection. The Kauravas will not be able to harm them."

Akrura remained in Hastinapura for some months, wanting to get a full understanding of the whole situation. When he was finally ready to return to Mathura, he spoke with Dhritarastra. The intelligent minister from Mathura had seen that everything ultimately depended upon the blind king. Although not openly sinful, as Kamsa had been, Dhritarastra was nevertheless covertly encouraging his evil-minded sons. It was in his power to prevent a conflict by checking Duryodhana, perhaps by sending him off to some distant country.

Dhritarastra listened in silence as Akrura spoke. "O king, the throne has only become yours by default. It was rightfully Pandu's and thus his sons have the first claim, or at least an equal claim with your sons. You should therefore deal equally with all the princes. Indeed, a wise man deals equally with all living beings, seeing them all as equal parts of the supreme spirit, Krishna. Affection for family members arises from illusion. As a great monarch it is your duty to rule impartially, always keeping in mind such eternal spiritual truths."

Dhritarastra made no argument as Akrura offered his advice. The Vrishni minister made it clear that the blind king was courting disaster by opposing morality. If he did not deal virtuously with the saintly Pandavas then in the end he would reap only sorrow.

Dhritarastra sighed. "I accept all this, O wise Akrura. If only I was able to follow your advice. My attachment for my own sons is too strong. Perhaps I want them to be what I could never be."

Dhritarastra had always cursed his blindness. Born in Kuru's line, he was a powerful warrior, but had never been able to display his prowess. It had been Pandu who had gone out and established the supremacy of the Kuru dynasty. And it was Pandu who had won the people's love and admiration. They had not been happy when Pandu went to the forest, leaving the blind Dhritarastra in his place.

The king continued, "What can I do? I am a mere man, influenced by desire and hate. The Lord has made me what I am. Everything moves under his supreme will. Now he has appeared among us to remove the earth's burden and that will surely happen. Who can prevent the course of destiny?"

Dhritarastra had heard the sages describe how Krishna had appeared to destroy all demonic elements on earth. Maybe Duryodhana and his brothers were in that category. If so then what could be done? And why should anyone worry? Krishna would no doubt rectify the situation—if indeed he was the Supreme.

Akrura could see that his advice was falling on deaf ears. Dhritarastra's blindness was made doubly pernicious by a refusal to see the facts and act responsibly. There could only be one outcome, a truth which Dhritarastra must surely realise. By his intentional policy of favouring the Kauravas over the Pandavas he would cause a conflict that would ultimately destroy the whole Kuru house. Akrura took his leave from Dhritarastra and then left for Mathura.

After Akrura's departure Dhritarastra felt anxious. Perhaps there was more he could do. Pandu's sons certainly had first claim to the throne. As well as it being their rightful inheritance, they were virtuous, powerful and well-loved by the people. Yudhisthira was especially qualified, showing a remarkable understanding of religion and law. The king had to admit that his own sons were inferior. Yet he could not bear to think of them standing aside to let the Pandavas take over the kingdom. If that did happen it would mean that he himself would need to stand down.

Torn by his duality, Dhritarastra took counsel from Bhishma, Vidura and the brahmins. All of them were unequivocal. Yudhisthira should be installed as prince regent. Bhishma said, "This is the only virtuous course, O king. Representatives of the people have come to us many times asking that the prince be made heir to the throne. He is now fully trained and highly capable. Do not delay in his installation."

Dhritarastra could not argue. He soon had the ceremony performed. To the people's joy and Duryodhana's horror, Yudhisthira became the heir apparent. The Kaurava prince was astonished. How could his father have done this to him? Seeing his anger and dismay, Bhima sneered at him, mocking his miserable expressions. Taking Karna and Dushasana with him, Duryodhana stormed away to see Shakuni.

When the four of them were alone, Duryodhana exclaimed, "I cannot take any more, Uncle! Bhima is vicious and vile. Yudhisthira is now prince regent and I have become a nobody in the palace. What can be done?"

As the angry Duryodhana raged on, Shakuni appeared thoughtful. After some moments his face lit up. "I believe the great festival in Varanavata will occur soon. The king always sends a representative to that distant city for their yearly celebrations. Why not this year the Pandavas be the ones who go?"

Duryodhana looked mystified. Shakuni's mouth twisted in a slight smile. "Fires often start in these hot places. Would it not be a tragedy if the Pandavas were caught in such a conflagration?"

Duryodhana eyes widened. He nodded in understanding. Dushasana laughed and shook Shakuni's hand, but Karna was doubtful. He jumped to his feet. "I cannot condone any treachery. We are warriors who possess strength of arms. If we have enemies then let us march out onto the battlefield and settle the score in the proper way."

Shakuni went over to him and placed a hand on his shoulder. "Dear child, you are doubtlessly heroic. Yet you seem to have forgotten the Pandavas' power. It is never wise to confront those of superior strength. Do you not recall what happened at Kampilya? Have you not seen how effortlessly Bhima tosses the Kaurava princes about?"

Karna scowled. He would prefer to forget about Kampilya. They had been caught by surprise. Drupada had been more powerful than expected—and, unlike the Kauravas, the Pandavas had been given the opportunity to see that before they attacked him.

"Say what you will, Shakuni. I for one do not fear Bhima or any of his brothers. I favour open combat and cannot join with any cowardly schemes to attack them covertly."

Karna strode out of the room. Duryodhana tried to stop him, but Shakuni told him not to worry. "Let him be. He is headstrong and impetuous, but he will never leave your side. Doubtlessly you will have need of his power and heroism before long."

Shakuni then revealed his idea to Duryodhana. The prince should use his influence with his father to ensure that the Pandavas be sent to Varanavata. The cunning Shakuni had carefully analysed the situation. He could understand Dhritarastra's mentality. "If you press him your father will certainly agree to this proposal, my dear prince."

Trusting Shakuni's judgement, Duryodhana readily agreed. Sitting alone with his uncle he carefully worked out the details of their plan, then left to see the king.

* * *

Dhritarastra sat alone in his chamber, his chin resting on his hand. After Yudhisthira's installation he had seen how Duryodhana was fuming. The prince had hardly spoken to him since the day of the ceremony. Upset by this, Dhritarastra had spoken with Shakuni. His brother-in-law had then suggested that he speak with a brahmin called Kanika, who was an expert in statecraft and politics. This brahmin was also a friend of Shakuni and shared his devious mentality. When the king asked for his advice, he told him that he should immediately destroy the Pandavas. "If you view these brothers as your enemies you should have no compunction, O king. Do not hesitate. Before they become too strong, they must be rooted out. Otherwise your position will be threatened."

Kanika suggested that the king employ some secret means to dispose of them. Externally he should maintain a friendly disposition toward them, but as soon as an opportunity arose, he should strike. "You will not have the support of your ministers for a direct confrontation. Nor will the people be happy if they see you harm the Pandavas."

Dhritarastra pondered Kanika's advice. How could he ever hurt Pandu's sons? What sense was there in seeing them as his enemies? What harm had they ever done him? Thinking of Duryodhana, the king's mind wavered. His son would never be happy in the Pandavas' presence. Nor would he ever assume the throne. That much was clear. There was no question of the people or indeed the Kuru elders choosing Duryodhana over Yudhisthira, or even any of his brothers. Already he was hearing reports of what the people were saying. "Let Yudhisthira be given the throne now. Why should we be ruled by the blind Dhritarastra?"

The king knew he had to decide one way or the other. Either he took Duryodhana in hand, making him accept the fact that Yudhisthira would be the next king, or he would have to follow Kanika's advice. Neither course seemed attractive.

As the king sat thinking, he heard Duryodhana's heavy steps approaching. Dhritarastra could sense his agitation. He asked what ailed him and Duryodhana replied, "I am hearing worrying reports. It appears the people want Yudhisthira installed as king immediately. They are not happy with you, dear father, and it seems they do not care for me either."

As he spoke the prince paced back and forth, his golden ornaments jangling together. "Ignominy will soon be ours. With Yudhisthira as king our line will be cast into misfortune. How do you think the harsh and inimical Bhima will treat us? We will be the butts of ridicule. Rejected and despised by everyone, we will have to abandon our family home."

Duryodhana told his father that he had thought of a means of saving the situation. He carefully revealed the plan that he and Shakuni had discussed. The prince watched his father's reactions closely as he was not sure how the king felt toward the Pandavas. He first suggested that they be sent to Varanavata. Duryodhana spoke in a low voice, looking around the king's chamber to see if anyone else was present. "Once the brothers are in that distant city, who knows what may happen? Perhaps they will never return."

Dhritarastra immediately understood. Quickly raising a hand, he checked his son, exclaiming, "No! Such thoughts are wicked. I cannot allow you to harm Pandu's sons. My brother was kind and generous toward me. He gave me this very kingdom which I now enjoy. I bear neither him nor his sons any ill will. Indeed, I loved Pandu and his sons are equally dear to me."

Even as he spoke Dhritarastra again felt the uncertainty he had been wrestling with since Yudhisthira's installation. His voice became more subdued, "Besides, what would the people say if we sent the Pandavas away? They may well rise up and remove us by force. And I am sure that Bhishma and the other Kuru elders would favour Pandu's sons."

Duryodhana smiled. He had already considered this possibility. "There need be no such fear, O king. Let us begin winning the people's favour by bestowing upon them wealth and honours. Once our position is established, we can send the brothers away. In their absence we will continue to reinforce our standing with the citizens until the time is right for my coronation. When I have become king the Pandavas could even return."

Dhritarastra leaned forward. "This very thought has already crossed my mind, dear child, but I have kept it to myself out of fear of the implications. Such a course of action would find no favour with either

Bhishma, Vidura, Drona or Kripa. Those wise and virtuous men see no difference between the Kurus and the Pandavas. If they realise we are trying to deprive the Pandavas of their rights—even by harming them— will they not consider us worthy of punishment?"

Duryodhana was unconcerned by this objection. He had spent some time carefully discussing every possibility with Shakuni. He moved closer to his father. "O king, Bhishma always remains neutral, favouring neither ourselves nor the Pandavas. He has also sworn to protect the Hastinapura throne—and you now occupy that throne. As far as the others are concerned; Drona's son Ashvatthama is my staunch supporter and Drona will certainly not oppose his own dear son. Kripa is our paid employee and his sister has married Drona—we are therefore assured of his support. Vidura may oppose us, but what can he do? He too depends upon us for his livelihood and anyway he possesses little power."

Duryodhana repeatedly exhorted his father to send the Pandavas away. He described how in their presence he was suffering intensely. The king still felt reluctant, but his attachment for his son finally prevailed. Agreeing to the prince's proposal, he said, "Ensure that this is kept a secret from all but your most trusted counsellors."

Duryodhana assented and then happily left the king's chamber to immediately begin making his arrangements, leaving his father still consumed by doubts.

CHAPTER FIVE

ON THE RUN

By giving continuous charity, the Kauravas began to gain favour among the people. They arranged for various ceremonies in which recognition and honour was given to many leading citizens. Gradually their popularity increased.

As the time for the festival in Varanavata approached, Dhritarastra had his ministers praise the city in the Pandavas presence. They mentioned its beauty and ideal climate, as well as describing the wonderful festival soon to be celebrated.

The young Pandava princes were attracted. Seeing this, Dhritarastra said to them, "I have lately been hearing a lot about Varanavata and its many attractions. Normally we send a delegation to their festival. I thought this year that you brothers might like to go. It would be a pleasant vacation."

Yudhisthira immediately realised what was happening. He had already noticed how the Kauravas were trying to win over the people. Now it was clear why. Some devious plan was afoot, but the prince knew there was little he could do. He and his brothers were not strong. The king was plainly a party to Duryodhana's schemes. He had control of the treasury, army and ministers. It would be pointless and perhaps dangerous to oppose him. Concealing his feelings, Yudhisthira replied, "Let it be so. I think we would enjoy a holiday in Varanavata."

Duryodhana was thrilled to hear that the Pandavas had agreed to go away. He spoke in secret with a close confidante named Purochana, instructing him to go at once to Varanavata. "Construct a house of highly flammable materials, making it appear perfectly normal. Bring the Pandavas in there, and when they are settled and at their ease..."

He trailed off and made a sign indicating fire. Purochana smiled in understanding and Duryodhana said, "This world and all its wealth are at my command. You shall want for nothing. Go now and carry out my order. I am fully depending on you."

Purochana gathered a few trusted artisans and left at once for Varanavata. A few days later the Pandavas prepared to leave. They said their farewells to the elders and aggrieved citizens, who did not want them to go. Despite the Kauravas' many contrivances, the gentle Pandavas were still most loved by the people. Many of them even suspected some evil doing by the Kauravas.

As the Pandavas mounted their chariots to leave, Duryodhana stood by with his brothers to see them off. "Farewell brothers, may the gods bless you on your way. May not the slightest evil befall you."

The Pandavas, along with their mother, went out of the city followed by crowds of people. The citizens implored them to remain in Hastinapura, censuring Dhritarastra for sending them away. But Yudhisthira checked them. He stopped his chariot just outside the city gates and said, "Dear friends, Dhritarastra is the king. He is our father, preceptor and superior. We must follow his commands without question. This is the eternal law laid down by God. Return now to your homes. When the time is right you may render us service."

The people reluctantly turned back, but Vidura came forward to speak with Yudhisthira. He addressed him in a language that only the two of them could understand. Through his spies the minister had come to know of Duryodhana's plan, but, like Yudhisthira, did not feel it wise to openly oppose the king. Taking hold of Yudhisthira's arm and speaking softly, he said, "Fire cannot harm one who hides in a hole or in the deep forest. By the stars one can find his way at night. Even though oppressed by enemies, he who conquers his own senses will never be defeated. Indeed, he will come to rule the world."

Yudhisthira nodded in understanding. The Kuru minister then blessed the brothers and bid them farewell. When they were some way out of the city Yudhisthira told his mother and brothers what Vidura had said. "He confirmed my own suspicions. It is plain that Duryodhana has somehow contrived to have us killed, seemingly by fire. Our uncle has given me a clue how we can escape."

Feeling apprehensive, they travelled to Varanavata, arriving by early evening. The citizens came out to greet them in large numbers, pleased to see Pandu's famous sons. There was a festive scene as thousands of people appeared on many kinds of chariots, waving flags and playing on instruments. The city elders greeted the brothers and led them into the city, where they were met by Purochana. He told them that, on the king's orders, he was arranging for a mansion to be specially constructed for their stay in the city. The brothers looked at each other but said nothing.

Within two weeks of their arrival the mansion was complete. With a flourish, Purochana showed them around the large building. "Everything has been arranged for your comfort, O princes. You will not want for anything. I shall also stay here as your obedient servant."

When Purochana had gone, Yudhisthira went over to one of the walls and tapped it lightly. "This house consists entirely of highly flammable materials," he said to his brothers. "Can you not detect the odour of oil and lacquer? Without doubt the sinful Purochana intends to burn us to death. He is nothing more than Duryodhana's instrument. The greatly intelligent Vidura has properly warned us of this danger."

Bhima snorted. "Then let us leave here at once. I've had enough of Duryodhana's plots. We should deal with him."

Yudhisthira shook his head. "No, the time is not right. What can we five do against the state of Hastinapura, now effectively under Duryodhana's control through his weak-minded father?"

Yudhisthira also dismissed the suggestion that they flee from Varanavata. "If we run Duryodhana will know that we have discovered his plot. He will dispatch spies to seek us out and have us killed by any means possible. Better we stay here for now and say nothing. Be especially careful about Purochana. If he suspects that we have discovered him he may do anything."

The other Pandavas, always obedient to their elder brother, agreed. Yudhisthira remembered Vidura's words. "We need to dig a tunnel under this place. If it is set ablaze, we can shelter there."

Yudhisthira said they should spend their days exploring the surrounding area. Then when the opportunity came for them to escape they would know their way around.

A couple of days after they had moved into the house, which Purochana had named 'Blessed Abode', a strange man appeared there asking to meet with them. "I am an expert miner. Vidura has sent me here, saying you will have use for my skills."

Speaking in the same tongue used by Vidura when he warned Yudhisthira, the miner reminded him of that incident. Yudhisthira, at first suspicious that this may be yet another of Duryodhana's tricks, was reassured. He greeted the miner warmly. "It is good to see you, noble sir. Any friend of Vidura is also our friend."

Yudhisthira told him about the house and Purochana's plan to burn them to death. The miner said he would be able to build a tunnel that led from the house into the nearby woods. "It can be completed in a month. I think Purochana will wait longer than that before he attacks. He will want to be sure that you are completely at your ease."

Yudhisthira agreed and the miner started at once, digging from a concealed place within the house. As the days and weeks passed, the Pandavas spent much of their time wandering in the surrounding countryside. They ascertained a route away from the town, marking it with pieces of white cloth that would be visible at night.

More than a month went by. The brothers and their mother gave the appearance of being peaceful, but they were always alert, waiting for Purochana to make his move. One of them would remain awake at night, listening out for any unusual sounds, and they always had their weapons at the ready.

Seeing that Purochana suspected nothing and was confident that they were well settled in, Yudhisthira one day said to his brothers, "I feel we should act now before Purochana has a chance. Let us set fire to this place ourselves, burning that wicked man along with the building. The tunnel is now complete and we can make good our escape, leaving everyone to think that we have perished."

Yudhisthira knew that news of their supposed deaths would soon reach Hastinapura. They would thus be able to travel through the country without fear of being pursued. Remaining incognito, they could get right away from Varanavata and consider their next move.

The following day a festival was celebrated. Kunti arranged for food to be distributed from her house for the poor and needy in the city. By the arrangement of providence a tribal woman and her five sons came to the house. They ate heartily and drank a large amount of wine. Gradually they became drunk and fell asleep. Unable to rouse them, the servants left them where they lay.

When everyone had left the house that night, the Pandavas retired to their room. Purochana also slept in his usual place in the room by the door. Outside a storm blew up. The Pandavas sat silently, till they were sure that Purochana was deeply asleep. Then, one by one, they entered the tunnel, carefully protecting their mother. Bhima waited till they were all in the tunnel, then he took a torch and set light to the house, starting with the door. He ran back to the tunnel and within minutes the house was blazing fiercely.

Purochana had no chance to escape. The whole house became an inferno. Crowds of citizens, roused by the noise of the blaze, came out onto the streets. When they saw the Pandavas' house ablaze they cried out in distress. As the flames gradually subsided, they threw water over the embers and began searching around. They found the charred corpses of the tribal woman and her five sons. Believing them to be the remains of Kunti and the Pandavas they lamented loudly. "Alas, this is surely an act of the wicked and heartless Duryodhana. Envious of his godly cousins he has arranged for their destruction. No doubt his blind father was also a party to this, otherwise how could it have been possible?"

The citizens had noticed the flammable materials used for the house's construction. None of them detected the tunnel as the miner had helped them search through the ashes and had kept it concealed. Messengers were then sent to Hastinapura to inform the Kurus of the tragedy.

* * *

Out in the woods the Pandavas emerged from the tunnel into the blackness of the night. Carrying torches, they searched out their cloth markers and began to follow the path they had laid through the woods. Tired from lack of sleep and from the effort of making their way through the long tunnel, they stumbled through the forest. After walking for over an hour Kunti fell to the ground, unable to continue. The brothers gathered around her and gently fanned her face with large leaves. They looked around fearfully at the thick woods. Then, to their amazement, Bhima lifted all of them onto his huge frame. He placed his mother on his shoulders, the twins on his sides, and Yudhisthira and

Arjuna on his arms. Keeping all five of them in these positions, he began to run through the forest, trampling down the foliage.

Bhima soon reached the banks of the Ganges, where he set down his mother and brothers. They drank the clear water and splashed it on their faces, relieving their fatigue. They then started following the river to the south, looking for a shallow place to cross. As they made their way along the riverbank they came across a large boat. A man on board called out to them, again speaking in the same dialect Vidura had used in his warning to Yudhisthira. Like the miner, the boatman said that he had been sent there by Vidura. "He told me to stay here, awaiting your arrival. I have been here for over a month, expecting you at any time."

Greeting the boatman warmly, the five brothers and their mother boarded the boat, which was propelled by sails and an engine. It set off, cutting swiftly through the dark waters. The Pandavas lay down to rest and by sunrise the boat had carried them a long distance away from Varanavata. They disembarked on the opposite side of the river and, after thanking the boatman and giving him a message of gratitude for Vidura, they made their way into the thick forest.

Travelling south, the brothers struggled through the dense undergrowth. Kunti found it especially difficult. Prickly bushes grew everywhere. Tangled creepers and roots lay across the ground and she repeatedly stumbled and fell. Bhima and Arjuna walked by her side, supporting her as they slowly went deeper and deeper into the forest. They walked throughout the morning and by the afternoon all of them except Bhima were exhausted. Yudhisthira stopped them in a clearing and they sat down to rest. Looking around in despair, he said, "What could be more painful? Here we are utterly lost in these desolate woods. We do not know where to go or what to do. It is not even certain that Purochana perished in the fire. Perhaps he has informed the Kurus that we survived, and even now they may have spies searching for us."

The sounds of birds and various forest animals echoed around them. Frequently they had heard the growls of tigers in the distance as they walked. They had seen snakes coiled on tree branches and great apes moving through the treetops.

Yudhisthira looked at Bhima. "O hero, only you are free of fatigue. Born of the ever energetic Vayu, and blessed by the Nagas with their *rasa*, you possess limitless strength. Dear brother, we depend on you to save us now. Take us again on your arms and shoulders and carry us through this forest."

Bhima stood up with a smile. Another opportunity to serve his mother and brothers. The second Pandava resembled a young oak tree. His shoulders were as broad as a door and his whole body rippled with muscles. Following his brother's instruction, he again lifted everyone. He then rushed straight into the forest, caring nothing for any obstacle. Like a great elephant he broke down trees with his chest and made a road through the woods. The wind created by the speed of his movement blew over bushes, and his mother and brothers practically fainted. He swam across wide streams, still carrying everyone and keeping them above the water.

When night fell Yudhisthira told him to stop. Bhima saw a large banyan tree and he placed them down beneath its branches. Kunti slumped exhausted to the ground. Parched with thirst, she asked Bhima if he could find water. Bhima stood up, craning his neck. "I hear waterfowl in the distance. There must be a lake nearby. Wait here while I go and see."

Bhima ran off into the wood. A mile away he found the lake. Taking off his upper cloth he soaked it and ran back to his mother and brothers. When he got back he discovered that they had all fallen asleep. As he looked down at their faces he began to lament loudly. "Alas, what more painful sight could there be than seeing my noble mother and brothers asleep on the bare ground? They who could not sleep on the best of beds in Varanavata are now sunk in slumber on the cold earth."

Bhima bewailed at length, and then began to curse the Kauravas. "Wicked minded ones, rejoice now while you can. Surely the gods are favouring you, otherwise I would already have sent you and your followers to Death's grim abode. What though can I do while Yudhisthira does not become angry?"

Breathing heavily and clenching his fists, Bhima looked at the dark woods around him. They had travelled a long distance and he felt sure there must be a town nearby. Resolving to remain awake till morning, he sat on a log close to his brothers.

Not far from the banyan tree lived a Rakshasa and his sister. The demon had heard Bhima crashing through the forest and he sat high in his tree, sniffing the air. His huge mouth broke into a twisted smile, revealing rows of yellowish fangs. He shouted to his sister, "Hidimbi, I smell men. It has been too long since we feasted on human flesh. Go and seek them out. Rip out their throats and bring them here. We shall drink our fill of their frothing blood and rejoice together."

Hidimbi cackled and dropped down from the tree. She padded silently through the woods and approached the Pandavas. Peering through the trees she saw Bhima sitting on the log. Her heart was at once attracted to the handsome youth, with his golden complexion, leonine shoulders and lotus petal eyes. The demoness had never seen such an attractive man. Any thought of killing him left her mind. There might be some momentary pleasure in eating his flesh, but there would be far more pleasure if she were able to enjoy conjugal union with him.

Hidimbi exercised her mystic power and transformed herself into a beautiful maiden. Bedecked with celestial ornaments, a tight fitting silk sari wrapped around her thin waisted body, she moved slowly toward Bhima, glancing down bashfully.

Hearing her steps Bhima started up but when he saw the beautiful woman he sat back down again. Smiling at the surprised looking Pandava, Hidimbi said, "O best of men, who are you and why are you here? Who are these godlike men asleep on the ground? And that lady of transcendent beauty there; who is she?"

Bhima looked at Hidimbi suspiciously. He knew that demons were able to appear in any form they liked. Seeing his apprehension, Hidimbi reassured him. "Do not fear. I wish you no harm. Indeed, you have captured my heart. Know that I am Hidimbi, the sister of Hidimba, a wicked Rakshasa who controls this region. That demon wishes to eat your flesh and has sent me here to fetch you. However, I would rather sport with you in wedded bliss. Become my husband and I shall save you from my cruel brother."

Bhima shook his head. "Here lies my beloved mother and brothers. How can I abandon them, leaving them as food for a Rakshasa while I gratify my lust? It is not possible."

"Then wake them and I shall save you all. Carrying you through the skies, I shall take you to some celestial region where we may enjoy in peace."

Bhima could not agree. "I shall not awaken them out of fear of your brother. Dear girl, no Rakshasa can withstand my prowess, nor can any man or even celestial. O timid one, stay or go as you please. Or if you like bring your brother here. It is all the same to me."

While they were speaking Hidimba became impatient. What was his sister doing? He jumped down from his tree and made his way after her.

Hearing his heavy steps Hidimbi spoke urgently. "Here comes my brother now. Doubtlessly you are brave and powerful, but I have many times seen the superiority of Rakshasas over men. Quickly wake your family and I shall take you all away.

Bhima laughed derisively. "You should not fear. Do not consider me weak, like an ordinary human being. I possess great power. Watch now as I crush the life out of this cannibal."

Suddenly Hidimba burst into the clearing where they stood. As tall as two men, with pointed ears and bright red hair, he was a frightful sight. Seeing his sister standing before Bhima in her voluptuous form, he let out an angry roar. His eyes reddened in fury. "Foolish woman, how dare you disobey me? Do you not fear my anger? It seems you are ready to sacrifice all Rakshasa honour for the sake of lust. I shall kill you along with these humans, for whom you wish to do me a great injustice."

The demon rushed with outstretched arms at his sister. Bhima stepped in front of her and exclaimed, "Stop!" Smiling scornfully, he said, "Wretch! Why are you disturbing my peacefully sleeping brothers and why do you attack this innocent woman? Sent here by you, she has been overpowered by desire upon seeing me. For this you should blame the god of love, not her."

The demon halted in his tracks and stared in disbelief at Bhima. How could any mere human be so rash as to defy him?

Bhima went on, keeping his voice down so as not to disturb his mother and brothers. "Fight with me, wicked minded one. I will not stand by and watch you attack a woman. Step into the woods with me and I will send you to the land of the dead, pounding your head to pieces. Birds of prey will then gleefully feast on your flesh. By slaying you I shall render this forest safe for men to enter."

Hidimba laughed, throwing back his hideous head. "O human, these are bold and boastful words. Make them good and then you may vaunt of your power. You think yourself strong, but today you shall learn the truth. These ones here may sleep at their pleasure till you are killed. After drinking your blood, I shall kill them, followed by my sinful sister."

Hidimba ran straight at Bhima, who seized hold of his arms. He violently dragged the struggling Rakshasa well away from his sleeping family. Infuriated, the demon broke free and clasped Bhima in his massive arms. Sending forth a terrible yell he squeezed the Pandava with all his power. Bhima dragged him still further away. Expanding his great chest, he broke the demon's grip. A fierce fight ensued. The two combatants aimed terrific blows at each other. They grasped and threw each other about with full force. Trees were smashed and broken down as they cannoned into them.

The roars of the fighters woke the other Pandavas and their mother, who sat up and looked around in surprise. Seeing the beautiful Hidimbi standing nearby, they were astonished. Kunti asked, "Who and whose are you, most fair maiden? Are you an Apsara or some other celestial girl? Tell me why you are here."

Hidimbi replied, "This great forest is the abode of me and my brother, Hidimba, chief of all the Rakshasas in this region. I came here on his behest, seeking to kill you. However, upon seeing your golden-hued son I have been brought under Cupid's control. I cannot suppress my passion."

The demoness pointed to where the fight was raging. "Your mighty son dragged my brother off to a distance. See them now, the roaring rivals, man and Rakshasa engaged in a frightful combat."

Yudhisthira and his brothers jumped up. They saw Bhima grappling with the demon, sending up a cloud of dust that hung suspended in the rays of the moon. Arjuna immediately ran over and smilingly said to Bhima, "Dear brother, fear not. We are now here. We did not realise that you were becoming tired in this fight. Stand off now and I shall soon finish this demon."

Jibed in this way, Bhima blazed up in anger. "Do not worry Arjuna, you are not needed here," he growled. "Having come into my clutches this wretch will not escape with his life."

"Then act quickly," Arjuna urged. "Dawn is approaching and demons gain strength from the twilight."

Bhima gazed at Hidimba, his eyes crimson with rage. The Rakshasa charged him and Bhima ducked down, tripping him. As the demon toppled over, Bhima seized him and lifted him over his head. He spun him around, yelling, "After living a vain and sinful life, feeding on other's flesh, you deserve an unholy death. Smashing you and reducing you to nothing, I shall today free this forest of its thorny bush."

Whirling him furiously, Bhima dashed the Rakshasa to the ground. All Hidimba's limbs were shattered and he let out a terrible howl. Bhima then broke his back in two.

Seeing the demon slain, Bhima's brothers joyfully surrounded him, embracing and congratulating him. Arjuna said, "Great hero, I never doubted your ability to kill this one. Let us now depart. I believe there is a town near here."

The sun was rising and paths through the forest were visible. Deciding to head south, the brothers set off, with Kunti in their midst. As they walked away, Hidimbi began to follow them. Bhima turned to her and said threateningly, "Rakshasas revenge themselves on their enemy by alluring deceptions. Desist, Hidimbi, or you shall go the way your brother has gone."

Bhima wanted only to scare her away, but Yudhisthira reprimanded him. "You should never kill a woman, Bhima. Virtue should be preserved even at the cost of your body. Anyway, what can this woman do? You have slain her far more powerful brother. She is no threat to us."

Hidimbi stood with her head down. She folded her palms and looked up at Kunti. "Most noble lady, surely you know the agony of a love stricken woman. I am feeling that pain now for your son Bhima. I have abandoned everything for his sake—my family, friends and even my *dharma*. If I am forsaken by this hero and yourself, I will not be able to live. Have no doubt."

Hidimbi glanced at Bhima, who caught her eye and looked away quickly. She went on addressing Kunti, begging that she be allowed to marry the Pandava. She asked that she be allowed to go with Bhima to celestial regions where they could enjoy together. "O illustrious lady, pray have compassion on me, considering me your most obedient servant. After we have spent some time together I will bring Bhima back to you."

Hidimbi argued that her marriage to Bhima would be quite in accord with virtue, especially as it would save her life. "Protecting one's life by whatever means possible is always considered a prime virtue. Indeed, virtue itself protects life. He who keeps his virtue even amid great distress is the foremost of virtuous men."

Hidimbi looked hopefully at Kunti and Yudhisthira, who stood by his mother's side. Pleased to hear Hidimbi speaking about virtue and seeing that both Kunti and Bhima were not objecting to her suggestion, Yudhisthira replied, "Dear lady of slender waist, you have spoken well. It must be as you say. Marry Bhima then, and take him with you to heavenly regions, but he must be returned each night."

Hidimbi's face blossomed into a great smile. She looked over at Bhima, who said, "Blessed lady, I agree to this union on one condition only. As soon as a son is born to you, I shall leave you."

Hidimbi agreed and they were married there and then in the forest according to the Gandharva rites, by an exchange of garlands. Hidimbi took all the brothers and Kunti to a delightful place high in the Himalayas. They constructed a wooden hut and dwelt peacefully, living on the celestial fruits that grew all around them. By day Hidimbi went away with Bhima, showing him numerous heavenly regions. They sported together on the soft banks of crystal-clear streams and by the sides of lotus filled lakes. In meadows covered with many coloured flowers, and in fragrant woods frequented by the denizens of heaven, they walked together hand in hand. Hidimbi poured forth the sweetest music and dressed herself like a goddess. She gave constant delight to Bhima, who felt the days pass as if they were moments.

After some months Hidimbi became pregnant. In the way of celestial women, she very soon gave birth to a son, who immediately grew into a youth. He stood before his parents glowing like a god. His head was completely bald, his features fierce, and he had a powerful physique like his father. He bowed before his mother and father and they went with him to see the other Pandavas. That boy, who was named Ghatotkacha, spent some time with the Pandavas, serving them in every way. The brothers soon became affectionate toward him.

Finally, Yudhisthira said, "We have tarried long in this region. Now, as agreed, it is time for Bhima to leave Hidimbi. We must continue on our way."

Kunti and her sons said their fond farewells to Hidimbi and Ghatotkacha. Before leaving, Bhima's son said, "The very moment you think of me I shall come before you. Always consider me your servant."

Hidimbi embraced Bhima tearfully. "Shall we meet again?" she asked.

Bhima said they would be reunited when he and his brothers were free from danger and had settled in their own kingdom. They then parted and the Pandavas continued making their way to the south. With their beards and matted hair, they resembled five ascetics. Although they passed through many towns and forest ashrams, no one recognised them. They spent much time hearing Vedic knowledge from the forest sages.

One day while they were seated in an ashram, Vyasadeva came to see them. Appearing there by his mystic power, the sage accepted their obeisance and blessed them. When they were seated before him, he said, "O best of the Bharata race, I have known for some time of your situation. You are being unjustly treated by the Kurus. I have therefore come here desiring to help you. Do not lament for your misfortune. In due course you will understand. Everything is under the Lord's supreme control."

Vyasadeva advised them to enter a nearby town called Ekachakra. He told them to remain there for some time. In due course he would advise them further. The rishi consoled Kunti, "My dear daughter, take heart. Your son Yudhisthira will become the lord of this earth, virtuously ruling over all other kings. Assisted by his brothers he will perform great sacrifices and distribute much charity to the brahmins."

After showing them the way to Ekachakra, Vyasadeva left. The brothers then travelled to that village where they found accomodation in a brahmin's house. They began to live there peacefully, undetected by anybody.

CHAPTER SIX

THE FIRE-BORN PRINCESS

In Hastinapura the messengers from Varanavata brought news of the Pandavas supposed deaths. Dhritarastra wailed in sorrow. Genuinely upset by the news, his grief was compounded by feelings of guilt. He held his head and cried. "Today my illustrious brother Pandu, who had lived on through his sons, has died. This is a black day for the Kurus."

The king instructed that a funeral ceremony be performed. Thousands of grieving citizens entered the Ganges to make offerings to the departed souls. They lamented terribly, calling out the names of Kunti and her sons. Bhishma was particularly afflicted and he went to his rooms to grieve alone. Duryodhana and his brothers made a show of sorrow, but inwardly they rejoiced. Vidura also did not grieve much, but he knew he could not reveal the truth to anyone. Even Bhishma, although favourable to the Pandavas, would likely inform the king and there would be much tension and disturbance in Hastinapura. It would be best to wait till a more opportune moment.

The Pandavas lived for some time in Ekachakra. Presenting themselves as brahmins, they gleaned their livelihood by begging. By day they would go around the village collecting alms. They would return in the evening and Kunti would prepare their meal, dividing the food in half, one portion for Bhima and the other for everyone else.

While the Pandavas lived in Ekachakra a travelling brahmin stayed for a night in the same house as them. He told them stories he had heard on his travels. They learned that there would soon be a *swayamvara* ceremony in king Drupada's capital, in which his daughter would choose a husband. They listened as the brahmin described Drupada's daughter, Draupadi. "This noble lady is incomparably beautiful. She was not born of any mortal woman; all the kings of the world will attend her *swayamvara*."

Fascinated, the Pandavas asked the brahmin to tell them more about Draupadi. "This story really begins with Drona's birth," the brahmin replied. "It is rooted in the relationship between that great acharya and the mighty king Drupada."

The brahmin told them the history of Drona and Drupadas' disagreement, which the Pandavas knew so well. They sat silently as he described how they had overpowered Drupada. "After this the king went away seething with indignation. He wanted revenge on Drona. Realising that only another powerful brahmin would be able to match Drona's strength, he entered the forest to search one out.

"He came across two brahmin brothers named Yaja and Upayaja. When he asked them if they could arrange for him to beget a son who could kill Drona, they agreed to perform a sacrifice on his behalf. The king and his wife sat in the sacrifice, watching as the two brahmins made offerings into a great fire. Then, before their astonished eyes, a youth rose out of the fire. Dressed in golden armour, that effulgent warrior immediately mounted a chariot and rode about, roaring and brandishing a bow. A voice was heard from the heavens announcing that he was born for Drona's destruction. He was named Dhristyadyumna.

"After this a girl also rose from the fire. With the complexion of a blue lotus, she was as beautiful as the Goddess of Fortune. Her eyes were dark and her hair hung down in long black ringlets. She emitted a sweet fragrance, her waist was thin, her hips broad, and her limbs were exquisitely formed. A voice was again heard from the heavens; 'This divine beauty will be the best of all women. Accomplishing the gods' purpose, she will cause the destruction of countless warriors.'"

The brahmin told them that Drona, even knowing that Dhristadyumna had been born for his death, accepted him into his school and taught him the science of arms.

When the brahmin had finished speaking the Pandavas sat silent. Their minds were bewildered. Hearing that their beloved guru Drona was to be killed, and also the description of the celestially beautiful Draupadi, they felt stunned and unable to speak.

49

That evening, after they retired for the night, Kunti spoke to her sons. Seeing their anxious state, she said, "We have lived here long enough. I feel we should now leave and make our way to Drupada's kingdom, Panchala."

Yudhisthira agreed. He and his brothers dearly wanted to attend Draupadi's *swayamvara*, but he remembered Vyasadeva's instruction. "The rishi asked us to wait here for his return," he said to his mother.

Even as he was mentioning Vyasadeva's name the sage suddenly appeared before them. They immediately bowed at his feet and he said, "I understood your minds, and thus have I come here to see you. You should certainly go to Panchala for Draupadi's *swayamvara*."

The sage said that Arjuna should enter the contest to try for Draupadi's hand. "The princess is a worthy bride. Indeed, she is destined to marry you brothers."

Yudhisthira said, "O all knowing rishi, we shall go at once to Panchala."

Vyasadeva then took his leave from the brothers, and the next day they set off for Drupada's city, Kampilya, the capital of Panchala. Walking on the roads by day and night, they travelled in a northerly direction. After three days' journey they reached the Ganges. It was night and they walked by the light of a torch held by Arjuna. As they approached the river they were suddenly accosted by someone who shouted at them from out of the darkness.

"Halt! You men should not go any further. Know that I am Chitraratha, the Gandharva chief. Night is the allotted time for celestials like us to sport in the river. Men should bathe only during the day. If you come any closer you will be in grave danger. I am powerful and will not tolerate any abuse."

Arjuna held up his torch and peered ahead. He saw the Gandharva before him, seated on a shining chariot. Stepping forward, he laughed. "Fool, how can anyone be barred from using the Ganges at any time? This is not in accord with religion. Only one bereft of power would heed your warning. As for us, we care nothing for your words."

Chitraratha became furious. He drew back his bow and released a succession of arrows that hissed like poisonous snakes. Arjuna was unperturbed. He fended off some of the arrows with his shield and struck down others with his torch. Laughing again, he called out, "O

Gandharva, do not try to frighten those who are skilled in weapons. You are wasting your time. As you are a celestial, I shall fight you with celestial weapons. Stand ready to receive the Agneyastra, the fire-god's missile."

Lifting his torch, Arjuna recited the mantras to invoke the celestial weapon. He then hurled the torch at Chitraratha. Charged by mystic power, it exploded against his chariot and reduced it to ashes. Stunned, the Gandharva fell headlong to the ground. Arjuna seized him by the hair, which was adorned with flower garlands, and dragged him over to Yudhisthira.

Chitraratha's shocked wife then ran forward with folded palms and begged Arjuna to release him. Yudhisthira smiled at Arjuna and said, "Who would kill an enemy who is vanquished in battle, deprived of his fame, defenceless and moreover, protected by a woman? Let him go."

Arjuna released Chitraratha and his wife ran over and sprinkled water on his face. He revived and got to his feet, addressing Arjuna in a subdued voice. "Henceforth I shall give up my pride for I have been humbled by a man. Still, I consider it my good fortune that I have met you heroes, whom I know to be the sons of king Pandu. You have spared my life and I desire to give you something in return."

Arjuna held up his hands. "I cannot accept anything in exchange for your life. The Vedas ordain that one in distress should never be slain. Furthermore, my brother ordered me to release you. It was therefore my duty."

Arjuna asked why the Gandharva had seen fit to challenge them. "We are all learned in the Vedas, virtuous and powerful wielders of weapons. What was our fault?"

Chitraratha replied that he had felt unable to tolerate their transgression. "No one possessing power should brook any insult in front of his wife. As well as this, you are not accompanied by any priest, nor do you carry sacred fire. Therefore, did I censure you."

The Gandharva went on to explain that he had heard much about the Kuru race from the rishi Narada. He also personally knew all the gods who had fathered the Pandavas. "I know that you men are all virtuous heroes. By the power of that virtue you were able to overcome me, a celestial. However, it is essential that you find a qualified brahmin to be your guide. kings without brahmins are soon overpowered, while those with them can conquer the whole earth and finally attain heaven."

Arjuna asked him if he could give them any advice about how to find a priest. Chitraratha replied, "Go north to the hermitage known as Utkacha. There you will find an effulgent rishi named Dhaumya. If he consents, you can accept him as your guide."

Thanking the Gandharva for his advice, the Pandavas took their leave from him and began following the path to the north. Before long they reached Utkacha. Going before Dhaumya, they bowed at his feet. The rishi received them with offerings of water and wild fruits. He was impressed with their humility and could see that, like himself, they were Vaishnavas, worshippers of Vishnu. Thus, when they requested him to become their priest he readily agreed.

The brothers were overjoyed. With Dhaumya as their guide they felt their kingdom was already regained, their enemies defeated, and the Panchala princess won. For his part, Dhaumya, looking upon the five heroes, felt that by virtue of their own feats they would soon be the lords of the earth.

* * *

The morning after they met, the Pandavas and Dhaumya set off for Kampilya. On their way they saw crowds of brahmins who were also going to the *swayamvara*. Travelling with them, the brothers themselves appeared like five young ascetics. With their matted hair and long beards, no one could recognise them amidst the throngs of brahmins walking on the road. After a few days journey they reached a village on the outskirts of Kampilya. There they found accomodation in a potter's house, where they began to live as they had in Ekachakra, begging for alms.

The brothers heard from the villagers about the *swayamvara*. king Drupada had set a stiff test for winning his daughter. A special bow had been made, huge and fashioned of seasoned oak. Anyone hoping to win Draupadi's hand would have to string that bow, in itself a near impossible task, then use it to hit a barely visible target. A small wooden bird had been placed at the top of a long pole. Beneath it a metal plate rotated with a single hole punched in it. The successful archer would have to shoot his arrow through the hole at the exact moment it passed over the target.

Hearing this Arjuna felt his bodily hairs stand up. He prayed he would get the chance to try his hand at the test. If he could win Draupadi and thereby secure Drupada's alliance, it would greatly strengthen Yudhisthira's position. He waited eagerly for the day of the ceremony.

In Kampilya kings and princes were arriving from many countries. Drupada had made lavish preparations. A vast stadium had been erected with one hundred broad gates set in its tall white walls. On the day of the ceremony a stream of colourfully dressed people poured through those gates and gradually filled the sloping terraces, sending up a sound like the ocean. Jewel-encrusted seats stood on golden platforms in the front rows, and one by one the visiting monarchs took their places. Kettle drums resounded and thousands of conches were blown. The air was filled with fragrant incense and within the arena brahmins chanted Vedic hymns. Crowds of ascetic brahmins entered the stadium, seeming to illuminate all sides with their bodily radiance.

Leaving their mother at the potter's hut, the Pandavas and Dhaumya entered the arena along with the brahmins. Unnoticed by anyone, they sat amid the ascetics and looked around the arena. At the head of all the kings sat Duryodhana, surrounded by his brothers, all of them dressed in brilliant gold armour and ornaments. Seeing the prince with his head thrown back, looking arrogantly around him, Bhima clenched his fists. He wanted to rush forward right away and grab Duryodhana by the neck, but he kept himself in check. They could not risk discovery yet.

On one side of the arena sat Drupada with his sons and ministers. Before the ceremony began, he distributed heaps of gold and jewels to the brahmins, desiring to invoke auspiciousness for his daughter. The Pandavas kept their place as the brahmins all around them went up to receive the charity. When they had received sufficient wealth, Drupada's son Dhristyadyumna stood up to announce the start of the *swayamvara*. His powerful voice reverberated around the arena.

"The princess Draupadi will now choose her husband. Anyone desiring her hand must pass the test."

Dhristyadyumna pointed to the awesome looking bow on a table next to the target. "Here is the bow and there is the target. Any man of noble birth who can string this bow and with it shoot down the target will win Draupadi's hand. I say this truly."

As he took his seat again, Draupadi came into the arena. A gasp went up from the crowd as they saw her astonishing beauty. She resembled a goddess. Her faultless features resembled a blue lotus, her thin-waisted body was perfectly formed, and she seemed to glow like the full moon. All eyes followed her as she slowly made her way to her place on the royal platform.

Seeing the transcendentally beautiful princess, the kings and princes leapt up from their seats. They glared at one another and made loud declarations. "Draupadi shall be mine!" "Go home all of you—I shall win this princess!" "Consider her already won by me!" Afflicted with desire, they felt envious of even their friends.

As they boasted and vaunted their power, the monarchs made a great noise and Dhristyadyumna again stood to silence them. When everyone was settled once more, they saw above the arena numerous gods and other celestials arriving to witness the proceedings. Those divine beings stayed in the sky, seated upon their golden conveyances, and they dropped showers of celestial flowers on the arena.

Among the many kings sat Krishna and his brother Balarama. Glancing around the crowd he spotted the Pandavas. He smiled to himself and turned toward Balarama, speaking to him in a whisper. "Dear brother, just look over there. Do you see Yudhisthira and his brothers?"

Balarama looked carefully at the five men sitting together, then turned to Krishna with a smile. Both were joyful to see the Pandavas safe and well.

Drupada then indicated that the competition should begin. He looked around at the kings. None of them looked like worthy husbands for Draupadi. Only Krishna and the other monarchs from Mathura seemed qualified, but they were not competing. There was only one person that Drupada wanted to have as his son-in-law—Arjuna. Hearing rumors that the Pandavas had survived the fire in Varanavata, the king had devised a test that he felt sure only Arjuna could pass. He had even been told by the brahmins at Draupadi's birth that she would become Arjuna's bride. Would those words prove false? Where was Arjuna? The king looked around anxiously.

Seeing at last the divine Draupadi, the Pandavas were struck by Cupid's arrows. They gazed at her with wide open eyes. Surely, she would not be won by Duryodhana or any of his cronies. How did those wretches deserve such a prize? Arjuna looked intently at the massive bow. He doubted that any of the Kauravas would succeed. No doubt he would soon get his chance to try for the princess.

Dhristyadyumna began to call out the monarchs' names and they stepped up to the bow, but when they tried to string it they were utterly confounded. Some could hardly lift it an inch. Of those who could it took their full strength to bend the great bow even slightly. Straining and struggling to the limit of their power, they were hurled to the ground as it sprang back and they lay there groaning. One by one the kings and princes were humiliated and returned slowly to their seats, their hope of winning Draupadi shattered.

After more than twenty monarchs had tried and failed, Karna rose up and marched forward. A gasp of admiration went up as he lifted and strung the bow in a matter of moments. He placed an arrow on the string and took aim. Seeing him resolved to shoot the target, Yudhisthira and his brothers felt that it had already been struck down. Suddenly Draupadi stood up and called out, "I will not wed a charioteer's son." Karna's humble origins were by then widely known.

Karna turned angrily toward her. There was nothing he could say. The princess had exercised her prerogative, and Dhristyadyumna had already stated that the test was meant for those of noble birth. Throwing the bow aside, he glanced up at the sun and laughed in vexation. The crowd was silent as he stormed back to his seat.

Duryodhana then stood up. He strode to the table were the bow had been replaced by Drupada's servants. Like Karna, he deftly strung it and placed a golden shafted arrow on the string. The crowd held their breath as he took careful aim. Draupadi was seized with apprehension. She had heard all about Duryodhana. What would she do if he succeeded? How could she marry that arrogant prince? She glanced around at the other monarchs. Seeing Krishna, she prayed to him that Duryodhana might fail. Krishna watched with a smile as Duryodhana stood motionless, aiming the fully stretched bow at the target. There was a great twang as he released the arrow. It shot upwards and passed cleanly through the hole missing the target by a hair's breadth.

The prince angrily threw the bow down. Seeing even the great Hastinapura prince fail, everyone else remained in their seats. The princes who had come from Mathura with Krishna had heard from him that Draupadi was destined to marry Arjuna, so they did not attempt the test. Drupada looked around in complete anxiety. Would Arjuna come? Was he even still alive?

Krishna and Balarama looked over at the brahmins' compound. If Arjuna was to attempt the test it would have to be now. Realising this, the Pandava turned toward Dhaumya, who nodded in assent. Arjuna then stood up and strode out into the arena. Seeing him make straight for the bow, the brahmins cheered and waved their shawls. Some were dismayed, fearing that this brash young brahmin would bring ridicule on their order. "How will he ever succeed when men like Duryodhana have failed?" they exclaimed.

Others were confident. "Just see his stride, like a powerful lion. Look at those broad shoulders. Why should he not succeed? A brahmin's power is always greater than a warrior's."

Going before the royal platform, Arjuna bowed to Drupada and asked, "Is it permissible for brahmins to try this test?"

The king looked at him curiously. "Brahmins are always superior to the royal order," he replied. "Indeed, we depend upon your power for our protection, even as the gods depend upon Vishnu. You may try the test."

Arjuna turned and walked over to the bow. He folded his palms and walked around it in respect, then he lifted the bow and weighed it in his hand. In one skilful movement he bent and strung it, swiftly placing an arrow on the string. The whole stadium was absolutely silent as the unusual brahmin stood stock-still; the stretched bow held firmly in his powerful hands. Suddenly he released the golden shaft and it shot upward, piercing the target right through its middle. With a great clatter it fell to the ground.

The stadium burst into an uproar. Brahmins danced around in glee, throwing their garments into the arena. The crowd roared in joy and thousands of musical instruments sounded. From the sky the celestials rained down flowers and beat their drums. Draupadi's heart beat excitedly. Could this be Arjuna, as her father had so fervently hoped? He hardly seemed like a brahmin, with his broad shoulders and his expertise with the bow. The princess went slowly forward with the nuptial garland in her hands. She placed it over Arjuna's head and, catching his eye, she looked down shyly. He was now her husband and the formal ceremony would soon follow. Drupada looked closely at Arjuna. There was no shame in his daughter marrying a brahmin. But who was he?

With their pride smashed by a brahmin, the monarchs were horrified. They stood up in a body and looked at each other in dismay. "How has Drupada allowed this?" they exclaimed. "Does he have no respect for the royal order? By bestowing his daughter on a brahmin he has simply insulted us. How can it be tolerated?"

Seeing the kings rising up in anger, Yudhisthira began making his way out of the stadium, followed by his brothers and Draupadi. The kings were shouting and arguing among themselves. Some suggested they attack Arjuna, but others declined, saying that a brahmin should never be assaulted. Drupada was the real culprit, they argued. On account of his disrespect for them he deserved to be killed.

With weapons at the ready the kings advanced menacingly toward Drupada. Seeing this Yudhisthira quickly turned to Bhima and Arjuna and said, "Drupada is now our father and worthy of our protection. You two should check these belligerent kings, even as the shore checks the ocean."

The two princes ran back into the arena. Arjuna took up the bow with which he had struck the target and called out a challenge to the kings. By his side stood Bhima, who had pulled up and stripped a tree and was brandishing it like a colossal club. The kings looked at them in surprise. What kind of brahmins were these?

Krishna had remained unmoved as the kings advanced against Drupada. Seeing the two Pandavas in the arena he said to Balarama, "These two are undoubtedly Bhima and Arjuna. Only Bhima could have uprooted that tree, and who but Arjuna could have passed Drupada's test?"

Krishna indicated the other Pandavas waiting by the gate. "That one there, a full four cubits tall, with eyes like lotus petals, a fair complexion and prominent features, who bears himself with all humility—that is Yudhisthira. By his side are the handsome sons of the Ashvinis, Nakula and Sahadeva. As sure as I am Vasudeva's son, this is the truth."

Balarama agreed, "How wonderful that our cousins have survived the fire."

The kings had turned to face Bhima and Arjuna. "Although brahmins should not be attacked, if they are aggressors there is no sin in fighting them," some of them declared, raising their weapons.

Drupada quickly had his soldiers provide Arjuna with a sheath of long shafted arrows. Karna, particularly angered that he had been refused the opportunity to compete, stepped forward and shouted, "O brahmin, stand ready to receive my shafts." He sent a stream of arrows at Arjuna, who immediately countered all of them. A fierce exchange took place between the two warriors. Their arrows collided in mid air and fell shattered to the ground. Penetrating Karna's guard, Arjuna stunned him with a cluster of forceful shafts that struck him all over. Karna was astonished to witness Arjuna's speed and power. He stepped up his own attack, letting go many hundreds of silver-winged shafts that filled the air like a flock of birds. He invoked celestial weapons that caused a vast number of arrows to fly from his bow. Arjuna expertly resisted the attack, invoking other weapons to check Karna's. He stood unharmed, laughing at his opponent.

As the duel went on, king Shalya from Madras rushed at Bhima. The powerful monarch caught hold of Bhima's tree and hurled it aside. The two men began grappling in furious hand to hand combat. They resembled a pair of angry elephants contending for a female. They wrestled for some time, throwing each other about and shaking the earth as they stamped around the arena. With his superior strength Bhima gained the advantage. He lifted Shalya above his head and slammed him to the ground, leaving him dazed. The prince did not use his full power on the king, knowing him to be Madri's brother.

All the other kings watched in amazement as the two so-called brahmins exhibited the strength and skill of heroic warriors. Realising that he could not gain the upper hand, Karna lowered his bow and called out to Arjuna, "O brahmin, I am pleased by your prowess. It is without compare. Who are you? Very few warriors could resist my attack. I think only my guru Parasurama, or Indra, or the infallible Vishnu are capable—or perhaps Arjuna, the son of Kunti. Are you by chance any of these?"

Arjuna smiled tightly. "Know me to be a simple brahmin who has become expert in arms by his guru's grace. I am ready to vanquish you in battle. Attack me if you dare."

Karna found it hard to accept that this was an ordinary brahmin. But he knew that a brahmin's power was always to be respected. It would be better to desist from battle. Draupadi was already won and there was nothing left to gain from fighting. Bowing slightly to Arjuna, he turned and walked away.

Duryodhana had looked on in amazement as both Karna and Shalya had been matched in prowess by the two brahmins. Turning to the other kings he said, "These two are no ordinary men. They must surely be either great rishis or heroes from some mighty line of kings. Let us first establish their lineage and then the fight may continue."

Krishna then stepped forward and spoke. "O rulers of the earth, I see no point in any further conflict here. Draupadi has been fairly won in a wonderful fashion by this brahmin. Let us not blight this auspicious occasion by bloodshed—and especially by assaulting brahmins."

Arguing persuasively, Krishna managed to calm down all the kings. One by one they lowered their weapons and made their way out of the arena. Taking their opportunity, Arjuna and Bhima rejoined Yudhisthira at the gate. Along with Draupadi they quickly went back to the potter's hut.

CHAPTER SEVEN

A KINGDOM DIVIDED

Kunti waited alone at the hut for her sons to return. She felt anxious. What if they had been discovered? Duryodhana and his brothers would be at the *swayamvara*. If they saw the Pandavas alive they would certainly try to have them killed. Kunti remembered Vyasadeva's predictions. Surely that illustrious sage could not have been wrong, but the course of destiny was always difficult to fathom. God was the ultimate controller—and no one could know his plan.

Kunti busied herself in preparing her sons' evening meal. As she bustled about the hut, she suddenly heard Arjuna's voice greeting her. "Dear mother, we are back. Come and see the wonderful alms we have got today."

Feeling a surge of relief, Kunti called back, "I am so glad you are safe. Share the alms equally among you."

Arjuna then entered the hut with Yudhisthira. Draupadi came between them and when Kunti saw her she was shocked. "Oh! What have I said?" The Kuru queen felt her religious principles threatened. She valued truth above everything. Even in jest she would not speak a falsehood, but she had said that all her sons should share Draupadi. How was it possible? No woman could have five husbands. She looked anxiously at Yudhisthira.

"Do not worry mother," Yudhisthira replied. "You shall doubtlessly be saved from sin."

Yudhisthira turned to Arjuna, "You have won this maiden and thus you should now take her hand in sacred marriage."

Arjuna looked at his brother in horror. "Please do not cast me onto the path of wicked men. What virtuous man would accept a maiden's hand in the presence of his unmarried elder brother? You should be the one to marry her, not me. After that should come Bhima, and only then myself and finally the twins."

By now the other Pandavas had entered the hut and hearing Arjuna's words they all glanced at Draupadi, who smiled and returned their looks. All five brothers felt their hearts leap and their minds became bewildered. The Panchala princess glowed with beauty and she filled the hut with her natural bodily fragrance. The brothers could hardly take their eyes away from her.

Seeing the condition of his brothers, Yudhisthira feared that Draupadi may cause disunion among them. After reflecting for some moments, he said, "This chaste girl shall become the wife of us all. This is our mother's order and in my view it is what Vyasadeva meant when he told us of her destiny."

The brothers had wondered about the sage's words, but now they understood. All of them beamed with happiness. Draupadi was a prize beyond compare.

At that moment there was a knock on the door and Krishna entered. Seeing Yudhisthira seated on the floor and surrounded by his brothers, like Indra amid the chief gods, he went over and touched his feet. "I am your cousin Krishna. Here too is my brother Balarama."

Krishna and Balarama both offered their respects to Kunti by bowing before her and touching her feet. Yudhisthira was surprised to see them. "How did you find us," he asked.

Krishna smiled. "Fire is easily detected, even when covered. Who other than yourselves could have performed such feats in the *swayamvara*? By good fortune you have escaped the fire in Varanavata, and by good fortune have Duryodhana's evil intentions been thwarted. Be blessed. May you grow in prosperity like a fire in a cave that gradually spreads all around."

The brothers folded their palms and thanked Krishna who said he had best leave at once, before anyone noticed he had come there. Along with Balarama he went furtively out of the hut. After seeing their cousin from Mathura, and hearing his reassuring words, the brothers felt sure they would soon recover their kingdom. Like their mother they all had faith in him as the all-powerful supreme person.

Not far from the hut Dhristyadyumna had observed Krishna and his brother come and go. Curious to know who had won his sister, the

Panchala prince had followed the Pandavas from the stadium. He crept up to the hut and peered through the window. Inside he saw the five brothers and Kunti being served their meal by Draupadi. He watched as she gave equal portions to four of the men, and a huge portion equal to all the others put together to the one who had thrown down Shalya. As they ate, the brothers began to discuss arms and warfare. Dhristyadyumna listened as they spoke in the language of warriors, laughing together as they described the fight at the *swayamvara*, and how they had routed the monarchs.

The Pandavas then lay down to rest. Draupadi smiling in great happiness, lay humbly at their feet, and Kunti at their head. Dhristyadyumna had seen and heard enough. These men were clearly not brahmins. They were certainly great warriors, probably royalty in disguise. Were they the Pandavas? The prince slipped away and went quickly to the palace to inform his father of everything he had seen.

* * *

Drupada sat anxiously in his palace. It had been some hours since his son had gone after the brahmins. Where had they taken his daughter? Why had they not stayed in the city? There still had not been a proper marriage ceremony. The king bit his lips and gazed out from his balcony. Soon, to his relief, he saw Dhristyadyumna hastily approaching. He ran down to greet the prince, immediately quizzing him about Draupadi. "Where is my beloved daughter now? Who was it who won her? Was it indeed a high born brahmin—or perhaps a great warrior from the royal order? Tell me she has not been taken by a low born man. Dear son, my deepest desire is that she has been won by Arjuna. Alas, where now are the Pandavas? Do those heroic men still live?"

Dhristyadyumna spoke with a smile. "Father, I saw those five men take Draupadi with them to a potter's house near the city. There they were greeted by a lady as beautiful as a goddess who I think is their mother. Draupadi was joyfully serving them and took her place at their feet."

As they spoke Drupada and his son made their way into the palace. The prince described how he had heard the five brahmins speaking on martial subjects. "Their voices are deep like thunderclouds and they resemble five effulgent gods. I am sure they belong to the royal order. From the way in which the target was struck down, from the fact that they are five and travelling with their mother, and from their language and appearance, I believe that your desire has been fulfilled. They can only be Kunti and her sons."

Drupada looked up at a painting of Vishnu hanging from the palace wall. He prayed that his son's words were true. The king hardly dared believe that it had been Arjuna who passed the test; but who else could have succeeded?

Drupada looked thoughtful. "When morning comes send our priest to the potter's hut. He should try to ascertain their identities. Meanwhile, have a great feast prepared and ask the brahmins to calculate an auspicious day for the marriage."

Early the next day Drupada's priest went to the Pandavas. Yudhisthira received him with respect. When he was seated in the hut the priest, accepting the brothers as brahmins, said, "O venerable ones, having seen his daughter won in the assembly by a wonderful feat of arms, Drupada's joy is boundless. Still, he is anxious to know who you are. The king believes you may be the Pandavas in disguise. Is this true? His ardent desire has always been that Arjuna would marry his daughter. Has it been fulfilled?"

Yudhisthira turned to his brothers. "Bring water and wash this man's feet. He is Drupada's holy priest and worthy of our respect in every way."

Bhima quickly followed Yudhisthira's instruction, who then said, "O brahmin, the king set a price for winning his daughter. That price has been paid and he therefore has nothing to say about our lineage. All his questions have been answered by the striking down of the target with his bow."

Hearing Yudhisthira's firm rebuttal the priest's eyes opened wide, but Yudhisthira reassured him. "Do not fear, gentle sir. The king's long cherished desire will soon be fulfilled. Could any low born or unqualified man have passed his test? Go back and tell Drupada that he need not grieve."

As the priest was leaving another messenger from the palace arrived to announce that a feast had been prepared in the city. "The king requests that you all attend. He said that a proper wedding ceremony can now be performed, if it so pleases you."

Yudhisthira smiled and nodded in assent. The messenger showed them to a fine golden chariot, and they climbed aboard with their mother and Draupadi. Soon they reached the great white palace in Kampilya where they were led into the hall where the feast was waiting. Headed by Yudhisthira they walked into the great chamber, which was spread with costly rugs and decorated all around with fine paintings. Golden seats furnished with silk had been set out for the feast. Obviously comfortable with their opulent surroundings, the brothers took their places without any hesitation. Well dressed servants immediately attended them and began to lay out gold and silver dishes containing fine food of every description.

After eating their fill, the Pandavas washed their hands and stood up. They saw that tables were set out along the walls. Some were spread with paraphernalia used by brahmins in sacrifices, others held items used by traders and merchants, while on other tables there were weapons and armour.

The brothers immediately went over to the weapons and began examining them with interest. Obsrving this and noting their lion-like gait as they strode across the chamber, as well as their powerfully built bodies, the king felt joyful. There was no doubt that these men were warriors of the royal order. Drupada walked up to them and, with a broad smile, asked, "Are we to know you as warriors or brahmins? Or are you perhaps celestials disguised as brahmins who have come to win my daughter's hand? Truth is the highest virtue, dear sirs. Please therefore settle my doubts."

Yudhisthira looked the king in the eye. "O Panchala monarch, be of good cheer. Your desire has been fulfilled. Know us to be *kshatriyas*, warriors of the royal order. We are the sons of the illustrious Pandu. I am Yudhisthira, this one is Bhima, he who won your daughter by a stupendous feat of archery is Arjuna, and these two here are the twins Nakula and Sahadeva. The lady who accompanied Draupadi to the inner chambers is our mother Kunti. O king, like a lotus flower transplanted from one clear lake to another, your chaste daughter has gone from one royal house to another. You are now our revered father-in-law and our guru. I speak the truth."

Drupada was unable to reply for some moments. Tears flowed from his eyes and his limbs trembled with ecstatic emotion. Suppressing his joy with difficulty, he finally said, "What greater good fortune could there be? Hearing about the fire we had feared the worst. Now we see that our prayers have been answered. Tell me, great hero, how you escaped from Varanavata."

Yudhisthira explained everything in detail. Drupada angrily censured Dhritarastra. "How could the blind king allow this?" He assured the Pandavas that they could live with him for as long as necessary. Looking at Arjuna he then said, "Let this mighty hero take Draupadi's hand with all due rites. Today is an auspicious day."

Yudhisthira replied, "O king, as the eldest brother I must marry first."

"Then you should take her hand or let her be given to any of you whom you deem fit." The king surveyed the five brothers. Each of them was equal to Indra himself.

Yudhisthira shook his head. "Draupadi shall not marry any one of us. She shall be the wife of us all."

Drupada caught his breath. He took a step back. "Is this consistent with virtue? O descendant of Bharata, I have never heard of a woman having five husbands."

Yudhisthira spoke reassuringly. "I have considered this carefully, O king. My mind always turns from sin and I find no fault in Draupadi's becoming the joint wife of us all. Our mother the sinless Kunti also approves. You have nothing to fear. It is certainly in line with virtue."

Drupada was still doubtful. "Pray forgive me, but I would like further consultation on the matter. Let us speak with learned brahmins and decide what should be done. Tomorrow I will do whatever is proper."

As the discussions took place Vyasadeva arrived at the palace. Seeing the effulgent rishi, everyone stood up and then bowed before him. Holding up his hand in blessing, he acknowledged everyone present and took his seat.

Drupada immediately asked him about Yudhisthira's proposal and the sage replied, "I have come here specifically to clear up this doubt. In my opinion there will be no sin in your daughter accepting the five brothers as her husbands. I shall explain why."

Vyasadeva asked to speak alone with Drupada. They went into the king's chambers and the sage began to narrate an ancient history. He described how the five Pandavas had all been powerful gods in their previous lives. They were destined to marry an incarnation of the goddess Laxmi, and Draupadi was that incarnation. She had also been blessed by the great god Shiva that she would have five husbands. "There cannot be any fault in the acts of such gods," concluded Vyasadeva. "Therefore, permit your daughter to marry the Pandavas."

Drupada felt his doubts dispelled by the all-knowing rishi. He cheerfully agreed and arranged for the ceremony at once. The palace was decorated with countless flower garlands and adorned everywhere with precious stones. Troops in spotless armour lined the courtyard as the sacred fire was kindled by Dhaumya. Sacred mantras were melodiously chanted to the accompaniment of music and the people cheered as the Pandavas, now again adorned with the resplendent dress of the royal order, accepted Draupadi's hand. On five consecutive days she married each of the brothers amid much celebration throughout the city.

Krishna, hearing of the occasion, sent vast amounts of wealth as wedding gifts for the brothers. Gold, jewels, costly robes, soft blankets and skins, horses, elephants, chariots and all sorts of other valuable items arrived from Mathura. Wishing to please Krishna, Yudhisthira accepted all those presents and sent a message of thanks to him.

Feeling great happiness, the five brothers and their wife and mother began to live comfortably in Kampilya.

* * *

News of the Pandavas survival soon travelled around the world. Learning of the Kurus' treachery toward the brothers, many kings censured Dhritarastra and the other Kuru leaders. Why could they not show any love to those virtuous heroes?

Spies brought the news to Duryodhana even as he was still travelling back to Hastinapura. He struck his head in disbelief and horror. How had they survived the fire? They seemed to lead charmed lives. Not only had they evaded death, but now they had even become stronger by forming an alliance with the powerful Drupada. Duryodhana cursed Purochana. "The fool! At least he was killed."

Dushasana criticised Arjuna. "He cheated in the test by disguising himself. If he had revealed his identity he would never have succeeded, for we would have captured him. Surely destiny is supreme and man's endeavours useless."

Duryodhana pressed his fingers against his forehead. "We have cause for concern now, dear brother. Our cousins have mighty warriors on their side. We have already witnessed Drupada's might, and his son Dhristadyumna is predicted to be Drona's slayer. We need to speak to Father." Entering the city, the Kauravas hastily made their way to the palace.

Elsewhere in Hastinapura feelings were different. Bhishma and Vidura rejoiced when they heard the news. Vidura went at once to Dhritarastra and said, "O king, by good fortune the Kurus are prospering."

The blind king sat up. Duryodhana must have succeeded in winning Draupadi. How wonderful! He exclaimed, "What good luck!" He called out to his servant, "Have ornaments made for the Panchala princess. Use the very finest jewels."

The king reached out for Vidura's hand. "Bring Duryodhana and Draupadi before me in great pomp. This is indeed a joyous day."

Vidura laughed. "My dear king, you do not understand. The princess has been won by Arjuna. He and his brothers survived the fire and are now in Kampilya."

Appearing even more delighted, Dhritarastra sat back in his throne and clapped his hands. "Oh, what good tidings! Pandu's sons are dearer to me than they were even to him. This news fills me with joy."

Vidura looked intently at his blind brother and said, "May this feeling stay with you for a hundred summers."

As they were speaking, Duryodhana and Karna had entered the room. They smiled at Vidura and bowed their heads slightly. They greeted the king but stayed silent until Vidura left. When Duryodhana was sure he was out of earshot, he said to the king, "Father, how is it that you are joyful to hear of our enemies' success? O best of men, their good fortune is our great danger. We should act quickly to ensure that we are not soon swallowed up by them, along with our wealth and followers."

Dhritarastra reached out for his son's hand. "My desires are the same as yours, dear child. I did not want to reveal such feelings to Vidura. Tell me, what is your plan?"

Duryodhana glanced at Karna with a smile. "Here is what I think we should do: Let us immediately send trusted and skilful brahmins to Kampilya who can sow seeds of dissent among the five brothers. This will foment a quarrel between Kunti's and Madri's sons. Or let us offer vast wealth to Drupada so that he will abandon the Pandavas and come to our side. Or we could incite Draupadi against her husbands—that cannot be difficult with a woman who has five husbands. Perhaps we could even tempt the Pandavas with beautiful women, causing Draupadi to spurn them."

Duryodhana became enlivened as he went on suggesting his ideas. As he spoke he slashed at the air with an imaginary sword. "If we can somehow have Bhima killed then our problems are solved. Without him the Pandavas are nothing. There must be some spies who could find a way to eliminate him."

Duryodhana cackled at the thought of Bhima's death. He went on, "If all else fails we could just have them brought back here and then use our immense resources and power to wipe them out. Who could check us? What do you think, Karna?"

Duryodhana turned to his friend, who was shaking his head. He said, "I do not think your ideas are well considered, my friend. No intrigue will work against the Pandavas, nor any machinations or treachery. You have already tried this without success, even when they were young boys without a friend or ally. Then they were living right here in the city. Now they are grown up, powerful, living at a distance, and allied with the mighty Drupada."

Karna went on dismissing Duryodhana's other proposals. In his view there was no chance of creating disunion among the five brothers— they were like one person. As for Draupadi, she had accepted them when they were in poverty and near exile; how would she reject them now? "She has five powerful husbands, what more could she desire? And her father is virtuous and truthful. He will not forsake his sons-in-law for the sake of wealth."

Karna strode back and forth as he spoke. He stopped in front of Dhritarastra, his hands on his hips. "Here is my idea, great monarch.

Gather your army and order it to march on Kampilya now. With Duryodhana and I at their head your vastly superior forces will soon crush the Pandavas and Drupada. Forget any more trickery. Only prowess can succeed here. It must be done soon, before Krishna can come with the fearsome Yadava hosts to support his cousins. If that happens, we will face a difficult task. Let us display our strength now. After killing your enemies, you will rule this wide world as its undisputed emperor."

Dhritarastra praised Karna. "You are a mighty hero, without doubt. Only one of your great prowess could speak thus. Still, before I can undertake any such move I must consult Bhishma and the other Kurus. We cannot possibly enter into open hostilies with powerful foes without their support."

Karna's head fell. He looked across at Duryodhana who grimaced. Neither Bhishma nor Drona would ever agree to attack the Pandavas. He tried to argue, but Dhritarastra was firm. He would call an assembly to discuss what should be done.

When all the leading Kurus were seated in the hall looking like so many gods, the blind king told them what Karna had suggested. Bhishma immediately got to his feet. Tears flowed from his eyes as he spoke. "Pandu's sons are our own. They are as dear to me as your sons, O king, and equally deserving of our protection. I can never agree to a fight with them. We should make a treaty with them and hand over half the kingdom. This is the only virtuous course. If they have no claim to the kingdom, neither do the Kauravas. In fact, the truth is that because their father Pandu had first claim to the throne they are its rightful heirs."

Bhishma paused and looked around the assembly. No one could argue. They all remained silent as he continued to make it clear that there should be no delay in restoring the Pandavas to their rightful position. "Otherwise sin and degradation will be our lot. Since I heard they had perished in the fire I could not face any living being. Their survival exonerates our house from a terrible stain. By God's grace our reputation is saved. Let us not forfeit that grace. Embrace the Pandavas. Do not confront them in battle. They are virtuous and they are united. Not even Indra, king of the gods, could deprive them of their paternal kingdom by force."

Drona then stood up and added, "A true friend when consulted will always speak the truth, whether or not it is agreeable. O king, I share Bhishma's opinion. Pandu's sons should be given their kingdom. This is eternal virtue."

Drona suggested that messengers be sent at once to Kampilya, bearing many valuable gifts for the Pandavas and Drupada. "Your own sons should go. They should bring the Pandavas back to Hastinapura. Receive them with love, O king, for they are just like your sons."

Hearing this Karna's face darkened. He jumped to his feet, gesturing toward Bhishma and Drona. "These two are not to be trusted. O king, although maintained by you they show no gratitude. Siding with the enemy, they speak as if they were your friends. You should certainly ignore their advice."

Drona laughed. "You are a wicked man, Karna. Your desire is simply to harm the Pandavas. My advice was meant only for the Kurus' welfare. If it is ignored, then in my view the Kuru house will be destroyed."

Karna snorted and started to reply, but Vidura stood up and silenced him by raising his hand. The Kuru prime minister then said to Dhritarastra, "My lord, you should pay heed to Bhishma and Drona. Even after careful consideration I cannot think of a better friend than these two. They are equally disposed to both the Kauravas and Pandavas. They are wise and learned in all scriptures. Their words are meant only for your good. Those who disagree with them, seeking to excite your attachment for your sons, offer advice fraught with evil."

Vidura looked across at Duryodhana as he went on. "Who but one cursed by the gods would try to achieve through war that which can be had by peaceful means? The Pandavas can never be vanquished in battle. They are equal to the celestials and have on their side the all-powerful Krishna. Know for certain that wherever there is Krishna there will be victory."

A murmur of approval came from the assembly as Vidura spoke. Only Duryodhana, Karna and Dushasana disapproved, turning their heads away from Vidura and scowling.

Everyone looked at Dhritarastra. The blind king stayed silent for some moments, then said, "In my view Bhishma, Drona and Vidura have spoken the truth. There is no doubt that those great heroes, the Pandavas, are as much my sons as they are Pandu's. Their survival has removed my great grief. It is fortunate indeed that they and their mother are alive, and that Purochana is dead. Fortunate too is their alliance with Drupada. O Vidura, go to Kampilya and bring them here. They are certainly entitled to the kingdom, no less than my own sons."

The king dismissed the assembly. His decision was final. Duryodhana and his brothers stormed out of the hall, striding across the wide mosaic floor with their silk robes flowing behind them. As everyone dispersed, Vidura helped the king down from his throne and led him toward his chambers.

* * *

The next morning Vidura left for Kampilya. He carried with him numerous jewels and all kinds of other riches. Accompanied by a division of soldiers, he travelled along the forest paths to Drupada's kingdom. Vidura had heard that Krishna was in Kampilya to visit the Pandavas. The Kuru minister felt excited at the prospect of seeing him. Many times he had heard from the rishis about Krishna's divine identity. He had no doubt that Krishna was God, come to the earth for his own inscrutable purposes.

After a three day journey he saw the tall buildings of Kampilya in the distance. With the sun reflecting from its golden temple domes, the city resembled a great cloud pierced by lightning bolts. When he reached the outskirts of the city, messengers ran to inform Drupada. The Panchala king personally came out with the Pandavas to greet him. They received Vidura with affection and respect, worshipping him with offerings of *arghya*, and the Kuru minister presented them with all the valuable gifts from Hastinapura.

When at last they were all seated in Drupada's chambers, Vidura said, "Great king, Dhritarastra sends you his warmest greetings. He and all his ministers were overjoyed to hear about our alliance with you. Every one of them, and indeed all Hastinapura's citizens, long to see Pandu's sons again. They also very much desire to see the virtuous Queen Kunti and the divine Draupadi. Kindly permit them to come back with me."

Drupada smiled and nodded. "O greatly learned man, I too am pleased by our alliance. It is proper for the princes to now return to their ancestral kingdom, but it is not my position to order it. Here is Krishna, the greatest authority. If he permits, and if Yudhisthira and his brothers so desire, then they may go."

Drupada was unsure what kind of reception awaited the Pandavas in Hastinapura. If it was anything like the treatment they had so far received, they had best keep away. But Krishna would surely know what was right. Drupada looked over at him. Vidura followed his gaze, seeing Krishna for the first time. He was struck by the Yadu prince's beauty. Krishna's complexion was blackish, framed by curling black locks of hair. He wore yellow silks with many golden ornaments. Catching Vidura's eye, he smiled and nodded in greeting. He then turned toward Yudhisthira, gesturing for him to speak, and the Pandava said, "My dear Krishna, we depend fully on you and shall gladly do whatever you consider right."

Krishna, who sat next to Drupada on a tall seat encrusted with gems, said, "In my opinion they should go. My dear king, you are the eldest and most learned man here, tell us what you think."

Drupada agreed with Krishna. "There can be no better well-wisher of the Pandavas than you, O Krishna. Your decision will certainly be in their best interests. Let preparations be made for their departure in the morning."

After saying fond farewells to Drupada, the Pandavas mounted a great golden chariot with Draupadi and left the city, headed by Vidura and the soldiers from Hastinapura. The king and his wife followed them on foot. They shed tears and called out, "Our dear daughter, dear Draupadi, go now with God and serve your husbands well."

Krishna accompanied the princes on his own splendid chariot and a contingent of powerful warriors marched behind him. The procession went out of Kampilya like a line of celestials leaving Indra's capital Amaravati.

When they entered Hastinapura they saw citizens lining the streets. The people crowded around the Pandavas, joyfully greeting them. "Welcome back! Today king Pandu has returned to life."

Brahmins blessed them as they went by. "If we have ever performed any religious acts then let the Pandavas live in our city for one hundred years."

The people bowed their heads to the ground as Krishna passed. They threw flower petals and rice grains on the ground and wealthy people threw gems from the balconies of their houses.

Standing on the terrace of their chariot, the Pandavas waved at the citizens. The brothers wept with joy to see their city again. Dhritarastra sent out Drona, Kripa and other important ministers to meet the procession on the road. They escorted the Pandavas and Krishna to the great palace assigned to them by Dhritarastra, informing them that there would be a royal assembly the following morning. The king would then make his decision about the kingdom.

The next day the Pandavas took their places in the vast assembly hall. Krishna was given a seat of honour near the king and he sat comfortably, seeming to light up the hall with his bodily effulgence. When everyone was settled, Dhritarastra spoke. "Surely we are favoured by the gods to have Pandu's sons with us again. So that no further dispute may arise between them and the Kauravas, I wish to divide the kingdom into two parts. Yudhisthira, dear child, go to Khandava. This shall be your half of the kingdom."

The assembly remained silent after the king had spoken. Bhishma and Vidura looked at one another. Dhritarastra had certainly given half the kingdom, Khandava was a huge area of land, but it was completely unoccupied. Cursed long ago by a rishi, it had been abandoned and now consisted of nothing more than jungle and desert.

Yudhisthira was not concerned. He was happy to accept any settlement if it would mean peace. The Pandava had seen Krishna smile when he heard the name of Khandava. He would know what to do. Furthermore, Dhritarastra was the ruling monarch and as such his decisions represented the will of the Almighty. Yudhisthira would never question his order. Folding his palms, he said, "It shall be as you desire, my lord. We shall leave tomorrow."

The next morning Dhritarastra crowned Yudhisthira as king of Khandava. Vyasadeva performed the rituals, and when it was time for the Pandavas to depart, he went with them. Krishna also accompanied the brothers. Reaching the vast Khandava region, he asked Vyasadeva to select an auspicious site to establish a city. Krishna then summoned Indra. When the deity appeared, shining like the sun, Krishna said,

"Great king of the gods, sprinkle your heavenly nectar on this land. Make it rich and fertile. Then construct a celestial city for the Pandavas."

Indra set about the task. He called for the heavenly architect Vishvakarma to begin building the city. Soon many great mansions were standing along the sides of broad highways. Tall palaces of white marble rose up from the centre of the city. There were beautiful gardens and orchards everywhere. The god built hundreds of temples dedicated to Vishnu and the principal deities. Vast granite walls surrounded the city, with a wide moat all around them. By the power of Indra's nectar, the surrounding country became green and fertile. Delightful woods filled with blossoming and fragrant trees spread out around the city. Within those woods were lakes filled with lotuses and frequented by swans, ducks and cranes.

The Pandavas took up their residence in the central palace, which resembled the heavenly Mount Meru, abode of the gods. The city soon attracted many thousands of saintly brahmins, who began to live in houses built for them around the royal quarters. People from all the other orders also came in great numbers to populate the city, which became known as Indraprastha.

Out of friendship for the Pandavas, Krishna remained in the city for some weeks. He and Arjuna were especially close and they spent much time together. Draupadi also took every opportunity to serve Krishna, thereby obliging him to her.

CHAPTER EIGHT

THE CELESTIAL HALL

Some time after moving to Indraprastha, the Pandavas were visited by the celestial sage Narada. He was served by Draupadi and seeing her divine beauty he feared that dissension might arise among the five brothers. He told them an ancient history about two Asuras, celestial demons, who had come to blows over a woman. Although they had been inseparable and devoted to one another, out of envy they had finally killed each other in a terrible fight. Narada cautioned the Pandavas. "Do not let this happen to you. Establish a rule concerning Draupadi so that no disagreement may arise."

The brothers then reached an agreement. They would each have a certain amount of time with Draupadi. If any of them intruded upon another who was alone with Draupadi there would be a severe consequence; the offender would have to go to the forest for one year, having no contact with Draupadi during that time.

As time went by Indraprastha became famous even among the gods. They saw how the virtuous rule of the Pandavas kept all the citizens on the path of piety. Always guided by the brahmins, Yudhisthira ensured that all his people were cared for in every respect. His kingdom flourished and many other kings accepted his leadership.

Draupadi served her five husbands with unswerving devotion. According to their agreement they each had their allotted time with her. One day it so happened that it was Yudhisthira's turn. As he sat alone in his rooms with Draupadi, a brahmin came to the palace in distress. He cried out to Yudhisthira, "O king, king! Save me! Wicked robbers have taken my cows. Do not allow virtue to be destroyed in this way. It is always the king's duty to protect his citizens."

Yudhisthira did not hear the brahmin's cries, but Arjuna heard them and immediately called out, "Fear not, gentle brahmin. I shall quickly apprehend the robbers."

When he ran to fetch his weapons, he discovered that Yudhisthira was alone with Draupadi in the room where they were kept. He hesitated at the door. How could he break the rule? But if he did not catch the thieves then Yudhisthira's virtuous reputation would be marred. People would censure the king for failing to protect a brahmin. Arjuna winced at that thought. If he entered the room it would simply mean that he would have to go to the forest for a year, but Yudhisthira's reputation would be saved. Even if he died there it would be better than allowing sin and calumny to touch his brother.

Arjuna knocked hard on the door and entered. Looking straight ahead of him he went toward the weapons. Yudhisthira sat up in surprise and greeted him warmly. Saying he would explain later, Arjuna quickly took his weapons and went after the robbers. Before long he caught them and recovered the brahmin's cows. He then returned to the city and went before Yudhisthira. Bowing at his feet, he told him why he had entered his room, then said, "Permit me now to go to the forest, in accord with our agreement."

Yudhisthira raised his hands. "Why? You have not committed any sin. You were simply wishing to uphold virtue. Do not go."

Arjuna was firm. "You have often told me that virtue should be practised without quibbling. I must adhere to truth, for it is my greatest strength. The agreement was broken, and I must go."

Tears fell from Yudhisthira's eyes, but he could make no argument. His brother was right. The Pandava king nodded in assent and Arjuna immediately left to prepare for his departure. Soon he was ready and, watched by his sorrowful brothers, he walked out of the city followed by many ascetic brahmins who took the opportunity to go on a pilgrimage with him. On Yudhisthira's order many servants also accompanied him, bearing wealth to distribute in charity to the rishis he met on his way.

Arjuna decided to follow the coastline, visiting all the many holy places that lay along that route. Eventually he came to Krishna's own city Dwaraka, which lay on the western coast, where he stayed for some while. With Krishna's assistance he was able to win the hand of

Subhadra, Krishna's exquisitely beautiful sister. At the end of the year he returned to Indraprastha, taking the princess with him. His delighted brothers surrounded him as he entered the city. They congratulated him on winning Subhadra and listened in wonder as he told them about his adventures during his travels.

A few days after Arjuna's return, Krishna and Balarama came to Hastinapura. They were accompanied by the leading personalities from Dwaraka. They entered the city in state, admiring its wondrous architecture. Indraprastha appeared like a jewel among cities. The streets were washed spotlessly clean and sprinkled with perfumed water. Tall white mansions stood on all sides, adorned with garlands of wildflowers and decked with rows of brightly coloured flags. As the procession from Dwaraka passed by, wealthy men threw sparkling gems on the road. Thousands of conchshells were blown and brahmins chanted auspicious hymns, praising Krishna and his associates.

The Pandavas greeted their guests with respect and love. Yudhisthira had them housed in his own magnificent palace. Krishna and Balarama then presented him with the wealth they had brought as Subhadra's dowry. Heaps of gold bricks were laid out, along with countless precious stones and many costly rugs and blankets. The two Yadu chiefs also gave thousands of cows decorated with gold ornaments, a thousand horses white as the moon, a thousand mules and a thousand first class war chariots. They had also brought a thousand great elephants, each raised on the sea beach and resembling a hill, decked with bells and ornaments. The wealth presented to the Pandavas looked like a sea stretching in all directions.

Yudhisthira graciously received the gifts. He and his brothers spent many days with the Yadus, sporting and talking together in great happiness. Finally, the Yadus returned to Dwaraka, but Krishna decided to stay on a little longer. He wanted to spend more time with Arjuna. The two friends went on hunting trips together in the forest surrounding Indraprastha, laughing and joking together as they tracked the wild animals that posed a threat to the rishis who lived in the forest.

On one particularly hot day they were sitting together in the shade of a large banyan tree when, to their surprise, a strange looking brahmin emerged from the woods. He had a copper-coloured complexion with bright yellow hair and beard. His reddish eyes were like lotus petals and his body was powerful and well-formed.

Seeing this brahmin, who shone like fire, Krishna and Arjuna immediately stood up in respect and folded their palms. "What can we do for you?" Krishna asked.

"I know you two to be the best of men," the brahmin replied in a resonant voice. "I have come to beg my food. However, I am not an ordinary brahmin. Know me to be Agni, god of fire. I wish to eat this entire forest in which we stand. Please assist me."

The god explained that he had made numerous attempts to consume the forest, but it was protected by Indra. "There is a Naga living here who is Indra's friend. Each time I blaze up to swallow this wood Indra sends down torrents of rain. Only you two can prevent him. I must eat this forest, for it contains many medicinal herbs."

Agni told them how he had become ill after consuming too much ghee in a great sacrifice performed by king Swetaki, an ancestor of Arjuna. Eating the forest herbs would cure him. The great creator, Brahma, had told Agni that he should ask Arjuna and Krishna to help him. "These two were formerly Nara and Narayana, the divine rishis," said Brahma. "Now they have appeared on earth to accomplish the gods' purposes. Therefore, ask for their help."

Arjuna folded his palms and addressed the god. "I would surely like to help you, and indeed I possess many powerful weapons with which I can check even the celestials. However, I have no bow capable of bearing their strength. And even if I had such a bow, I would also need an inexhaustible supply of arrows and a suitable chariot on which to stand as I do battle."

Agni smiled. "It shall be done." He thought of Varuna, god of the nether worlds and the waters. The deity at once appeared and Agni said, "Lord of the deep, please give me the bow and quivers which formerly belonged to king Soma, as well as his ape-bannered chariot. Arjuna needs them in order to achieve great deeds on behalf of the gods."

Varuna was the custodian of all kinds of celestial weapons, which he kept hidden in the ocean depths. He immediately made the chariot and weapons appear, and Agni gave them to Arjuna. The Pandava gazed in wonder at the bow, which Agni said was called the Gandiva. As tall as a man, it shone like a rainbow and was studded with sparkling gems. It was flawless, with no sign of weakness in any of its ornately formed parts. After bowing down to Agni, Arjuna took up the bow and approached the great chariot that Varuna had summoned. It was filled with celestial weapons, including two inexhaustible quivers of arrows. The chariot was yoked to a team of silvery steeds from the land of the Gandharvas. Resembling an evening cloud reflecting the splendour of the sun, it was dazzling and was furnished with a tall golden flagstaff. Its flag bore an image of Hanuman, Rama's famous monkey servant, who emitted fierce cries from atop the staff.

As Arjuna mounted the chariot and donned the suit of celestial armour he found there, Varuna presented a discus weapon to Krishna. "Here is your eternal weapon, Sudarshana," he said, handing him the effulgent disc, which looked like a circle of fire. "Hurled from your hand, this razor-edged weapon can slay any creature within the three worlds. Here too is your club, the Kaumodaki, which is capable of crushing the hordes of Daityas and Danavas."

After giving the two weapons to Krishna, Varuna bowed before him and vanished from the spot. Standing on the chariot encased from head to toe in his armour, Arjuna shone brilliantly. Krishna climbed into the driver's seat and took up the reins, saying he would take control of the chariot for Arjuna. In heroic tones, Arjuna said to Agni, "O great deity, blaze up to your full extent. With Krishna as my charioteer and the Gandiva as my weapon, I am ready to withstand even the entire celestial host."

Agni at once assumed his fiery form and engulfed the forest. Huge flames leapt upward and dense clouds of black smoke spread throughout the sky. The crackling of burning wood was deafening and the air was filled with a choking stench. The lakes and ponds in the vast forest were boiled dry and the rocks glowed white hot.

In the heavens Indra became alarmed. His Naga friend Takshaka was in dire danger. The king of the gods sent massive clouds over the forest which began to thunder and release volumes of water. But the conflagration was so intense that the rain simply turned to steam in the sky. Indra caused even larger clouds to appear, and great columns of water began to douse the flames.

Arjuna invoked the Vayavya wind weapon. He fired it upwards and dispersed all the clouds. Indra's eyes turned red with fury and he summoned many celestial fighters to challenge Arjuna. Thousands of Asuras, Gandharvas, Yakshas and Nagas all appeared in the sky and hurled their weapons at Arjuna.

The Pandava countered their attack with consummate skill. With the Gandiva constantly twanging, he released streams of arrows charged with the force of celestial weapons. By Krishna's expert driving, his chariot wheeled about and evaded the missiles that rained down on him from the sky.

Seeing Arjuna successfully holding off the heavenly army, Indra then appeared personally, accompanied by all the principal gods. Although impressed by his son's power he was determined to show his own superiority.

One by one the deities threw their personal weapons at Arjuna. Yamaraja his death-dealing staff, Surya his dart, Varuna his noose and Indra himself took up his fearsome thunderbolt. Dozens of other gods also released their weapons, but Arjuna stood unmoved on his chariot. With his swift arrows he checked those missiles. So many shafts were fired by Arjuna that they seemed to be leaving his bow in one continuous line. By the strength of his arms and the Gandiva he checked the gods' attack and they praised his prowess.

Then a voice was heard in the sky saying, "Indra, your friend Takshaka is not here. Desist from battle. The burning of this forest and the sinful beings within it has been ordained by fate. You will not be able to overpower Arjuna and Krishna."

Recognising the voice to belong to Brahma, the gods retired from the fight. Agni continued to devour the forest for fifteen days. As it burned, hordes of Rakshasas and other demons rushed out in terror. Arjuna cut them all down with his arrows. Krishna drove the chariot round the forest with such speed that it seemed to be on all sides at once. No demon was able to escape from Arjuna.

Living in the forest was a leader of the Danava race of demons named Maya who had hidden himself underground during the fire. When the flames began to die down he came out and tried to make his escape. Using his powers of illusion, he evaded Arjuna but was seen by Krishna, who raised his discus weapon to kill him. The intelligent demon then ran to Arjuna and fell at his feet, saying, "O hero, I seek your protection."

Bound by his principles, Arjuna could not refuse. He raised his hand to stop Krishna from killing Maya. The demon thanked him with folded palms and said, "You have saved my life, Arjuna. What can I do for you in return?"

"I will not take payment for doing my duty," Arjuna replied at once.

Maya insisted. "You need not see it as payment. Let me just do something to please you."

"O Danava, if you wish to please me then kindly do something for Krishna."

Maya turned expectantly toward Krishna, who said, "There is one thing you can do which will greatly please me. Construct a celestial assembly hall for Yudhisthira in Indraprastha. Let it be the finest hall within this world."

Krishna knew that Maya's building skills were incomparable. He had constructed many wonderful edifices in the netherworlds where the demons resided. Agreeing to Krishna's request, the Danava accompanied him and Arjuna back to Indraprastha. After some thought, he drew a design for the hall and then left for the Himalayas to collect the materials he would need. "I have left there large amounts of celestial gems unknown to this world," he explained. "I will soon fetch these and then begin work."

After Maya had gone, Krishna approached Yudhisthira and asked his permission to leave. The Pandavas were sorrowful at the prospect of his departure. Krishna embraced them with love and said that he would come again before long. He affectionately bade farewell to Kunti, Draupadi and Subhadra. They all fought back their tears as they watched him go, not wanting to cause any inauspiciousness at the moment of his leaving.

As Krishna went out of Indraprastha, the Pandavas accompanied him for some way. Yudhisthira personally took the reins of his chariot, while Arjuna stood fanning him with a golden handled whisk. Bhima held a parasol over his head and the twins walked ahead, clearing a way through the crowds that had assembled to see him off. When at last they parted, the five brothers stood watching the chariot till it was nothing more than a speck in the distance. They then slowly returned to the city, thinking only of their friend from Dwaraka.

* * *

Within a few days Maya returned with thousands of Rakshasas carrying the materials for the hall. As well as the gems he brought with him a great club which he presented to Bhima, and a celestial conchshell known as the Devadatta, which he gave to Arjuna. "This club is equal to a hundred thousand other clubs, and the sound of this conchshell will instil terror in any enemy."

Then, on a day favoured by auspicious stars, the Danava began work. He marked out an area of five thousand square cubits and, using his celestial powers, started construction. It took him over a year. Thousands of golden pillars were erected to support the splendid hall. It resembled a mass of new clouds rising in the sky. Giving off both terrestial and celestial light, it seemed to be on fire. It was spacious, cool, charming and soothing to the mind. Adorned with jewelled walls and gates, it was decorated with countless pictures and heavenly ornaments. With its crystal stairways, golden arches and beautiful ponds, the hall surpassed even the Sudharma hall of the Yadus, which had been brought from the heavens.

Yudhisthira then entered the hall. To invoke auspiciousness, he distributed charity to thousands of brahmins. A festival was declared in the city, with athletes, actors, bards, wrestlers and musicians all displaying their skills. Many ceremonies were performed in which Vishnu and all the gods were worshipped with costly paraphernalia.

When Yudhisthira was sitting in state in the great central hall, many celestial rishis came there from all over the universe. They were given seats of honour and they looked like so many moons lighting up the hall. Foremost among them all was Narada, who was worshipped by Yudhisthira and his brothers with all respect.

After taking his seat next to the Pandavas, Narada inquired from Yudhisthira, "O king, are you properly protecting the people? Is your mind fixed in virtue? Do you pursue life's four aims—religion, profit, pleasure and liberation—each at its proper time?"

Narada questioned the attentive king at length, his questions effectively constituting instructions on the art of kingship. The rishi's wisdom and knowledge were famed throughout the universe. He was also famous as a great servant of Vishnu and he knew the Lord's divine plan. His movements were always arranged to assist that plan. The Pandavas and their whole assembly remained silent as he spoke. Narada explained that the essential duty of a king was to protect all living beings within his jurisdiction, not just by providing them with their material necessities, but also by ensuring that they advanced toward life's goal of spiritual emancipation.

When Narada finished speaking, Yudhisthira replied, "O all knowing sage, you have perfectly described true religion and morality. I shall do all that you have said. My knowledge has increased by your teachings. By the Lord's grace I am endeavouring to do my duty, striving to follow in the footsteps of my noble ancestors, but I do not possess the same ability as them."

Seeing Narada admiring the celestial hall, Yudhisthira asked him if he had seen any to equal it anywhere in the universe. He knew the sage was a frequent visitor to the higher planets of the gods. Narada then began to describe the assembly halls he had seen, starting with that of Indra. In the course of his descriptions he mentioned the names of many of Yudhisthira's forefathers who had ascended to heaven. Yudhisthira heard how his father Pandu was living in the great assembly hall of Yamaraja. Hearing also that the great king Harischandra was dwelling with Indra, Yudhisthira became curious. He asked Narada, "How is it that my father did not attain the abode of the king of gods, as did Harischandra? What pious acts did that king perform which my father did not?"

Narada explained that Harischandra had performed the great Rajasuya sacrifice, which entailed subjugating all other kings and establishing its performer as the world emperor. During its performance vast charity had to be distributed to hundreds of thousands of brahmins. A king who successfully performed this sacrifice, setting the whole world on the path of virtue, became qualified to attain Indra's abode.

Narada then said, "Your father asked me to pass you a message. He desires that you perform the Rajasuya. You will thereby elevate both yourself and him to Indra's heavenly planet."

Both Narada and Pandu knew that the gods wanted Yudhisthira to perform the sacrifice. It was part of a divine plan meant to free the world from demonic influences. Since Pandu's demise evil kings had been growing in power and were exploiting the earth for sinful purposes. Yudhisthira would need to overpower them before he could perform the Rajasuya. Narada understood that Yudhisthira and his brothers were dear to Krishna, who wanted to use them as instruments in his plan to reestablish religion in the world.

The sage concluded, "Consider then the performance of the Rajasuya, O king. But be warned; it will not be easy. Darkly powerful spirits will oppose you. A war may result which will destroy all the world's kings and warriors. Knowing this, do what you feel is best."

Narada said that he would soon be visiting Dwaraka to see Krishna. Fearing that he did not have the power and resources to perform the Rajasuya, Yudhisthira said, "Please ask the infallible Lord to soon come again to Hastinapura. More than ever I need his help and guidance."

Narada assented and then got up from his seat. Along with the other rishis he rose up into the air and vanished.

From his wonderful assembly hall, which was called the Mayasabha, Yudhisthira ruled over Indraprastha with justice and compassion. His virtuous rule attracted the cooperation of the gods, and thus it was seen that his kingdom was not even afflicted by any natural disturbances. The rains fell in proper time and the earth gave forth abundant produce. Men lived to a full age, free from disease and anxiety, and they had everything they desired. Everyone properly followed their religious duties and were devoted to God. No one entertained any hostility toward Yudhisthira and he became famous as Ajatashatru, one without an enemy.

The years passed by as the Pandavas ruled from Indraprastha. Draupadi bore each of them a son, who, like their fathers, grew up like the gods in heaven.

But Yudhisthira was not content. He thought continuously about the Rajasuya. Recognising that it was the desire of the gods, and thus of the Lord himself, he intensely desired its performance. Narada's caution, however, had made him apprehensive and he bided his time. When at last he felt that he had sufficiently established his rule, he decided to go ahead. He called a full assembly to discuss what had to be done. When everyone was present, he said, "I think I must perform the Rajasuya. Although I do not long for dominion over this earth for myself, I wish to carry out the Lord's desire."

Yudhisthira considered that the sacrifice would be an opportunity to establish Krishna's supreme position throughout the world. If everyone recognised Krishna's supremacy and thus worhipped him, their ultimate liberation would be assured. This was the only proper aim for an emperor.

The ministers were all in full agreement. They could think of no better person than Yudhisthira to become emperor. If his virtuous rule could be extended across the earth, it would become exactly like heaven. Dhaumya stood up and spoke in response. "Great king, you are surely fit to perform this sacrifice, which will bestow upon you universal sovereignty. First though you must gain the acquiescence of all other kings."

Yudhisthira at once sent his four brothers in the four directions in order to win over the kings. Those who would not accept his rule would have to be overpowered. The Pandava knew there would be some who would put up a fight. He discussed with his ministers the best way to proceed. Everyone agreed that they should first consult with Krishna. Yudhisthira prayed within his heart. Krishna would certainly understand his desire and Narada would also have informed him. If he wished to come, then he would no doubt soon arrive in Indraprastha.

CHAPTER NINE

VIRTUE ESTABLISHED

News reached Dwaraka about the Pandavas' incomparable hall and increasing opulence. Krishna heard with pleasure how Yudhisthira was righteously ruling his people. Hearing also that Subhadra had given birth to a son named Abhimanyu, Krishna desired to go again to Indraprastha.

Each day Krishna would go to his own assembly hall, the Sudharma, to meet with the citizens. This hall had been constructed for Indra by Vishvakarma, the architect of the gods, and it had been presented to Krishna when he built Dwaraka. It had the special quality of being able to free the people within it from all material suffering. Krishna would enter the hall and bow before king Ugrasena, who ruled over Dwaraka. He would then take his seat on a jewelled throne near the king. Although not the king himself, Krishna was respected as the most important person present. Everyone in Dwaraka accepted his divinity and they saw him as their natural leader, especially after he had personally slain Kamsa, Ugrasena's evil-minded son who had seized the throne of Mathura from his father.

When everyone was settled in the hall they would be entertained by jesters, dancers and musicians. Brahmins would recite Vedic hymns, and the sounds of *mridanga* drums, flutes and bells could be heard throughout the hall. After the various performances, the day's business would commence.

One day a messenger arrived at the hall from a distant country. After being respectfully received, he introduced himself as a king who had escaped from Jarasandha, the ruler of the Magadha province. Jarasandha, in alliance with other kings, had been attacking all his surrounding kingdoms. Defeating the monarchs there, he would capture and imprison them. The messenger explained, "This evil man intends to offer all the captive kings as human sacrifices to the the goddess Kaali. I have therefore come here to seek your shelter and protection. O Krishna, all powerful Lord, please save these kings and end Jarasandha's reign of terror for once and for all."

It was well known that Krishna had fought and defeated Jarasandha many times, but the Magadha king had somehow managed to escape with his life. Jarasandha hated Krishna for having killed his friend Kamsa, who had also been the husband of his two daughters. Taking a vast army, he had marched on Dwaraka repeatedly, but he had always been crushed by Krishna.

Krishna consoled the messenger and offered him a seat in the hall. He turned toward Ugrasena and his ministers to discuss what action they should take, but just as he was about to speak, Narada entered the hall. Everyone in the assembly stood in respect. Narada was given a seat of honour and personally worshipped by Krishna. When the ceremony was complete, Krishna said, "O godly sage, welcome is your presence here. Surely everything is known to you. Please tell us how Yudhisthira is faring. What are his plans?"

Narada smiled. "My Lord, what can be beyond your knowledge? Yet you come to this world and act just like an ordinary man. I can therefore tell you that Yudhisthira is flourishing in every respect. He resembles Indra in Amaravati. Now he desires to perform the Rajasuya and is praying that you will assist him. He has asked that you go soon to Indraprastha."

Krishna thanked Narada for the information. He turned to his chief advisor, Uddhava. "What do you think, wise one? How can we satisfy this distressed king and the pious Yudhisthira?"

Uddhava stood. "I think, O Krishna, that both things can be achieved at once. If you go to Indraprastha you will enable your cousin Yudhisthira to perform the Rajasuya. For this he will have to defeat Jarasandha. Thus, the kings will also be released."

Uddhava cautioned that Jarasandha would not be easy to conquer. "We have intelligence that he has amassed an immense army. To avoid a difficult encounter in which millions will die I suggest that he be challenged to a one-to-one fight. In my view the person to defeat him is Bhima. He should go to Jarasandha disguised as a brahmin and beg a fight from him. Jarasandha is proud of his charitable nature. He never refuses a brahmin's request, and if you go with Bhima I am sure he will be victorious."

The Yadu assembly voiced their approval. They had been considering how to deal with Jarasandha. It could only be a matter of time before he again marched on Dwaraka with yet another army.

Krishna said, "I shall immediately leave for Indraprastha."

He told the messenger to return to the imprisoned kings and reassure them that they would soon be released. After taking permission from Ugrasena, he prepared to depart.

A great procession left Dwaraka the next day. Krishna travelled in state with all the principal Yadus and their wives. Thousands of soldiers went with them, protecting them on all sides. The slowly moving procession resembled the sea rolling onto the shore. When they reached the outskirts of Indraprastha, messengers informed Yudhisthira and he cried out in joy. He ran out of the city with all his brothers to greet the visitors. As the royal musicians played and brahmins chanted hymns, the procession made its way along the crowded city streets.

When all the Yadus had been settled in various palaces, Yudhisthira approached Krishna to ask him about the Rajasuya. Sitting with Krishna on a broad golden couch, Yudhisthira said, "Although I strongly desire to perform this great sacrifice, I am apprehensive. It will not be easy. Do you think I should go ahead? My dear Krishna, your advice is always impartial and full of sublime wisdom. Please tell me your opinion."

Krishna looked round at Yudhisthira and his brothers, who sat surrounding them. It was a warm day and servants fanned them with long-handled peacock feather fans. The sounds of brahmins worshipping in nearby temples drifted in, creating a soothing air of auspiciousness. Raising his hand, which was adorned with brilliant gems, Krishna said, "king Yudhisthira, with your four powerful brothers you are worthy in every way to perform the Rajasuya and become emperor of the earth. I think the chief obstacle will be Jarasandha. That dark-hearted man has formed an almost invincible alliance with other similarly inclined monarchs. His influence is now spread throughout the middle portion of the world and he has designs on the rest. You will need to curb him without delay."

Yudhisthira turned to his brothers. "How shall we deal with Jarasandha?"

Bhima said, "In my view it would be unwise to engage in warfare with this wretch—especially in his own land. Too many lives would be lost. When dealing with a strong enemy one needs to employ cunning strategies. Between Krishna's skilful diplomacy, my strength, and Arjuna's ever victorious nature, I think we can finish the wicked Jarasandha."

Krishna agreed. "Jarasandha must indeed be checked by whatever means possible. He too desires to become emperor. He now has more than eighty kings held captive. When that number reaches one hundred, he will offer them in sacrifice, aiming to establish himself as supreme in this world."

Yudhisthira was still apprehensive. He did not like the idea of sending just three men to face the highly powerful Jarasandha, even if Krishna was among them. Yudhisthira looked over at Krishna. His love for him overpowered any thought of his divinity. The Pandava king voiced his concern. "How can I risk your lives for the sake of my own selfish desires? Bhima and Arjuna are like my two eyes and you are like my mind, dear Krishna. I could not possibly live without you. In my view Jarasandha would be hard to overcome even for Yamaraja, what to speak of ourselves."

Arjuna then spoke, his voice filled with heroic determination. "Why should we cower before Jarasandha? We have energy, strength, weapons, allies and dominions. We belong to a race famous for its valor. What can be achieved by one lacking courage? Our fame and virtue will surely perish if we do not challenge Jarasandha. On the other hand, simply by confronting him, even if we are defeated, both will be enhanced."

Krishna applauded Arjuna. "This is the proper mood for one born in the Bharata race. We should either kill Jarasandha, or being killed by him, ascend to heaven."

Yudhisthira asked Krishna about Jarasandha's history. Krishna described how he had been born in two pieces from the two wives of king Brihadratha. "The king was blessed by a rishi to get a son, and the rishi gave him a charmed mango for his senior wife. The king cut it in two and gave it to both wives, desiring two sons. When he saw the two half-babies he threw them in the forest where a Rakshasa woman named Jara found them. She joined the parts into one baby, who then came to life with a great roar. Jara returned the child to his father, and he was named Jarasandha, 'joined by Jara'.

Krishna said, "Let us leave at once. Jarasandha's time has come. I am sure Bhima will defeat him in single combat."

Yudhisthira relented. "Seeing your determination, Krishna, I consider him as already killed, the imprisoned kings as released, and the Rajasuya completed. What is impossible for one who has you as his guide? Leave with my brothers whenever you wish."

Krishna decided to go at once. On his suggestion the three heroes dressed themselves as brahmins and began to make the journey on foot. They walked for some days, begging their meals as they travelled and sleeping on the ground. At last they reached the Goratha hill, from which they saw in the distance Jarasandha's capital, Girivraja. Sitting amid beautiful parkland and woods, it appeared splendid, with many mansions and palaces.

Pointing toward the city, Krishna said, "This unassailable city is protected on all sides by five hills. Let us enter it now by passing over the largest of them, called Chaityaka, which stands before the main gate."

Krishna led them to the top of the hill, and they began to tear down its peak with their bare hands, hurling down boulders and creating a landslide. They then ran down its slopes with loud shouts. At the bottom of the hill was a great drum made from the skin of a Rakshasa that Jarasandha had slain. When struck it would vibrate for a full month and Jarasandha had it continuously sounded to warn off any potential attackers. Arjuna and Krishna smashed the drum to pieces.

The three of them then clambered over the city wall and made their way toward the king's palace. The guards stood back in surprise as the three apparent brahmins strode along the main highway. Awed by their obvious power, the soldiers made no attempt to check them. Even the palace guards froze in astonishment as they burst in, marching fearlessly into the courtyard where Jarasandha was seated. The king had been warned by his brahmins of fearful omens and was performing a sacrifice to ward off evil. When he saw the three brahmins approaching he hastily rose up and said, "Welcome. Please be seated and accept my worship."

Jarasandha immediately arranged for his visitors to be worshipped with a footbath and various offerings. He also offered them much charity but Krishna held up his hands and refused it, saying, "We cannot accept your charity, O king, but we wish you well. May you soon attain salvation."

Jarasandha looked carefully at his unusual guests. They did not resemble any brahmins he had seen before. Powerfully built and fearless, they bore the traits of *kshatriyas,* princely warriors. Noting the bowstring scars on their forearms he felt sure they must be warriors, but as they had appeared before him as brahmins, he said, "I cannot allow you to see me without giving you something. It is always a king's duty to bestow charity on brahmins."

As Jarasandha spoke his guards came and quietly informed him what his visitors had done before seeing him. The king became even more curious. "I do not think you are brahmins. You bear all the signs of warriors. Why did you enter my city by climbing the wall? This is how enemies enter. Your acts of violence outside the city were also inimical. Who are you? What do you want?"

Krishna replied, "We are here representing one who desires the imperial dignity. It is true that we consider you an enemy. If you will not acquiesce peacefully, accepting our demands, then you shall witness our prowess today."

Jarasandha was surprised. "What have I ever done to you, or indeed anyone else? I always follow my duties as a king. What injury have I done to any living being?"

Krishna smiled and shook his head. "This is not true. You have captured many men and intend to make human sacrifices of them. Even now they are suffering in captivity, persecuted by you. How is this not sinful? If you are virtuous you should release them at once. Otherwise you will have to stand to fight. You offered us charity, but all we desire from you is battle. We shall soon despatch you to Death's abode. Know me to be Krishna, and these two are Bhima and Arjuna."

Jarasandha laughed. "Of course! My old enemy Krishna. So, you have been forced to resort to trickery, having failed to slay me in any other way. I disagree with you that I am sinful. All the kings held by me were first defeated in a fair fight. Their lives are forfeit to me. I will certainly not release them from fear of you. Rather I will fight. Whatever you prefer—troops against troops, one on one, or me against two or even all three of you together."

Krishna laughed. "Your pride will soon be crushed. We ask from you a fight in single combat. Choose any one of us you please."

Jarasandha nodded slowly, carefully eyeing his three antagonists. Finally, he said, "I select Bhima, for only he is a suitable match for me."

Bhima bit his lips and glared at Jarasandha. "I am ready."

The Magadha king had two huge maces brought out and he allowed Bhima to choose one. Then he led him to an arena on the edge of the city. Many citizens followed them and crowded round, eager to watch the fight, which soon began in earnest.

They came together with upraised maces, creating showers of sparks as the weapons collided. Before long the maces were smashed and the combatants fought hand-to-hand. Both men were expert wrestlers and they displayed wonderful moves, dexterously seizing and throwing each other around the arena. First Bhima and then Jarasandha seemed to have the advantage. They roared and smashed each other with their palms and fists, causing great cracking sounds to reverberate around the city. Both greatly enjoyed fighting and they laughed in delight as they grappled together, appreciating each other's strength and skill. They fought throughout the day and when evening came, they retired, agreeing to meet again the next day.

The fight went on for twenty eight days. Neither showed any sign of fatigue. By the twenty-eighth day Bhima began to wonder if it would ever end. They seemed to be equally matched in every respect. Noting this, Krishna thought about how he could help Bhima. There was no question of assisting him in the fight, but he could offer him some useful advice. Taking up a blade of grass, Krishna waited till Bhima was looking at him and then he bifurcated it, throwing the two pieces aside.

Bhima immediately understood Krishna's sign. Of course. Jarasandha had been joined at birth and would surely be weak along the join. When an opportunity came, he threw Jarasandha to the ground and quickly grasped one of his legs, standing on the other one. With a great roar he tore his opponent in two.

The onlooking citizens cried out in sorrow. "Our king is slain!"

Arjuna and Krishna cheered loudly and embraced Bhima. They went with him back into the city and consoled Jarasandha's son, Jayatsena, whom they then installed as king of Magadha. Jayatsena agreed to accept Yudhisthira's rule and said he would attend the Rajasuya. He had the imprisoned kings released and they came to offer their thanks to Krishna and the two Pandavas. Jayatsena then arranged for transport to take them back to Indraprastha.

When they arrived back Krishna went straight to Yudhisthira. He bowed at his feet and said, "O king, by good fortune Jarasandha is slain and your brothers are well."

Yudhisthira joyfully embraced Krishna, who asked for permission to depart, saying he would return when the sacrifice commenced. The Pandavas would first have to gain the compliance of all other kings. Krishna wished them well in that endeavour and then left for Dwaraka.

Yudhisthira spoke with his brothers. It was time for them to make their expeditions. Taking large numbers of troops, Arjuna went to the north, Bhima to the east, Sahadeva to the south, and Nakula to the west. As the brothers spread out from Indraprastha, they encountered hundreds of kings ruling over various provinces. Most monarchs happily acquiesced, aware of Yudhisthira's virtue and remembering fondly theirs or their fathers' previous encounters with the Kuru dynasty. Even Dhritarastra and his sons, seeing the glories of the Kuru house expanding, happily endorsed Yudhisthira. Some kings, however, were averse to Yudhisthira's rule. In those cases, the Pandavas first tried diplomatic means to win them over, but if this failed then a battle would ensue. Some kings, even though not antagonistic to the Pandavas, fought anyway as a matter of pride. Eventually all were subdued by the might of the four brothers and the Kuru armies. No one could stand before them and before long the entire globe was under Yudhisthira's control.

CHAPTER TEN

THE GREAT SACRIFICE

Yudhisthira received news of his brothers' conquests and he began making arrangements for the sacrifice. One by one they returned, bringing with them the vast wealth they had either been given or had won. Yudhisthira's treasury became like a shoreless ocean. It could not be emptied in even a hundred years.

As the time for the sacrifice approached, Krishna came again to Indraprastha. Accompanied by his wives and ministers, he was surrounded by the great Yadu and Vrishni armies. The clatter of their horses' hooves and chariot wheels filled the city. Krishna presented Yudhisthira with still more wealth and the Pandava received him with love. Embracing him warmly, he said, "Dear Krishna, for your sake only has this earth been brought under my control. Indeed, it has been possible only by your favour. By your grace I am now opulent beyond limit. I wish to engage my wealth in the service of the brahmins and in worshipping Vishnu. My Lord, install yourself in the sacrifice. If it is performed by you, I shall be freed from all sin."

Krishna praised Yudhisthira's virtues. "O best of kings, doubtlessly you deserve to become emperor. Let the sacrifice commence, led by the brahmins. Appoint me to some lesser office. I shall obey your commands."

Tears flowed from Yudhisthira's eyes. "When you are here and agreeable to my wish, I consider my success in this endeavour as certain."

When Vyasadeva arrived in Indraprastha he was placed in charge of the sacrifice. He appointed the many priests who were required to tend the six sacrificial fires and chant the sacred mantras. A great compound was marked out on the edge of the city and the altars carefully constructed. Many hundreds of kings arrived in Indraprastha and were accomodated in mansions which Yudhisthira had built especially for the occasion. Brahmins streamed into the city and they were given spacious living quarters, furnished with every desirable thing and attended by many servants.

When the Kurus arrived from Hastinapura, Yudhisthira greeted them personally. He was overjoyed to see Bhishma, Drona, Kripa and all his other beloved elders. He fell at their feet and said, "Everything I own is yours. Indeed, I am your servant. Please guide me."

Bhishma raised Yudhisthira and embraced him. His voice was choked with happiness as he praised the Pandava. All the Kuru elders were highly pleased that he was performing the Rajasuya. Even Dhritarastra, who could not attend, was happy and he had sent word of his approval. After all, the Pandavas were extending the glories of the Kuru dynasty, once more establishing their position as world emperors.

Bhishma said, "This is a fortunate day. Dear child, my heart swells with joy to see your success. We are here today to serve you. Give us some duty and we shall happily carry it out."

In consultation with Vyasadeva, Yudhisthira asked Bhishma and Drona to take charge of organizing the sacrifice. Duryodhana received the countless gifts brought for Yudhisthira. Dushasana took charge of distributing food and Ashvatthama looked after the brahmins. Other important jobs were given to the other senior Kurus. When all the tasks were assigned, Krishna volunteered to wash the brahmins' feet as they arrived. "In this way I shall receive their blessings."

The sacrificial compound was soon crowded with effulgent rishis. They chanted hymns from the Sama Veda and poured offerings into the blazing fires. Chief among them was Narada, who gazed around the arena in wonder. He knew that the divine plan was being enacted. The gods had come in person to witness the sacrifice and were seated on the gold platforms that had been set up around the arena. They saw that many of the kings present were celestial incarnations, and that Krishna, whom they accepted as the Supreme, was also there.

For many days the sacrifice proceeded, with offerings being made to all the chief gods. Tall columns of smoke rose up from the six fires as the ladles of ghee were poured in. Expert priests chanted the mantras, and they were checked by other brahmins who listened carefully to ensure no fault was committed, as that would allow evil forces to sully the sacrifice. Powerful warriors surrounded the compound, equipped with every kind of weapon and fully alert to any possible danger.

When at last the rituals were complete, Yudhisthira was crowned as emperor. The brahmins prepared the juice of the soma plant to offer to the great personalities in attendance. Traditionally the first offering was made to the most important person present, and when the time came Bhishma said to Yudhisthira, "O king, you should select the foremost of all personalities present. Offer him the first worship, then worship the others as they deserve."

Yudhisthira turned to his counsellors. "Whom do you consider fit to receive the first worship?"

There was some uncertainty. Some thought that Brahma, the powerful creator of the universe, should be first. Others suggested Shiva, while some thought it should be Vyasadeva or another of the great rishis. Yudhisthira knew who he wanted to worship, but he did not want to make an independent decision and be accused of favouritism. He turned to Bhishma. "O grandsire, who do you think is most worthy among all the luminaries assembled here?"

Bhishma at once said, "As the sun shines among all luminous objects, so Krishna shines among men. His effulgence, strength, knowledge and prowess are without equal. He should receive the first worship."

Yudhisthira beamed in agreement. He signalled to Sahadeva, who stood up and announced Yudhisthira's decision. He asked the gods and rishis for their endorsement, citing Krishna's glories. "By worshipping Krishna, who is the Lord in the heart of all beings, we will satisfy everyone."

A shout of approval went up from the gods and sages. "Let it be so!" they exclaimed.

Yudhisthira got down from his throne to personally worship Krishna, who said, "Out of my love for you, dear Yudhisthira, and knowing of yours for me, I will happily accept your offerings."

Among the monarchs present was the king of Chedi, Sishupala. He was an avowed enemy of Krishna, particularly hating him because he had kidnapped the beautiful princess Rukmini and married her on the day she was supposed to wed Sishupala himself. When he saw Krishna receiving the first worship, he scowled and jumped to his feet. Waving his arms he exclaimed, "Stop this ridiculous worship at once. Clearly, Bhishma, you lack any discrimination. How on earth can Krishna be the most important person here? He is not even a king. Nor is he the eldest, wisest, or anything else. There are so many others here who are far more worthy of worship than him."

Sishupala turned toward Krishna. "As for you, Krishna, how do you have the nerve to accept the worship? Like a dog that has stolen sacrifical offerings and licks them up in solitude, so do you sit there enjoying this misplaced honour that the ignorant Yudhisthira offers you. He has shown us what kind of man he is today—mean-minded and ill motivated. So too has Bhishma and indeed you yourself. I cannot stay here any longer."

Sishupala began to stride away from the sacrifice. A murmur went up from the assembly, some agreeing with him and others censuring him. Yudhisthira ran after him and tried to reason with him, pointing out how Bhishma was the most learned man in the assembly, and that his decision was supported by the many rishis present. Sishupala was unmoved. He looked round at Bhishma and laughed.

Bhishma described Krishna's transcendental position. There could be no doubt that he alone was worthy of the first worship. Keeping his anger in check, Bhishma said, "Blinded by envy of Krishna, Sishupala cannot understand his actual position. Therefore, he criticises him everywhere and always. The Chedi king is like a foolish child. No heed should be payed to him at all."

Yudhisthira returned to complete the worship as Sishupala watched in dismay. Turning toward the assembled kings he boomed, "How can you sit here and tolerate this madness? Rise up. With me as your leader stand in battle array against the Pandavas."

The kings appeared like an agitated ocean. Most had approved of Krishna's worship, but many had been incited by Sishupala. They began to argue together, slapping their powerful arms and reaching for their weapons.

Seeing his sacrifice about to be spoiled, Yudhisthira became alarmed, but Bhishma reassured him in a loud voice. "Fear not, O best of the Kurus. This Sishupala can rant only while Krishna does not act. Krishna is like a sleeping lion, and the kings who would challenge him are like so many barking dogs. Plainly he desires to take back the energy he has vested in Sishupala. Thus, has Sishupala's intelligence become so perverse. A man on the verge of death will say any foolish thing."

Sishupala exploded at Bhishma. He began to insult him with harsh language, at the same time continuously criticise Krishna, who looked on in silence. Sishupala was his cousin. Krishna recalled how he had made a promise to Sishupala's mother, who had heard a prophesy that Krishna would kill her son. "O blessed lady, I shall spare his life even if he insults me most grievously. Indeed, I shall tolerate one hundred insults from him."

Krishna silently listened to Sishupala's torrent of abuse. The Chedi monarch finally concluded, "I for one will not stand by as this injustice is perpetrated. You are a slave and a wretch, Krishna. No worship should be offered to you. Get up and fight with me. I shall send you, Bhishma and all the Pandavas to Death's abode."

Krishna spoke in a calm voice. "This man is my relative, yet he always wishes me ill. Once he came to Dwaraka while I was away and set light to the city. He killed and captured many citizens, even stealing some of their wives. On another occasion he cunningly disguised himself in order to rape an innocent princess. No virtue is to be found in him. I have promised to tolerate a hundred insults from him. He has gone beyond that number and will now die at my hand."

The assembly reproached Sishupala, who again rebuked Krishna. "Why should I fear one so weak. What harm can you do to me?"

Sushupala pulled out his sword, still hurling abuse at Krishna. In an instant Krishna raised and threw his *chakra* weapon. The brilliant disc streaked toward Sishupala who tried desperately to fend it off with his sword, but it caught him on the neck and severed his head. The slain king fell heavily, like a cliff edge falling onto a beach. Amid gasps of astonishment, a shining light left his body and merged with Krishna. Rain fell from the clear sky and claps of thunder were heard. The assembly was silent. Sishupala's supporters were angered, but out of fear said nothing.

The rishis broke the silence by praising Krishna. "Well done! Well done! This one thoroughly deserved to die. Now, by your grace, before our very eyes he has achieved liberation."

Gradually the assembly became peaceful. Yudhisthira ordered his brothers to perform Sishupala's last rites. Sishupala's son was then installed as the king of Chedi. The Rajasuya was thus brought to a successful conclusion, after which Yudhisthira distributed vast amounts of charity.

Gradually the kings left for their own kingdoms. Yudhisthira begged Krishna to stay on for a few more days and he agreed, sending his party on ahead of him. While in Indraprastha he was personally served by Draupadi and he developed much affection for the Pandava queen. One day he was paring some fruits she had served him when the sharp knife in his hand slipped and cut his finger. Seeing blood flow from the finger, Draupadi quickly tore off a strip of her fine sari and handed it to Krishna. Taking the cloth, Krishna said, "O blessed lady, I will surely repay this gift of yours."

Draupadi looked down modestly and thanked Krishna, who wrapped the piece of silk round his finger and then left the room.

* * *

Duryodhana had decided to remain in Indraprastha for a few days after the Rajasuya. He had been amazed to see the Pandavas' opulence. Burning with envy, he walked around the streets gazing open-mouthed at the hundreds of great palaces and mansions. The prince was especially fascinated by the wonderful assembly hall and he had the royal servants show him around. Shakuni had remained with him and the two men slowly toured the palatial building, stunned by its opulence. They felt as if they had entered Indra's mansion in heaven. The hundreds of rooms within the spacious hall were lit by countless celestial gems inlaid in the marble walls. Golden archways wreathed with fragrant garlands stood alongside crystal lakes. Exquisitely carved statues of gods and goddesses seemed alive, and everywhere the strains of heavenly music could be heard.

Seeing the celestial workmanship, Duryodhana felt his envy increase more and more. He snapped angrily at the servants and strode around with an air of indifference. Gradually he came to the large lake in the centre of the hall. Perfectly still, it was like a sheet of glass and had been designed in such a way as to reflect its marble bottom. It appeared like a continuation of the floor leading up to it, and Duryodhana fell for this illusion. Not noticing that the servants had gone to the sides, he walked straight into the lake, his golden helmet flying off as he plunged in with a loud shout.

The Pandavas were watching from a balcony nearby. Seeing Duryodhana disappear with a great splash, his arms and legs akimbo, Bhima guffawed. Many ladies were also present, and they too laughed out loud, with their hands over their mouths. Without looking up at them, Duryodhana hauled himself out of the lake and stood dripping by its side. Seeing his acute embrassment, Yudhisthira told his brothers not to laugh. He quickly arranged for dry clothes to be brought for Duryodhana. The Kaurava prince was seething. He could hardly bear the humiliation, especially the laughter of Bhima and Draupadi. He was still smarting from his failure to win the Panchala princess in the contest.

After changing his clothes, the prince completed his tour of the hall. Maya's deceptive designs caught him again when he came to an apparently open door which was actually shut. With his head held high he walked straight into it, cracking his head on the clear crystal. He then reached out to open another similar door which was already open, and he stumbled forward, cursing. The servants struggled to contain their laughter as the prince toppled through the door.

Yudhisthira ran up to console him, but Duryodhana simply laughed and stormed off. Krishna told Yudhisthira not to worry—Duryodhana had only got what he deserved. The Kaurava prince then left with Shakuni for Hastinapura, thinking only of revenge.

Krishna also decided to leave at that time. As he bade farewell to the tearful Pandavas, he said, "Cherish your subjects as if they were your own children. Be a refuge to them as a large tree is to the birds."

After Krishna's departure, Yudhisthira approached Vyasadeva and asked him if he felt the Rajasuya had been successful. "I heard previously from Narada that great danger can arise when this sacrifice is performed. Was this averted when Krishna slew Sishupala? Have you seen any other fearful portents?"

Vyasadeva replied that the signs were ominous. "It seems that in thirteen years from now there will arise a war which will destroy the world's warriors. Destiny will make you the cause, through Duryodhana's fault. Dear king, do not grieve for this, for none can surmount the inevitable influence of time. Know that it is God's will."

After blessing Yudhisthira, the sage took his leave and went to the Himalayas to practice asceticism. Alarmed at his words, Yudhisthira said to his brothers, "If I am to be the cause of so much death then perhaps I should end my own life now."

Arjuna replied, "Take heart, brother. The sage has said that it is God's will. Do your duty with a firm mind."

Yudhisthira was thoughtful. "From this day on I shall not make a quarrel with anyone, for that is always the root of war. I shall never use harsh words and shall always practice virtue. Ever obedient to the order of my elders, I will carefully avoid all conflict."

After making this vow, Yudhisthira felt a little more peaceful. No doubt some divine plan was unfolding. Many demonic kings had only reluctantly accepted his rule after being subjugated by his brothers. He had seen how they rose to support Sishupala at the sacrifice. Duryodhana also would not be happy in a subordinate position to the Pandavas—especially after his recent humiliation. It seemed Vyasadeva's words would prove true.

CHAPTER ELEVEN

EVERYTHING IS LOST

As he travelled back to Hastinapura, Duryodhana sat moping. Repeatedly sighing, he gazed distractedly at the passing countryside, hardly noticing the people who stood by the roadside waving at the royal procession. Shakuni touched his shoulder and asked, "What ails you, king? You appear greatly depressed."

Duryodhana turned his vacant eyes toward Shakuni. "My heart is on fire, Uncle. Seeing Yudhisthira's wealth and influence I cannot contain my jealousy. All the world now fears the Pandavas. When Sishupala was so unrightfully killed there were none who had the courage to challenge them. The kings of the world fetched them tributes, acting as if they were tax-paying citizens."

The Kaurava prince took off his jewelled helmet and tossed it on the seat of his chariot. He played with the many rings adorning his fingers. "I feel like ending my life. What man possessed of power could live like this, seeing his foes so prosperous? I will never equal the Pandavas. Nor have I found any way to destroy them. Surely fate is supreme and man's exertions useless."

Duryodhana sat sighing, tears of anguish running down his face. He asked Shakuni to present his plight to Dhritarastra. Shakuni placed an arm round his shoulders. "Why do you envy the Pandavas?" he asked, a slight edge of sarcasm to his voice. "By good fortune they have prospered, winning Draupadi as their wife and conquering the earth. What is there to be sorry about? All your attempts to subdue them have failed. Why then do you lament?"

Duryodhana looked curiously at his uncle. What was his point?

Shakuni smiled. "Dear king, their wealth, the Kuru wealth, can also be yours. You say there are none who have the courage to challenge them, but this is not true. On your side you have many mighty heroes; all your brothers, Drona, Karna, Kripa, Somadatta and so many others. With their assistance you could surely rule the entire world."

Duryodhana looked ahead. Hastinapura was visible in the distance, like a dark cloud on the horizon. Turning back to Shakuni he said, "Perhaps you are right, uncle. Who can defeat us? Let us challenge the Pandavas. By overpowering them we shall ourselves rule the earth and I shall own their wonderful assembly hall, so full of riches."

"No, this is not the best policy," Shakuni replied quickly. "The Pandavas, assisted by Krishna, are inconquerable. Some other means will be needed to dispose of them. Then you may hold sway over the earth." Shakuni fingered the dice he always carried, clicking them together as he spoke. "Indeed, O king, I know just the means."

Duryodhana leaned forward. "Then tell me, uncle. How can we get rid of my enemies for once and for all?"

"I believe that Yudhisthira is fond of dice," Shakuni replied, twisting the end of his dark mustache. "However, he is not so expert at the game."

Duryodhana smiled in understanding. No matter how good Yudhisthira might be at dice, he would be no match for Shakuni. The Gandhara king spent his whole time practicing with other experts at the game. He could make the dice do practically anything he wished. Duryodhana had even heard it said that Shakuni had been blessed by his father that he would never lose at dice. The prince could certainly not recall any instance where that blessing had failed.

"Just challenge him, king, and I shall do the rest," Shakuni continued. "Let me play on your behalf and I will win for you this whole world. Have no doubt."

The chariot had reached the city and the huge gates were swung back. The guards shouted respectful greetings to Duryodhana as he rode past. As the chariot sped along the main highway toward the palace, he suggested to Shakuni that they go at once to Dhritarastra. "Tell him what you have just told me. Let us get his permission."

Shakuni agreed and the two men went straight to the royal chamber, where Dhritarastra was seated alone. After bowing before him, Shakuni said, "Great king, your son is pale and afflicted with grief. If you think it fit, enquire from him as to the cause."

Dhritarastra looked surprised. "Duryodhana, my son, why are you depressed? What possible reason could there be for your sorrow? My vast wealth is at your disposal. Thousands of servants await your command. You have the best food, the best chariots and horses, finely furnished palaces and excellent gardens. Many beautiful damsels are ready to serve you. I think even the celestials do not have more opulence. Why then do you grieve?"

Duryodhana immediately told his father how he envied the Pandavas. Their wealth and influence far exceeded his. The prince described what he had seen in Indraprastha. "Yudhisthira received so much tribute at the Rajasuya that some had to be turned away. There was simply nowhere for it to go. Millions of elephants, horses, cows, and camels were given, as well as heaps of gold and gems piled up like mountains. One hundred thousand brahmins were fed at a sitting during the sacrifice, and this went on continuously."

Duryodhana said his mind had been completely stunned by the opulence he had seen. Even the gods had come to the sacrifice and offered gifts to Yudhisthira. There was now no limit to his wealth. Duryodhana's voice almost choked as he described it to his father.

Dhritarastra remained silent, and Shakuni then said, "I know a way by which we can win all this wealth, king. Challenge Yudhisthira at dice. He will not be able to refuse. Then let me play with him. I will win everything. You may then enjoy this earth without a rival."

Before the king could respond, Duryodhana immediately added, "Father, please grant your permission. Shakuni will not lose."

Dhritarastra pressed his hands together. "Perhaps but let me first consult with Vidura. He always knows what is best."

Duryodhana's face contorted. "You know Vidura favours the Pandavas. How will he agree? Father, I cannot live while my enemies are so prosperous. I would rather kill myself. Then you may live happily with Vidura. What need do you have for me anyway?"

Duryodhana knew he could manipulate his father. The blind king always gave in to him. As he expected, Dhritarastra was moved by his threats and he said, "Alright, I shall convince Vidura. You should order the royal builders to construct a hall equal to Yudhisthira's. Let me know when it is complete, then we shall arrange for the game."

When Duryodhana and Shakuni had left, smiling together, Dhritarastra summoned Vidura. He knew his brother would object to the dice game, but the king still could not do anything without first discussing it with him. When he arrived, Dhritarastra told him what he had in mind.

Vidura immediately protested. "O king, gambling always causes dispute. I cannot approve. You should be careful not to exacerbate the tense relationship that already exists between your sons and the Pandavas."

Dhritarastra held up his hands. "My mind is made up on this, dear brother. Whether right or wrong, the game will go ahead. Everything depends upon fate. If fate favours us, and the gods are with us, then no dispute will arise; and if fate ordains otherwise what can we do?"

Vidura rose from his seat and walked to the window, looking out at the beautiful palace gardens which the king had never seen. "This reasoning is false, king. We cannot deny responsibility for our acts, for we have free will. Surely everything lies in God's hands, but he gives us the consequences of our own acts. It is up to us how we act. Consider carefully why you want this gambling match. If you are acting out of impure motives, then the results will not be auspicious."

Dhritarastra said nothing and Vidura began to walk away, slowly shaking his head. He prayed that the king would see sense, but he was not hopeful. Although not a fool himself, Dhritarastra was virtually controlled by his foolish and covetous son. Disaster loomed. The dark age of Kali was imminent and if the gambling match went ahead it would almost surely usher in that fearful time, for it would lead to the annihilation of the world's rulers. Still, Dhritarastra's words were not entirely false. The Supreme Lord was ultimately controlling everything. If he wished for a great war, then it would happen without doubt. Trying to fathom God's mysterious will, Vidura left the room.

* * *

As the hall in Hastinapura was gradually built, Dhritarastra began to feel apprehensive. Disregarding Vidura's advice was always risky. It was true that gambling was fraught with danger—especially a match between his sons and the Pandavas. A war between them, involving as it would all the world's kings, would be catastrophic.

The king sighed. He would try one more time to change his son's mind. Sitting alone with him, he said, "My son, there is no need for playing dice. Vidura does not approve and I too am highly doubtful. Gambling leads to dissension, bringing in its wake terrible conflict. What need is there for you to gamble anyway? You have everything. A vast kingdom is at your command. What more could you want?"

Duryodhana sat kneading his hands. His father's anxiety was no surprise. Certainly, Vidura would have objected to the proposed match and the king never liked ignoring him. Duryodhana reached out and took his father's hand. His only hope of overcoming the Pandavas was slipping away. The prince spoke in a pitiful voice. "My existence has become wretched. How can I live while our enemies prosper like the gods in heaven? At the sacrifice it was my job to receive the offerings. Day after day I became completely exhausted from handling the gems and jewels that were given as tribute. I had never seen their like before. Our wealth is not a fig by comparison."

Duryodhana described the incidents in the hall when he fell into the lake and walked into the door. "After smashing my head on the solid crystal, I stood with my brains swimming. Those wretched twins then ran up and held me by my arms, saying, 'The door is over here, O king.' I could have died there and then."

Dhritarastra listened silently as his son went on describing the opulence of the Rajasuya. His voice became pleading, "I am practically losing my mind with envy. Is it not the accepted duty of *kshatriyas* to challenge their enemy? If we leave the Pandavas alone they will continue to flourish, eventually consuming us and all our wealth. However, if we challenge them to open warfare then our fate will likely be the same as Sishupala's. A dice game is the safest and surest means."

Dhritarastra spoke gently. "Enmity with the powerful is not sound policy, dear son. Nor do I like harbouring such feelings towards Pandu's sons. It cannot lead to any good. You think you will achieve your ends by gambling but mark my words it will result in a frightful war."

Duryodhana's tone was dismissive. "We are simply arranging for a friendly match. If Yudhisthira chooses to stake his wealth, then how will we be to blame? But believe me, Father, if he does stake he will certainly lose. Shakuni is undefeatable at dice."

"I know I will regret this," said Dhritarastra, rising from his seat. He rang a bell to summon his servants. As they entered the room, he said, "Do as you will, then, son. My doubts remain, for I cannot see how impious deeds will ever yield lasting prosperity, but I shall order Vidura to fetch the Pandavas here."

Duryodhana smiled and punched the air as his father was led out of the room by the servants. The prince went immediately to Shakuni to tell him the good news.

Vidura soon left for Indraprastha, his mind filled with foreboding. As he entered the Pandavas' city he saw that it had become unlimitedly affluent. Passing through jewelled golden arches, he marveled at the prosperity visible everywhere. The citizens, dressed in fine silks and decked with bright ornaments, moved about on shining chariots. Seven-storeyed mansions of diverse designs lined the long and smoothly paved roads, which sparkled with precious stones. Vidura saw teams of elephants, adorned with jewelled mantles, sprinkling the roads with perfumed water. He heard the blast of conches and the sound of bells and drums as brahmins worshipped Vishnu in great ornately carved granite temples. Seeing the Mayasabha from a distance he felt his bodily hair stand on end. It shone like a palace of the gods and emanated an exquisite fragrance. Servants led him in, and he was brought before Yudhisthira, who sat in the central hall surrounded by his brothers and ministers.

Seeing their beloved uncle, all the Pandavas jumped up and bowed at his feet. Overjoyed, Yudhisthira greeted him with tears in his eyes. Vidura embraced him with affection, but Yudhisthira could see that his expression was worried. He asked, "Something seems to be bothering you, Uncle. Do you come in peace? Is everything well in Hastinapura?"

Vidura looked down. "All is well with us, king. I have come here to invite you to see the assembly hall Dhritarastra has just had built. He suggested that you may like to play some dice with your cousins."

Yudhisthira glanced over at his brothers. Seeing this, Vidura said in a low voice, "I think that you understand his intentions well enough."

"Indeed, Uncle, and I know well how gambling produces quarrel and conflict. How then can I consent to play?"

Yudhisthira held his chin. This was a dilemma. On the one hand, how could he refuse Dhritarastra's invitation? He had vowed never to disobey his elders. How too could he ignore the moral code which dictated that a *kshatriya* not refuse any challenge, whether to fight or to play at dice? On the other hand, the game would surely result in disaster. Vyasadeva's words seemed all the more prescient.

Vidura raised his hands in a gesture of helplessness. "I tried to dissuade the king, but he was determined. Duryodhana and Shakuni have convinced him. Even now Shakuni is spending his time practicing dice with highly skilled players in preparation for the game. It is he you will have to face."

"If I am challenged, I can not refuse," Yudhisthira replied. "This is my duty. I am unwilling to gamble, but I will come with you to Hastinapura in obedience to Dhritarastra's desire."

Yudhisthira looked over at his brothers, who all appeared apprehensive, and said, "This whole universe moves by God's will. Bound by duties and obligations as if by a rope we are helplessly carried by fate. We shall leave tomorrow."

The next morning Yudhisthira mounted his blazing chariot along with his brothers and Draupadi. Appearing like the god of wealth leaving his celestial abode, he went out of Indraprastha with brahmins walking before him chanting sacred hymns.

When the party reached Hastinapura that evening they were greeted by the Kuru elders, who led them into Dhritarastra's palace where they rested for the night.

The following morning the five brothers were brought to the new assembly hall. Occupying the same area as the Mayasabha, it was supported by thousands of many-coloured marble pillars worked with gold leaf. Fine, handwoven rugs were laid out along the floor and beautifully carved seats were arranged in the many alcoves. Sunlight streamed in through countless windows and, as they were led in by the Kurus, the Pandavas admired the workmanship, although the building was obviously not the equal of theirs.

The hall was crowded with kings and princes who were visiting Hastinapura. The Pandavas greeted them, bowing before their elders and saluting their peers. They then sat down on fine seats covered with costly cloth and studded with gems. Seated opposite them were

Duryodhana and his brothers, along with Karna and Shakuni. When everyone was settled, Shakuni said, "O king, we have been waiting for you. Let us enjoy some friendly dicing together. Shall we establish the rules before we begin?"

Yudhisthira looked at the grinning Shakuni. "O Gandhara monarch, what virtue is there in gambling? Deceitful play is especially sinful and always avoided by the wise."

Shakuni laughed. "Those skilled in the game need not fear anything. In any event, it is excessive staking that leads to injury, not the game itself. Let the stakes be fixed and we need have no worries."

Yudhisthira shook his head, his face doubtful. "I have been advised by the rishis to avoid gaming with experts. Do not try to take from me the wealth with which I wish to serve the saintly brahmins. For myself I have no desire to win anything at gambling, therefore why should I play?"

Shakuni leaned back with a smile. "I understand. If you are afraid of losing, then we need not play. Obviously, one approaches a contest with a desire to win—that is only natural—but if you feel I am being dishonest in some way then we need not play."

Yudhisthira looked across to the Kuru elders. Dhritarastra sat at their head, hearing everything but seeing nothing. He made no remark. By his side sat Bhishma and Vidura, who both appeared uncomfortable. The whole hall remained silent as Yudhisthira looked around. Turning back to Shakuni he said, "When challenged I never refuse. I shall play, but who is a suitable match for me? Who can stake equally?"

Yudhisthira knew that Shakuni could not match him in staking, and thus could not fairly play against him, even though he may be more skilful at the game. But Duryodhana quickly spoke up. "Let my uncle play. I shall provide him with the stakes. Bet whatever you will, gems, gold or any other wealth."

The Pandavas looked at one another. This was what they had expected. Plainly it was no friendly game. Yudhisthira said, "I have not heard of one man playing while another stakes, but if everyone thinks it is acceptable then let us begin.

Yudhisthira looked again toward the Kuru elders, but still no one spoke. Shakuni took up his bone white dice. "What will you stake, great king?" he asked.

Yudhisthira took from his neck a long golden chain of immaculate pearls. "Here is my first bet."

"It is matched," said Duryodhana, fingering the heavy gold chains that hung round his own neck.

Shakuni closed his eyes and rubbed the dice together, then threw them across the large wooden board that had been set up for the game. "Kaali!" his voice rang out, invoking the Goddess as the dice skittered across the board. As they came to a stop on the desired throw he shouted, "Lo, I have won!"

"You should not be so proud of yourself, Shakuni," murmured Yudhisthira. "This game has been contrived only for my defeat, but it is not yet over. I will now stake my hundreds of thousands of jars of gold, each filled to the brim. Let us see if you win again."

Yudhisthira rarely played dice. He had no real liking for the game. It was a weakness of kings that often caused their destruction. Nevertheless, having accepted the challenge he would not back down. Powerful *kshatriyas* were always fearless, whether in battle or at gambling.

Shakuni looked over at Duryodhana. Yudhisthira had placed an immense stake. Duryodhana smiled and waved his hand. "It is matched again," he said.

Yudhisthira gathered up the dice and rolled them, calling out his intended throw, but they fell differently.

"Unlucky," said Shakuni, as he picked up the dice and made his throw. Again they landed according to his call and he cried out, "I win again!"

Looking pale, Yudhisthira said, "Then I shall stake my priceless celestial chariot, adorned with gems and gold, covered with tiger-skins and yoked to eight milk-white steeds. Make your throw, Shakuni."

Once again Yudhisthira lost, the dice falling as if commanded by Shakuni. The Pandava king seemed to be caught up in the fever of the game. He went on raising the stakes, losing every throw. Gradually he lost all his wealth. All that could be heard was the staking, then the clatter of the dice, followed by Shakuni's shout of, "I win again!"

Duryodhana and his brothers laughed and urged Yudhisthira to keep on playing. "What else will you stake, O emperor?" they taunted. "Your wealth is limitless."

Each time Shakuni shouted, Dhritarastra leaned forward and eagerly asked Vidura, "What has been won?" Vidura felt increasing distress as the game went on. He could hardly tolerate watching Yudhisthira being practically robbed. The Pandava had little chance of beating Shakuni at dice—that was obvious—but no one was protesting, least of all Dhritarastra. Everyone sat silently. Surely all-powerful destiny was moving them according to some higher plan.

Again and again the dice landed exactly according to Shakuni's call. Each time Yudhisthira remained impassive and made another huge stake. Playing with Shakuni's unfamiliar dice, he was unable to win a single throw.

Yudhisthira's brothers writhed in agony as they watched him losing. Bhima was especially suffering. He found Duryodhana's sneering demeanor unbearable. The powerful Pandava squeezed his hands together in frustration. He longed to jump up and challenge Duryodhana to an open fight, but without Yudhisthira's order he could say nothing. Arjuna and the twins also remained still, looking on in horror as their elder brother kept on losing.

Suddenly Vidura jumped to his feet. He could stand it no longer. The game had to be stopped. He spoke out loudly. "O great king, leader of the Kurus, listen to my words, which will be as disagreeable to you as medicine is to a dying man. Even when this sinful wretch Duryodhana was born I warned you that he would destroy our dynasty. That time is close. Act now before it is too late. Have Arjuna kill him at your command. This is the proper course of action. Otherwise you will sink into an ocean of grief. An unworthy son should always be abandoned for the good of the house"

Everyone looked at Vidura. Duryodhana frowned and ground his teeth together in anger, but the blind king said nothing. Vidura continued, "The virtuous Pandavas will provide you with far more happiness than the evil hearted Duryodhana. Purchase those five tigers at the cost of this jackal. Do not be like the king who once possessed a bird that could vomit gold, but out of greed cut it open and killed it."

Vidura further described the benefits of maintaining friendship with the Pandavas but seeing that this was having no effect on Dhritarastra, he began to describe the dangers of forming an enmity with them. "A great fire has blazed forth and you are about to enter it willingly. These five heroes are like enraged serpents with venom in their eyes. Do not provoke them further. When they stand in battle not even the celestials can face them. Driven by your covetous son, you are rushing toward a terrible conflict that will destroy the Kurus to their roots. Who will be your refuge in that hour of confusion?"

Suddenly Duryodhana exploded. Glaring at Vidura, who had never had a good word to say about him, he boomed out, "O Vidura, you are nothing but an enemy in the guise of a friend. You always praise our foes and criticise us. We are foolishly maintaining you, like a man keeping a serpent in his lap. Who do you think you are, offering us such vicious advice? Why do you find fault with me? I am what God has made me. If I am acting wrongly then it is God you should blame, not me, for I am under his control. You simply blather uselessly. Your opinion is not needed here. Go wherever you please. An unchaste wife, however well treated, always forsakes her husband."

Vidura shook his head. Duryodhana's outburst was nothing new, but his sarcastic words about God were particularly painful. The atheistic prince was mocking Vidura's faith. Now he sat looking at Vidura with a smug smile.

Vidura turned again to Dhritarastra. "O king, judge for yourself the merit of your son's words. I am trying only to offer advice meant for your good. Many men can be found who will speak agreeable words, seeking to win their master's favour, but rare are those who will speak disagreeable truths. O descendant of Bharata, act now with intelligence and humility. Cease persecuting the Pandavas and reject your son."

Still Dhritarastra remained silent. Vidura sat down, burying his face in his hands. What would it take for the king to see sense?

Duryodhana laughed and waved at Shakuni, who then said, "So, Yudhisthira, you have lost much wealth. Do you wish to stop now, or do you still have something left to stake?"

Yudhisthira looked steadily at Shakuni. "I have riches counted in the millions, tens of millions, billions and hundreds of billions. Even more. Why do you ask? With all this wealth do I play. Roll the dice."

Shakuni smiled. The dice once more clattered across the board as he made his call. Again, it fell as he desired, and again his laughing voice rang out, "I win!" Yudhisthira staked his land, animals, army, and servants, losing them all. When the entire kingdom was lost, Shakuni looked at him quizzically. "It seems you have lost everything, O king. How shall the game continue?"

Yudhisthira breathed heavily. He had lost every single throw. It was almost inconceivable. Nothing remained of his vast wealth; all of it now belonged to Duryodhana. Had it been willed by God? Was the Lord somehow testing him? Surely, he would not want to see his devotee lose everything. How would he be able to perform his duty as a king, protecting and serving the brahmins? He needed to win something back. What, though, could he stake?

Yudhisthira looked round at his brothers. Perhaps there was still a way back. He turned toward Shakuni. "These princes are also my wealth. With this fair-skinned Nakula then, the mighty-armed and virtuous son of Madri, do I play."

Seconds later Nakula was also lost. Yudhisthira shook his head in disbelief. Things had gone too far, but there could be no turning back now. His voice was strained as he made his next stake. "Here is Madri's other son, the equally powerful Sahadeva, so dear to us all. He should not be gambled, but I shall wager him."

Within moments Shakuni's voice was again ringing out in glee. "Lo, I have won!" He looked at Yudhisthira with a slight smile. "It seems that Bhima and Arjuna are dearer to you than the twins."

Yudhisthira blazed up. "Fool, do not try to create disunion among us, who are all of one heart. The game is not yet over. Here is Arjuna, who is ever energetic and who always takes us to the other shore of the sea of battle. He shall be my next stake."

The hall was completely silent as the dice were thrown again. Duryodhana leaned forward in eager anticipation. Winning Yudhisthira's wealth was one thing but taking possession of his brothers had been beyond his wildest hopes.

As the dice came to a halt Shakuni's monotonous voice was again heard. "I have won! O king, three of your brothers are now lost. Will you stop there?"

Yudhisthira thought of Krishna. What was his plan? It seemed incredible that the Lord could allow even his dear friend Arjuna to be lost. Could things still be turned around? He looked down as he spoke, "Although he does not deserve to be staked, although he is our leader and our shelter, still do I wager this lion-like Bhima, the foremost of all mace fighters and the grinder of foes."

Shakuni closed his eyes and made his throw and a few moments later Bhima was lost. Yudhisthira sat perspiring freely. There was only one thing left for him to do. He could not leave the hall with his four brothers lost into slavery to the Kauravas, which would no doubt be their fate. Taking a deep breath, he said, "I, the eldest of the Pandavas, am still left. Let me be the next stake. If I am lost, I shall do whatever a slave is obliged to do."

The kings watching the game gasped as Yudhisthira spoke. They watched in astonishment as the dice yet again practically obeyed Shakuni's command. "You are lost!" he exclaimed. "Surely an act worthy of a sinful man, for you still had wealth with which to bet. You still have one more stake dear to you. Why do you not bet Draupadi? By her you can win yourself back."

Yudhisthira sat in silent anguish. How could he bet Draupadi? It was his duty to protect her, not deliberately place her in danger. But what choice was left? Everything else was gone. If the Lord was going to save him, it could only be through Draupadi.

"She who is neither short nor tall, who is perfectly formed, who has eyes like lotus petals, who emanates the fragrance of lotuses, who has a wealth of beauty, grace and virtue, and who is possessed of every feminine accomplishment—with her I shall now play."

When Yudhisthira said this his brothers looked at each other in disbelief. The Kuru elders cried out, "Fie! Fie!" Many kings bowed their heads in sorrow, with tears flowing from their eyes. Bhishma, Drona and Kripa were covered with perspiration and Vidura sighed repeatedly, staring in hopeless despair at his blind brother. Dhritarastra leaned forward, eagerly asking, "Is the stake won? Is it won?"

Shakuni was flushed with excitement. By his side Duryodhana, Dushasana and Karna were all laughing loudly as he threw the dice with the inevitable result. His voice resounded through the shocked hall. "She is won! She is won!" He stood up and began to dance around, repeatedly saying in a sneering voice, "What now will you stake, O great emperor?" The griefstricken Yudhisthira sat mute, breathing heavily.

Duryodhana, relishing his moment of victory, turned to Vidura and said, "Come, Uncle, bring Draupadi here. Let that dear wife of the Pandavas be engaged in some menial work."

Vidura could hardly look at Duryodhana. He immediately retorted, "Wicked man, you fool, do you not see that you are standing on the edge of a steep precipice? Deadly snakes are on your head. Do not provoke them further and thus go to Death's abode."

Vidura turned to address Dhritarastra and the rest of the assembly. "In my view Draupadi cannot be lost as Yudhisthira had already lost himself when he bet her. Like a bamboo which bears fruit on the point of its death, this son of Dhritarastra wins treasures at dice, not seeing the frightful terrors that will soon follow. He will certainly cause the Kurus' destruction. When the words of wisdom spoken by friends are ignored, when temptation and lust hold sway, know for sure that a fearful and universal destruction is close."

Duryodhana waved his hand dismissively at Vidura, "Fie on you," he said with a snort. Looking round he saw the chief palace servant and he called out to him, "Pratikamin, bring Draupadi here. There is nothing to fear. It is only Vidura who raves crazily. He never wishes for our success."

The Pandavas sat with their heads bowed. Yudhisthira seemed stupefied with sorrow. He covered his face with his hands. How had he let himself get so carried away? He had gambled away everything, casting his brothers and even Draupadi into slavery. That had been a terrible mistake, but what could he now do? The Kuru elders, with the sole exception of Vidura, were silent. It seemed they did not disapprove of the gambling, nor of the fact that Draupadi was being brought to the assembly as a slave. Their silence amounted to tacit approval. What could he do? His own foolishness had brought about this calamity.

Seeing their elder brother subdued, and Dhritarastra also saying nothing, the other Pandavas kept themselves in check. They longed to challenge the gloating Duryodhana to open combat on the spot, but would never act without Yudhisthira's order. They watched in silent dread as the Pratikamin left the hall for the ladies' quarters.

CHAPTER TWELVE

EVIL TAKES A HOLD

Depressed at heart, the Pratikamin went quickly toward Draupadi's chamber. He stood before her with folded palms and said in a trembling voice, "O queen, you have been lost at dice by Yudhisthira. I have come here with Duryodhana's order to bring you to the assembly."

Draupadi put down the cloth she had been embroidering. Her mouth fell open. "How can this be true? Who would stake his own wife in a gambling match? Could he find nothing else to bet?"

"O queen, the king had already lost everything, including his brothers and even himself. He then staked you."

Draupadi stared at the servant. Certainly more Kaurava treachery must be afoot. Still it was strange that she should have been lost. She felt her anger rise. "Go back to the assembly, good sir, and ask one thing for me. Ask that gambler who he lost first; himself or me. Having ascertained this, you may then take me with you, if indeed it is my husband's desire."

The Pratikamin bowed and left Draupadi's room. Arriving back at the assembly, he addressed Yudhisthira with Draupadi's question. Yudhisthira made no reply. He sat sighing, his head hanging down, appearing like one deprived of his senses.

Duryodhana laughed. "Let Draupadi place her question directly to Yudhisthira so that we may all hear the words that pass between them. Go, Pratikamin, and fetch her here."

The servant slowly made his way back to Draupadi. With tears in his eyes he relayed Duryodhana's message. "O queen, it seems the Kurus' destruction is close at hand. When the weak brained Duryodhana is intent on humiliating you, he will not be able to maintain his good fortune for long."

Draupadi looked compassionately at the distressed servant. She spoke gently. "Surely the Lord has ordained this. In accord with destiny happiness and distress come, one after the other. We should therefore pursue only religion, seeing that as life's highest goal. If cherished it will pour blessings on us. Let not the Kurus abandon religion now by abusing me, a helpless woman in an embarrassed condition."

Draupadi was in the period of her menses. Wearing only a single cloth, she was keeping herself in seclusion, as was the custom. To be brought before a public assembly in that condition was unthinkable. "Go back to the assembly one more time and ask the virtuous Kuru elders their opinion. If they think it conformable to morality that I be brought before them, I shall go."

The servant returned to the hall and repeated Draupadi's words. Everyone sat with downcast faces. Duryodhana's eagerness and Dhritarastra's complicity left them feeling helpless. Yudhisthira looked up. "We are now under Duryodhana's command. He has ordered that Draupadi be brought here, so let it be so. Tell her to come here and stand before her elders, even though she is attired in a single cloth and should not be seen by anyone."

Yudhisthira looked across at Dhritarastra and Bhishma. The blind king was leaning forward slightly, but Bhishma appeared deeply pained. He slowly shook his head from side to side, but remained silent as Duryodhana again commanded the servant, "Go once more to Draupadi and bring here here. She now has her husband's order."

The servant shifted from foot to foot, perplexed. He feared Draupadi's anger, which he felt could burn the world itself to ashes, but did not want to disobey Duryodhana. The Kaurava prince became impatient. He turned to Dushasana. "This foolish servant is afraid of Bhima. Go, brother, and bring Draupadi yourself. What can the Pandavas do? They are now our slaves."

Throwing a smiling and disdainful glance at the Pandavas, Dushasana rose up and went out of the hall. Like a dog entering a lion's den, he went into Draupadi's quarters and said to her, "Come, princess, you are fairly won by us. Show yourself to your new lords, the Kauravas."

Draupadi shrank back from the leering prince. She got to her feet and ran from the room, calling out for Gandhari. Dushasana bellowed in anger and ran after her. Catching her by the hair, he began to drag her toward the hall. Draupadi trembled like a sapling caught in a gale. She cried out and struggled, but Dushasana pulled her even more forcefully, caring nothing for the fact that she had five invincible heroes as her protectors.

Seeing that she could do nothing to stop him, Draupadi spoke to Dushasana in a low and contemptuous voice. "Rude one, wretch, how dare you drag me before the assembly? Can you not see that I am indisposed?"

"So what?" Dushasana barked. "You are now our slave. What does it matter if you are attired in a single cloth or naked? Come and take your place among the serving women."

Dushasana dragged the piteously wailing Draupadi through the palace corridors and into the hall, where he threw her before Duryodhana. She lay with her cloth and hair disheveled, praying ardently to both Krishna and Arjuna.

Seeing Draupadi's pitiful condition, Vidura, Bhishma and Drona wept openly. They looked despairingly at Dhritarastra, but he only said, "What is happening? Is the Panchala princess here?"

Draupadi realised that not even her husbands were able to say anything. Gathering her cloth around her and covering her hair, she rose up like a flame, and began chastising the Kurus. "In this assembly are many learned men, devoted to sacrifice and possessed of godly virtues. Some of you are my elders and indeed my gurus. How then have you allowed me to be dragged before you in this state?"

She turned toward Dushasana, her eyes blazing. "Cruel rogue! Keep your hands off me. The Pandavas will not forgive you even if Indra and all the celestials protect you."

Turning back to the Kurus, she went on, "Yudhisthira is constrained by the subtle laws of morality. Only men of his high calibre can understand those laws. I will not admit even an atom of fault in him. Surely all you Kurus are of the same mind as Dushasana and his evil brothers, otherwise how could you sit silently as I am abused so? Alas! The Bharata race has been utterly disgraced today."

Draupadi threw a glance at her husbands, who sat like five enraged tigers ready to strike at any moment. Catching that glance, filled with modesty and anger, they felt more pain than they had by losing their wealth, kingdom and very selves.

Dushasana also saw Draupadi glancing at her husbands. Laughing loudly, he seized her again and dragged her even more violently. Duryodhana, Karna and Shakuni laughed along with him and applauded him. Apart from those four and the blind king, everyone else in the hall sent up loud cries of sorrow.

Draupadi pulled away from Dushasana and looked imploringly at Bhishma. The old Kuru leader took a deep breath and said, "Blessed lady, your question is difficult to answer. Surely a slave has no wealth of his own and cannot therefore stake anything. Yet a wife is always under her husband's control. Yudhisthira will abandon the world and all its wealth, but he will never abandon morality. He knew that Shakuni is matchless in dice, still he agreed to the play and lost everything. Knowing all this, I cannot decide on the matter."

Draupadi shook her head and her long braid moved about like an angry snake. "How can you suggest that Yudhisthira played voluntarily? Everything was arranged for his defeat. Although not expert himself, he was enticed into playing with skilful, wicked and deceitful gamblers. What virtue was there in this?"

Dushasana told Draupadi to keep quiet, rebuking her with harsh words. She fell to her knees and buried her face in her hands, weeping silently. Bhima could take no more. Afflicted with unbearable agony at seeing Draupadi's condition, he finally gave vent to his boiling anger. Looking toward Yudhisthira he said, "What gambler, however desperate, would stake his own wife? Even though you lost our wealth, kingdom and our own selves, I felt no anger, for you are our lord. But seeing the innocent Draupadi suffering as a result of your gambling, I am unable to control my wrath."

Bhima turned his broad shoulders toward the twins. "Sahadeva, bring fire. I shall burn the king's hands."

Arjuna was alarmed. He reached out and caught his brother's arm. "Bhima, in the association of immoral men you are losing your high morality. Do not fulfill the enemy's desire. Yudhisthira is without fault, and he is your venerable elder. Brought here and forced to play against his will, he has only added to his fame and virtue."

Arjuna's reproach made Bhima feel ashamed and sorry for his outburst. His head dropped and he replied, "You are right, Arjuna. Forgive me, my anger overpowered my reason."

Among Duryodhana's hundred brothers, one of them, Vikarna, was outraged. He could not believe what he was seeing and felt impelled to speak out. Seeing his chance, he stood up and said, "Draupadi's question deserves a proper answer. If we, as an assembly, cannot decide the matter then great sin will overcome us. Let us hear everyone's impartial opinion."

Vikarna looked around the assembly, appealing to Bhishma, Dhritarastra, Drona and Vidura to say something, but they remained silent. He then said, "If no one else has any opinion, then here is mine. I consider that Draupadi is not won. It is said that four vices afflict kings: hunting, womanizing, drinking and gambling. The actions of one under the influence of any of these four sins cannot be taken seriously. Mad with the fever of gambling, and urged on by the wicked Shakuni, Yudhisthira staked the Panchala princess. And even that was after he had lost himself. Therefore, how can she be considered as won by the Kauravas? It is not right."

Vikarna's words were received with uproarious acclaim. Many kings stood up and praised him, at the same time censuring Shakuni. Karna became furious. He jumped to his feet and waved his well-muscled arms to silence the assembly. His powerful voice filled the hall. "Vikarna, you speak like a fool. What do you know of morality? Many great personalities are here, all of them far more learned than you, and they are silent. Clearly, they consider Draupadi as fairly won. How then do you think otherwise? Obviously Yudhisthira lost her along with all his other possessions. This can hardly be doubted."

Karna looked down at the weeping Draupadi. Her words to him at her *swayamvara* were still vivid in his mind. He would never forget that humiliation. Feeling his anger rise as he recalled that moment, he said, "If you think this woman does not deserve such treatment, then consider these excellent words of mine. A chaste woman would never marry five husbands, contrary to the ordinance. She is practically a prostitute and it would not matter if she were brought here naked, never mind in a single cloth."

With a mocking sneer he then said, "Dushasana, remove her cloth. She is our property now."

Duryodhana cheered Karna and lifted a hand toward Dushasana, urging him on. Dushasana reached down and pulled Draupadi to her feet, taking hold of the end of her cloth. Before the eyes of the mortified assembly he began to forcefully strip her.

Draupadi tried to resist Dushasana, but it was useless. Her cloth slipped through her hands as he pulled even harder. She looked desperately at her husbands, but they did not move. The princess could understand that she had no protector in that assembly. She thought of Krishna. Surrendering fully to his shelter, she threw up her arms and prayed, "O Govinda! Krishna! Lord! Protector of the people and destroyer of all affliction, save me! Soul of the universe, see me sinking in the Kuru ocean. I am losing my senses in this wicked assembly. Please rescue me."

Hearing her piteous plea from where he was standing many miles away, Krishna immediately responded. He expanded himself by his inconceivable power and ran toward Hastinapura. Reaching the hall in a matter of moments he entered it invisibly. At once he began to supply an unlimited amount of cloth to Draupadi. As Dushasana pulled and pulled, he saw to his amazement that Draupadi remained fully clad. Her many-coloured dress piled up on the floor in an increasingly large heap. The prince kept on trying to strip her but after some time he gave up, exhausted. His efforts were useless.

The assembly was again in uproar. All the kings applauded Draupadi. They rebuked Dushasana, shouting at him to leave the Panchala princess alone. Perspiring heavily, he slumped down next to Duryodhana, shaking his head in astonishment.

Bhima glared at him steadily, as if to burn him with his very glance. As the assembly calmed down, he got to his feet and spoke out in a thunderous voice. "O kings, listen to my words. I shall now make a vow, the like of which has never before been made. If I do not tear open the chest of this wicked-minded scoundrel on the field of battle, drinking his life-blood, then may I not attain the path of my ancestors."

As Bhima uttered his terrible vow, Duryodhana and his brothers looked at him in horrified disgust, but all the other kings loudly praised him. They called for the Kurus to answer Draupadi's question. Their angry voices echoed round the hall. "Shame on Dhritarastra. Why is he silent? Where is his morality?"

Vidura then got to his feet and raised his arms to silence the assembly. He spoke again. "In this assembly religion is being persecuted. It is the duty of good men to relieve, by means of truth and morality, the suffering of any distressed person who approaches them. Those who sit in an assembly and fail to speak out against a sin are themselves afflicted by that sin. So far only Vikarna has spoken. Now it behooves everyone else to give their honest opinions in response to Draupadi's question."

Vidura looked pointedly toward Dhritarastra as he spoke. He cited an ancient story from scripture illustrating the importance of speaking the truth to a supplicant, but still the blind king said nothing. Seeing no one heeding Vidura, Karna said to Dushasana, "Take the servant woman Draupadi to the inner quarters where she belongs."

Dushasana again took hold of Draupadi and began pulling her out of the hall. Folding her palms, she looked up toward the Kuru elders and said, "Before I am taken away by this worst of men, I must offer you my respects. Forgive me for not doing so earlier, but I was sorely afflicted and deprived of my senses."

As Dushasana continued to violently drag Draupadi by the hair she beseeched the Kurus, "It seems that a dark age of evil has surely come. How do you tolerate seeing your daughter treated in such a way? Where are your morals? I should not even be seen by the sun or the wind in my present state, but here I am being cruelly persecuted before an assembly of kings."

Draupadi placed her question again. "O Kurus, tell me truthfully, am I a servant woman or not? I, the chaste wife of Yudhisthira, born in the royal order, Krishna's friend and your own relative. Tell me what is morally right, and I will cheerfully follow your order. I can no longer tolerate the touch of this destroyer of Kuru fame."

Bhishma, with tears running down his face, then said, "Blessed lady, noble one, that you should turn to religion even under such trying circumstances only adds to your great virtue and fame. The ways of morality are subtle and I find it difficult to answer your question. However, as the Kurus have given way to lust and ignorance I can say that their destruction will come on no distant date. Seeing them sitting here with downcast faces I think they will not give you a reply. In my view only Yudhisthira is able to respond."

All eyes turned toward Yudhisthira. He still appeared stunned and unable to speak. Everyone in the assembly remained silent, apparently afraid of Duryodhana's power. Smiling, the Kaurava prince waved at Dushasana to let go of Draupadi. He then rose up and said, "O Draupadi, I think Bhishma is correct. It is your husband who must answer your question. If he declares that he spoke falsely when he staked you, and that he is therefore still your lord, then you shall be free. And if his brothers declare the same thing, that they too were falsely staked, they shall also be free. The magnanimous Kurus are all grieving to see your condition, brought about by Yudhisthira. Now let him settle the matter."

A clamour arose among the assembly as many kings applauded Duryodhana. Others loudly lamented with cries of "Oh!" and "Alas". Again, they turned their eyes toward Yudhisthira, eager to hear his reply. Before he could say anything, Bhima, sorry for his previous outburst against Yudhisthira, jumped to his feet and said, "If this high souled son of Dharma were not our lord then we would never have pardoned the Kurus. He is our guru and the lord of our lives. If he considers himself won, then we are all won."

Bhima turned his reddish eyes toward Duryodhana and his brothers. "It is only because Yudhisthira does not command me that I have not slaughtered these wretches with my bare hands, even as a lion kills a number of small animals."

Seeing Bhima's fury about to explode, Bhishma, Drona and Vidura became alarmed and they exclaimed, "Forbear, forbear! O Bhima, you are capable of anything."

Karna criticised the three Kuru elders, accusing them of always supporting the Pandavas against the interests of their master. Turning toward Draupadi he said, "O beautiful lady, select for yourself another husband. The Pandavas are our slaves and cannot possess you any longer. The Kauravas are now your lords. Go to their servants' quarters and await their command. Clearly Yudhisthira considered his life, prowess and manhood as all useless, for he gambled you away in the presence of this assembly."

Bhima, still on his feet, glowered menacingly at Karna. He slowly took his seat again next to Yudhisthira, appearing like a smouldering fire about to burst into flames.

Duryodhana laughed and exchanged a glance with Karna. He turned to the Pandavas and said, "Come now, O heroes, tell us whether Draupadi is truly won or not."

Revelling in his moment of triumph, and wanting to encourage Karna, Duryodhana uncovered his right thigh, which resembled a tree trunk. He showed it to Draupadi with a smile, indicating that she should take her place on his lap as his wife.

Bhima roared in anger. His voice thundered around the hall. "If I do not smash that thigh in a great battle, then let me not attain the higher regions." He looked like a burning tree with sparks and flames emitting from every crevice.

The whole assembly was becoming agitated and Vidura rose again to address them. "A very great danger has now arisen from Bhima. O Dhritarastra, a calamity sent by destiny threatens to overtake us. Your sons have gambled in this assembly, disregarding every moral law. Now they are quarreling over a lady. Alas, the Kurus' prosperity is at an end."

Vidura reiterated that Draupadi was certainly not won by the Kauravas, as Yudhisthira had lost her when he himself was lost.

Duryodhana smiled at the painstricken Pandavas. "I will abide by the words of Yudhisthira's brothers. If they declare that Yudhisthira is no longer their master, then Draupadi will be free."

Arjuna at once retorted, "The son of Dharma was certainly our lord before the game began, but he has lost himself, so let the Kurus decide whose master he is now."

As Arjuna spoke inauspicious omens were suddenly seen and heard. A jackal cried in Dhritarastra's nearby sacrifical chamber. Asses brayed and fearful birds uttered fierce cries. Alarmed, Bhishma, Drona and Kripa cried out, "All peace!" Vidura urged the king to do something before disaster overtook him.

Realising at last that things had gone too far, Dhritarastra chastised his son. "Duryodhana, wicked minded wretch, by insulting Draupadi you are bringing certain destruction down on our heads."

The king turned his head toward where he had heard Draupadi speaking and said, "Dear Draupadi, you have suffered enough. Be peaceful. Chaste and devoted to virtue, you are the foremost of my daughters-in-law. Ask from me any boon you desire. I wish to make redress for the despicable treatment you have received."

Draupadi turned her tearstreaked face toward the blind king. "Best of the Bharatas, if you really desire to do me good then release Yudhisthira from slavery."

"It is done," replied Dhritarastra. "Now ask from me a second favour. My heart desires to give you something more."

"O king, release also the other Pandavas and give them back their chariots and weapons."

"Greatly blessed girl, it shall be so. Dear daughter, ask yet another boon and that too shall be granted."

Afraid of the omens, and of Vidura's repeated warnings, Dhritarastra was prepared to give everything back to the Pandavas, but Draupadi said, "O king, greed destroys virtue. I will not ask a further boon, for my husbands will be able to secure all prosperity by their own virtuous acts."

Karna laughed derisively. "What kind of men are the Pandavas? They have been saved by a woman."

Bhima flared up in anger, but Arjuna checked him, saying, "Desist, hero. Great men never take seriously the harsh words of inferiors. They always try to remember whatever little good may have been rendered them by the offending party."

Bhima's fury did not abate. He turned to Yudhisthira, "O king of kings, grant me leave to slay these foes here and now. Or shall I do it outside the palace? What consideration is required in the matter?"

Bhima glared at the Kauravas, like a lion casting its glance over a herd of deer. Arjuna held his arm and tried to calm him with appealing looks, but Bhima seemed as if he were on fire. Yudhisthira embraced him, saying softly, "Be peaceful, dear brother."

Yudhisthira then went before Dhritarastra and said, "O king, you are our lord. Command us now what we should do. We desire to always remain obedient to you."

The Kuru monarch replied, "Go in peace, Yudhisthira. At my command rule your kingdom with all your wealth. Live in peace and try to forget the harsh words that were uttered here today. Pious men such as yourself remember only the good deeds of their enemies, not their hostile acts."

Dhritarastra spoke at length to appease Yudhisthira. He begged him to maintain friendly relations with the Kauravas. "Have pity on me, your old and blind uncle, and on Gandhari, your aunt. Think of us as your father and mother. No malice was meant by me in this match. I merely wished to see the respective strengths and weaknesses of yourself and my sons. You have proved yourself to be highly virtuous. Return now to Indraprastha with my blessings. Let there be brotherly love between you and my sons."

Duryodhana glared at his father but remained silent. There was little he could say. Dhritarastra had accorded boons to Draupadi which he could hardly reverse now. The Kaurava turned his dark eyes toward Karna and Dushasana, who both sat shaking their heads.

After bowing before Dhritarastra and the other Kuru elders, the Pandavas ascended their chariot with Draupadi and headed back to Indraprastha. Dhritarastra rose to leave the hall and the assembly broke up. Some kings went away praising Yudhisthira, while others commended Duryodhana. The blind king was led away by Vidura. Thinking of the heinous treatment given to Draupadi by his sons, he was gripped by anxiety. How would the Pandavas ever forgive and forget such abuse? Especially Bhima. He had made terrible vows. It was unlikely he would forget those. The Kuru monarch entered his chamber and sat for his evening prayers, his mind filled with remorse. Why had he not acted sooner?

CHAPTER THIRTEEN

THE KURUS SEAL THEIR FATE

When everyone had dispersed after the dice game, Duryodhana sat alone with Shakuni, Karna and Dushasana. They condemned the king for his weakness. He had certainly blundered by showing favour toward powerful enemies, especially after they had already been subdued.

"The old man returned all that wealth which we had gained with so much endeavour," Dushasana lamented. "Now our hated foes are again strong."

Duryodhana appeared thoughtful. "You are right, brother, but I think we can still turn things around."

The prince had seen how his father had so eagerly asked about the gambling. He had clearly been enjoying his sons' success. It was only fear that had finally made him intervene. Perhaps they could play on that fear to make him think again.

"Let us go to the king at once," Duryodhana suggested. "We should point out the very grave danger he has created. By allowing the Pandavas to go back to their kingdom with all their wealth he has placed us in great peril."

"Then let us take up our weapons and pursue them," Karna exclaimed. "Taking them by surprise we can annihilate them before they reach their city."

"No, dear friend, the time is not yet right," Duryodhana replied. "We need to consolidate our position; gain more allies and build our armies. Only then should battle be joined with Pandu's highly powerful sons. Let us start by using strategy to weaken them."

Shakuni agreed. "This is intelligent, O king." He played with his dice, rolling them about in his hands. "I think you should speak with your father."

Duryodhana looked at the dice and nodded. This time there should be no mistake. Taking Karna with him, he immediately left for his father's chamber where he found him just finishing his prayers. The prince said, "Father, I am fearful. The Vedas clearly state that a dangerous enemy should be utterly destroyed. Any means whatsoever may be employed. The Pandavas are like five deadly serpents. By grievously offending them we have placed them on our heads. There is no doubt they now pose a dire threat. We must act quickly before everything is lost. If they are given time, they will assemble a vast force and crush us."

Dhritarastra said nothing. This was also his fear. The Kurus had ignited a fire at the gambling match which could well consume them to their roots. But what could now be done?

Duryodhana could see he had his father's full attention. He spoke softly. "Here is my idea. Summon Yudhisthira back for one final game. Let there be one decisive stake. The loser should be made to retire to the forest for twelve years. For one more year they may come out of the forest and live incognito in some town. If discovered, then a further twelve years exile will be their lot. Otherwise they may get their kingdom back when they return."

Dhritarastra immediately shook his head. The gambling had already produced fearful consequences. How could he permit another game? What would Vidura say?

Duryodhana was insistent. "This is the wisest policy, father. Shakuni will certainly win. Then we will have time to make our position strong—using Yudhisthira's wealth. While the Pandavas stay in the forest we can amass such a force that not even they will present any threat. Permit this final game and let us settle the issue now."

Dhritarastra again felt his mind pulled by his son's influence. Enmity had already been created with the Pandavas. It would be hard now to avoid a conflict. If they were out of the way then the danger would be gone. Maybe it would be best for everyone. Certainly, his own sons would be better off, as there seemed little doubt that Shakuni would win the game.

"Alright, have the Pandavas recalled. Arrange for the final game." The king spoke with a sigh. He still had misgivings but could not deny his son.

When the other Kuru elders heard that the Pandavas were being summoned for another game they were shocked. Every one of them disapproved. They tried hard to dissuade the king, but he would not listen. He had made up his mind.

Gandhari was also anxious. She went to her husband when he was alone and said, "Vidura long ago advised us to abandon Duryodhana, but you did not take heed. Now it seems he will destroy us all. My lord, do not approve the counsel of foolish men who are no better than boys. Do not rekindle a great fire that has been extinguished. Control your sons and become their leader, showing them the path of virtue. You are intelligent and must surely see the consequences of acting otherwise."

After hearing his queen's counsel Dhritarastra remained in thought for some moments. Finally, he said, "If the destruction of the Kurus has arrived then what can I do? If it is God's will then how can it be opposed? Let it happen at once. Noble lady, the match will go ahead. Consider it as ordained by destiny."

The blindfolded queen tried for some time to change her husband's mind, but he was determined. Finally, she gave up, shrugging her shoulders in helplessness. It seemed that the end of the Kurus truly was ordained by destiny. The king's attachment for Duryodhana had entirely overpowered his intelligence. Calling for her servants, Gandhari left for her room.

On Dhritarastra's order, a messenger was despatched on a swift steed to catch up with the Pandavas. On reaching them he bowed before Yudhisthira and said, "O son of Pandu, I carry the king's order. He requests you to come and throw the dice one more time."

Yudhisthira showed no surprise. It had been more of a surprise when Dhritarastra had returned his wealth and kingdom. Obviously, he had been influenced by Duryodhana, unable to see his ill gotten gains lost.

Yudhisthira turned to his brothers and said, "All creatures receive the fruits of their own work, good or bad, as ordained by God. Whether or not I play this game we shall receive those fruits. This is a challenge to play at dice, and it is also a summons by the king. How then can I refuse, even though I know it will be destructive to me? Surely mens' minds become bewildered when the hour of calamity approaches."

With heavy hearts the Pandavas retraced their steps back to Hastinapura. Seeing them returning, their friends and well wishers felt pain. It was plain what was about to happen. Entering the assembly hall, the brothers saw everyone seated as before. The blind king was on his throne with the Kuru elders by his side, and the dice game was set up in readiness.

When the Pandavas had again taken their places, Shakuni smiled and said, "Welcome back, Yudhisthira. The king has returned all your wealth and that is all well and good, but let us play one final game for a stake of high value."

Shakuni explained the rules. Hearing that the losers would be exiled for thirteen years, a great gasp went up from the kings in the hall. "This cannot be allowed!" some of them cried. "Duryodhana should be stopped before he destroys himself and his whole house."

Those cries went unheeded and the game began. Yudhisthira took up the dice and said, "How can one like me, who always desires to do his proper duty, refuse a challenge? I accept the stake."

A strange sense of fatality filled Yudhisthira's mind. He was about to lose everything and be consigned to the forest. Equally obvious was the fact that the Kurus would soon be destroyed due to their loss of virtue. Yudhisthira thought again of Krishna. Was this all his desire? What would he do when he discovered what had happened?

Filled with foreboding, Yudhisthira threw the dice. They clattered against the side of the board and yet again landed wrongly. The Pandava watched in silence as Shakuni made his throw. "I have won!" came the inevitable cry as the dice came to a stop.

Once more the watching kings cried out in distress, "For shame! For shame!" But Duryodhana and his brothers jumped to their feet in glee. Dushasana was completely overjoyed. "Now Duryodhana is the absolute sovereign of this world," he effused. "The Pandavas are defeated and plunged into misery. Whatever anyone may say about us the gods have favoured us. Proud of their wealth Kunti's sons laughed at Duryodhana in his suffering. Now they must enter the forest, deprived of everything."

Dancing around in great happiness, Dushasana railed at the Pandavas for some time. He told them to take off their royal robes and put on the deerskins which Duryodhana had ordered his servants to have ready. After hurling various kinds of insults at the Pandavas, who silently tolerated the abuse, Dushasana then turned to Draupadi and said, "Your father foolishly bestowed you upon these impotent men. What will you gain by serving them? Abandon them and select a worthy husband from among the Kauravas."

Bhima suddenly started toward Dushasana as a mountain lion might rush upon a deer. Seeing Yudhisthira's frown he checked himself with difficulty and loudly rebuked the Kaurava prince. "Crooked-minded wretch, thanks to Shakuni's skill at dice you arrogantly blather on. Know for certain that I will pierce your heart in battle, just as you now pierce our hearts with arrow-like words."

Dushasana burst out laughing. He again danced around and pointed at Bhima, calling out insults. Bhima, his mind fixed in virtue, restrained himself from killing the prince on the spot.

Having put on the deerskins, the Pandavas began to walk slowly out of the hall. Duryodhana walked behind them, caricaturing Bhima's powerful gait. Seeing this, Bhima coldly said, "I shall be Duryodhana's slayer. Felling him in a mace fight I will place my foot on his head. Arjuna will slay Karna and Sahadeva will kill the gambler Shakuni."

Arjuna fixed his gaze on Karna and said, "All this will surely come to pass. The promises of powerful men are not mere words. This malicious, vain and envious wretch will die at my hand, along with anyone who is foolish enough to support him."

Sahadeva then confirmed that he would kill Shakuni, and Nakula also uttered a vow to kill many of Duryodhana's followers.

After offering his respects to Dhritarastra and the other senior Kurus, Yudhisthira turned to leave. Vidura then came up to him and spoke consolingly. "Dear Yudhisthira, best of the Bharatas, do not feel any shame or guilt, for you have been defeated by sinful means. This has all been arranged by destiny for your ultimate welfare. You will be instructed there by the rishis and will also develop detachment from worldly affairs. Your power will thus greatly increase. O son of Kunti, be blessed. You have never committed any sin. We hope to see you soon return triumphant."

Before leaving Draupadi went to see Kunti. Bowing at her feet, she wept for some time and Kunti wept with her. In a choked voice Kunti said, "Be strong, child. You have adorned the Kurus with your shining qualities. It is fortunate for them that they were not burned to ashes by your wrath. Go now with my blessings. Protected by your own great virtue you will surely obtain all good fortune before long."

The Kuru queen embraced Draupadi who then joined her husbands. Kunti followed her out of the palace and when she saw her sons clad in deerskins, surrounded by grieving friends and rejoicing foes, she cried out in sorrow. She ran over and embraced them, one after another, and began to lament. "My sons, how could such reverses happen to virtuous men like yourselves? Oh, why did I bring you here from the mountains? Why did I not ascend your father's fire like Madri? Surely that princess saw this disaster looming, and thus she chose to follow our lord."

Kunti raised her arms to the sky and cried out to Krishna. "O dweller of Dwaraka, where are you? Why do you not save my sons and I? The wise say that you are without beginning or end, and that you always save those who seek you. Has that now proved false?"

Kunti wept uncontrollably. She berated the Kuru elders and called out to Pandu. Inconsolable, she shook with sorrow. Vidura took her arm and spoke soothingly. He led her away as her sons made their way along the street toward the city gate. The news of their exile had quickly spread and the roads were crowded with grieving citizens. Shocked at the sudden turn of events, they shouted out blessings and good wishes to the five brothers as they slowly walked out of the city, unable to say anything to anyone.

* * *

After the Pandavas had gone, Dhritarastra sat alone fretting. A terrible injustice had been perpetrated. He could have intervened at any time but had remained silent as his brother's children were robbed and insulted. The blind king called for Vidura and timidly asked, "Did you see how the Pandavas left the city? Please describe to me everything."

Vidura replied, "From the signs present when those heroes and their wife left Hastinapura it is plain we face great peril. Arjuna scattered sands that represented the innumerable arrows he will fire in battle against your sons. Bhima was slapping his powerful arms, no doubt thinking of how in due course he will crush the Kauravas. Yudhisthira himself kept his eyes down, knowing that his anger alone might consume those upon whom his gaze fell."

Vidura described how various threatening omens had been seen; lightning from the cloudless sky, the earth trembling, and jackals, vultures and ravens all uttering harsh cries. "All these signs portend a fearful destruction, king, as a result of your acts."

As Vidura spoke with Dhritarastra, the sage Narada suddenly appeared in the hall, surrounded by other great rishis. Looking at the king, he said, "In fourteen years from now, for Duryodhana's fault, the Kurus will be destroyed."

As the alarmed Kauravas looked on, the sage disappeared. Duryodhana and his brothers, as well as Karna and Shakuni, then went before Drona, considering him their best shelter. Folding his palms and speaking humbly, Duryodhana said, "Great brahmin, a grave danger has arisen from the Pandavas. Tell us now what we should do. You are our guru and a peerless warrior. Please guide us across the terrible Pandava ocean."

Drona gave a wry smile. Duryodhana had not cared for his advice when it was to give the Pandavas their rightful share of the kingdom. Yet it was still his duty to protect the Kurus, who after all maintained him. He said, "I will do whatever I can, although the rishis have said that the Pandavas, being of celestial origin, cannot be slain. When their exile is over, they will return in anger, more powerful than ever, to seek redress. With them will be Dhristyadyumna, who is destined to be my slayer. I see little hope. You should spend the next thirteen years performing sacrifice and enjoying life, for at the end of that period a great calamity will overwhelm you."

Hearing Drona's words, Dhritarastra felt even more anxious. He said to Vidura, "Dear brother, the Pandavas have gone and will not return until the agreed period is over. Yudhisthira will certainly see to this. However, you should arrange that they have every desirable thing. Soldiers, chariots, servants and whatever else they need."

Vidura shook his head at the blind king's empty gesture. The Pandavas would not accept anything now. Dhritarastra was trying to build a dam after he had let all the water run away.

As the king sat sighing, his charioteer and secretary Sanjaya came to him. He was Vyasadeva's spiritual disciple and despite his low social status was noted for his wisdom. Seeing his master sunk in worry, he said, "O great monarch, you have now obtained the entire earth and all its wealth. Why then do you grieve?"

"What worries are not theirs who have the Pandavas as their enemies?" said Dhritarastra.

"This, my lord, is due to your own great folly." Sanjaya had long served the king with affection and had his full trust. He spoke frankly. "With your consent, your wicked-minded and shameless son had the virtuous wife of the Pandavas dragged into the assembly and grievously abused. This act will destroy the world. A great hostility will arise to annihilate all the earth's monarchs. The gods deprive a man of his senses when his defeat is ordained. He thus sees evil as good and good as evil. How otherwise could such a heinous act of sin have been allowed in this very assembly?"

Dhritarastra hung his head. "I fear greatly Draupadi's wrath. Her afflicted glances could consume the world. When she was insulted everything became inauspicious. Gandhari and the palace ladies wailed loudly and are still weeping now. The brahmins refused to light the sacred fires that day. Terrible omens were witnessed in all directions. Therefore, did I grant her boons. Still my affection for Duryodhana made me deprive the Pandavas of everything and send them into the wilderness."

The blind king lamented for some time. He told Sanjaya he felt certain that the Pandavas would wreak an awful vengeance. All his counsellors were now warning him to prepare for that time. Vidura was especially full of foreboding. He came into the chamber as the king was speaking, and Dhritarastra asked, "Vidura, tell me what I should now do. What will be best for myself and the Kurus? How can we avoid total extermination?"

Vidura replied, "Dear king, the sages say that all good fortune ensues when one adheres strictly to virtue. Misled by Shakuni, your evil-hearted sons destroyed virtue when they defeated Yudhisthira at dice. The only way to make amends is to restore the Pandavas to their rightful position. Give them back their kingdom."

Dhritarastra grimaced. He had hoped Vidura would offer some counsel as to how the Kurus could secure their position. Perhaps his sons' acts were questionable, but the outcome had been that they, and indeed he, had achieved unrivalled prosperity. He was now effectively the Emperor. It had always pained him that, even though he was elder than Pandu, he had been denied the throne due to his blindness. He had only ruled by default when Pandu had retired. Now it seemed destiny had conferred upon him supreme rulership of the earth. Why should he just give it away?

Vidura saw Dhritarastra's disappointed expression and he spoke strongly. "If you do not follow my advice, king, you will be destroyed. Neither Bhima nor Arjuna leave any of their enemies unslain. You must act quickly. Abandon the wretch Duryodhana, send Shakuni away in disgrace, and embrace the virtuous Pandavas. Have Dushasana beg for Draupadi's forgiveness in the open court. Then install Yudhisthira on the throne with all due ceremony. What else can I advise? This is the only proper course for you now."

Dhritarastra clenched his fists. Yet again Vidura was telling him to reject his own sons in favour of the Pandavas. How could such advice be followed? Duryodhana was always saying that Vidura was really an enemy in the guise of a friend. Perhaps he was right. The king replied harshly to his brother. "Vidura, your words are not meant for my good. Why do you always favour the Pandavas? Do you expect me to abandon my own flesh and blood for their sake? Although I hold you in high esteem, I feel your advice is crooked. I cannot accept it. You may do as you please. Stay here or go, I do not care. However well an unchaste wife is treated she still forsakes her husband."

Dhritarastra rose suddenly and called for his servants. Waving his hand to dismiss his counsellors, he went to his inner chambers. Vidura watched in dismay. This was the worst possible outcome. Saying, "The Kurus are doomed," he went out of the hall and prepared to follow the Pandavas into the forest.

CHAPTER FOURTEEN

HEROES IN EXILE

After leaving Hastinapura, the Pandavas were followed for some distance by crowds of citizens who loudly criticised the Kuru leaders. They pleaded with the Pandavas not to go, praising the brothers' many virtues. All of them appeared greatly distressed. Yudhisthira, feeling compassion, turned to address them. "Hear me, pious citizens of Hastinapura. We feel blessed that you feel so much affection for us, crediting us with merits we do not possess, but we cannot return. For the sake of the love you bear for us, I ask that you go back and serve king Dhritarastra. Our friends and relatives in Hastinapura are filled with grief to see us leave. Do not abandon them now."

Seeing that Yudhisthira was determined, the citizens resigned themselves to going back without him. They shed tears and cried loudly. Slowly they began to head back to the city. The Pandavas then ascended chariots and went quickly away from Hastinapura. By evening they reached the edge of the forest and stopped for the night under a great banyan tree. Hundreds of ascetic brahmins came to see them and they lit fires that cast an orange glow into the black night. They chanted hymns and prayers which comforted the griefstricken Pandavas and their wife. Sitting around those sacred fires with the brahmins, the brothers appeared like resplendent gods surrounded by a concourse of celestial beings.

When morning came they made ready to enter the forest. The brahmins began to follow them, but Yudhisthira checked them. Peering into the dense woodlands, he said, "How will we maintain you in this terrible place? The forest is full of dangers. Please stay near the city where you will easily find your sustenance."

The brahmins were reluctant to let the Pandavas go without them. They told Yudhisthira that they would procure their own food without difficulty. "We are used to an ascetic life," said their leader, Shaunaka. "Allow us to accompany you and we shall do you good by our prayers and readings of holy scripture."

"Then let it be as you say," replied Yudhisthira. As he looked at the effulgent rishis who stood round him, he was seized with sorrow. In Indraprastha he had maintained hundreds of thousands of brahmins and now he could hardly look after a few. He sat down on the ground and wept. "Alas! Fie on Dhritarastra's sons. We are overcome by destitution. How shall I look upon you all, my well wishers and gurus, who deserve no suffering, scratching for food in the forest?"

Shaunaka spoke compassionately to the distraught Pandava. "O king, thousands of causes for grief and hundreds of fears overwhelm the ignorant day after day, but never the wise. Suffering and pain are afflictions of the body only. Learned men know that their real identity is different from the body and that misery is an illusion. Great hero, men like you are never subject to illusion. They are detached from the body and indeed from all material circumstances. Attachment is the root cause of suffering, dear child. This is well known to you. Fix yourself in that knowledge now and take heart."

The rishi instructed Yudhisthira for some time, gradually relieving his mind of its affliction. Yudhisthira listened with rapt attention. He always relished the rishis' words. That at least would be one consolation for him in the forest—he would get many opportunities to hear such instructions.

Shaunaka concluded, "You have achieved success in your householder life, O king, culminating in the great Rajasuya sacrifice. Now you should cultivate detachment. Practice yoga and meditation and you will achieve all spiritual success."

His grief assuaged, Yudhisthira got to his feet and thanked Shaunaka. The Pandavas then set off into the forest, with Draupadi in their midst. Behind them walked the brahmins, continuously chanting auspicious Vedic hymns. Travelling in a northwesterly direction they crossed over the great plain of Kurukshetra. When they reached the banks of the river Sarasvati, they saw ahead of them the Kamyaka forest. Numerous hermitages lined the riverbank, and the travellers saw many rishis standing in the gently flowing river, deep in meditation. The late afternoon sun reflected from the water, making the river appear like a long sheet of gold.

Yudhisthira decided they should stay in that beautiful, mind-soothing region, and they constructed several cottages for their residence. There they dwelt peacefully, hunting by day and spending their evenings hearing spiritual wisdom from the sages. The pain of what had happened in Hastinapura was still fresh, but the association of the rishis relieved them. They wondered if they would ever again see their friends and relatives. To their surprise, only a few days after they had arrived at Kamyaka, they saw Vidura approaching.

Yudhisthira jumped up and said to Bhima, "There is Vidura. What brings him here, I wonder? Does the mean-minded Shakuni desire to win from us even our weapons? Dear brother, if challenged I will be unable to refuse, but without Arjuna's Gandiva the recovery of our kingdom is unlikely."

The Pandavas greeted their uncle with love and respect. They sat him down and asked him why he had come. When Vidura explained how Dhritarastra had rejected his good counsel, the Pandavas shook their heads in despair. Dhritarastra's behavior did not bode well for the future. Vidura then said, "As the king will not heed my advice, I have left him and come here to offer you whatever counsel I can. O rulers of men, be patient. Tolerate silently the wrongs you have suffered. Increase your strength by spiritual practises and bide your time. Soon you will win back your wealth, without doubt."

The Pandavas were delighted to have Vidura with them. Yudhisthira replied, "I will be entirely guided by you, Uncle."

Vidura had spent some time in discussion with the Pandavas when they noticed another chariot approach. They saw that it was Sanjaya. Rising to greet him, they brought him into their midst and listened as he described what had happened in Hastinapura after Vidura's departure. "When the old king heard that Vidura had left, he fell down in a faint. When he recovered, he said to me, 'My wise brother is equal to the god of justice, Yamaraja himself. Alas, I have cruelly offended him. My heart burns in grief. Please go and bring him back.'"

Sanjaya turned to Vidura, "Your brother is consumed with repentance. Please return to Hastinapura and relieve his sorrow."

Vidura immediately agreed. Although Dhritarastra was loath to accept his advice, it would be better if he were near him. At least then there would be a chance that the blind monarch may see sense. Offering his blessings to the Pandavas, Vidura mounted his chariot and rode back to Hastinapura with Sanjaya. When he arrived there the king rose from his throne to embrace him, saying, "Please forgive me. When you left I felt like one lost. Surely you are sinless and have never done me the slightest harm. How could I have been so cruel."

Vidura spoke affectionately to the king. "Dear brother, I forgive you. My favour the Pandavas is natural, for one feels more for those in distress than he does for others. Both your sons and the Pandavas are equally dear to me, but the Pandavas are now in suffering."

Speaking apologetic words to each other, the brothers spent some time together, then retired for the night.

* * *

When Vidura left Hastinapura, Duryodhana had been delighted. When he again returned and was reconciled with the king, the Kaurava prince became depressed. He spoke with Shakuni, Karna and Dushasana. "I fear that sooner or later the intelligent Vidura will convince the king to bring back the Pandavas. If that happens, I shall certainly die. I cannot tolerate seeing them in prosperity."

Duryodhana pressed his bejewelled fingers together. He stood up and paced around the beautifully furnished chamber, pausing to gaze vacantly out of the window at the expansive palace gardens. Thinking only of the Pandavas, his eyes moved about restlessly. "They cannot be allowed to return. If the king brings them back, I will drink poison, throw myself into blazing fire, or fall upon my sword."

Shakuni came over to him and placed an arm around his shoulders. "O king, ruler of the world, what has come over you? How will the Pandavas return? They have agreed to spend thirteen years away. Yudhisthira will never break his word. Even if he does, why should we be worried? I still have my dice."

Duryodhana turned away from Shakuni and walked toward the table where his wine stood. He picked up the flagon and then put it down again. It seemed the Pandavas had taken possession of him. How could he enjoy life while they were alive?

Karna could understand his friend's mind. He stood up suddenly and drew his sword. Raising it high, he said loudly, "Here is my opinion. Let us go now in a body and fall upon the Pandavas. They are weakened, devoid of allies and in distress. We will soon crush them. Let us do it quickly before they again become powerful. Ridding the earth of our enemies, we shall live in undisturbed peace."

Hearing Karna's bold words, everyone cheered. They all agreed with him. Duryodhana said they should leave immediately, and they went out of the palace and mounted their great war chariots. The prince quickly assembled a phalanx of troops and was about to leave the city when he saw Vyasadeva ahead of him. The sage held up his hand and commanded him to stop. Duryodhana felt unable to defy the rishi, fearing the power of his curse. Reluctantly he turned around and headed back for the palace.

Vyasadeva then went to Dhritarastra and said, "Hear me king, I have not been pleased by your treatment of the Pandavas. You will face the consequences in thirteen years from now when they return to shower deadly arrows on the Kurus. Your wicked son seems bent on suicide, for he has rushed out to confront the Pandavas. Why do you not check him? You possess great intelligence. Surely you can see what will soon ensue."

Dhritarastra listened meekly as his father spoke. Vyasadeva suggested that he send Duryodhana alone into the forest to serve the Pandavas. Maybe then the prince would lose his envy for them, and they in turn may develop an attachment for him.

The king replied, "Without doubt I was deluded by ignorance when I allowed the gambling match. Everyone warned me against it, but being overly affectionate toward my son I would not listen."

"This is the truth, king. You have excessively favoured your sons over Pandu's. This is not surprising, as the son is the dearmost object to all men. Indeed, you are also dear to me. Out of affection only do I tell you that your best course of action is to have Duryodhana make peace with the Pandavas."

In the presence of Vyasadeva, Dhritarastra could understand everything clearly. He said, "O greatly intelligent rishi, it is exactly as you say. Vidura, Bhishma and Drona have also pointed this out to me. Still I seem unable to do what is necessary. Please therefore teach my son for me. Set him on the right path."

Vyasadeva stood up and everyone present also rose in respect. He pulled his shawl around his shoulders, made thin by extended fasting and austerity, and said, "I shall now depart, but the illustrious rishi Maitreya will soon come here. He will admonish your son for the Kurus' sake. O king, ensure that his advice is followed without delay. If it is not, he will curse your son in anger."

The sage left and, as he had predicted, Maitreya soon arrived. He was brought into the Kuru assembly and given a seat of honour. The rishi looked around the great hall, lit by shafts of sunlight that shone through the high windows. The light reflected from the jewels and ornaments decorating the Kurus and they resembled an assembly of celestials.

Informed that Maitreya was present, Dhritarastra asked after his welfare and then said, "Have you seen the Pandavas on your travels? Are they well? Will the brotherly affection between them and us remain unimpaired?"

Maitreya replied that he had seen the Pandavas not long ago in the forest. They were attired in deerskins and surrounded by rishis. "I learned from them of the danger that has arisen for the Kurus from gambling." Maitreya spoke gently and with obvious concern. He said he had come to Hastinapura for the welfare of the Kurus. Chiding Dhritarastra, he said, "Why, king, did you allow such sins to be perpetrated in this assembly? You are in full control here and must therefore take the blame."

Maitreya turned toward Duryodhana, who was frowning and looking away from him. "O mighty-armed Duryodhana, listen to the words I shall speak for your good. Do not quarrel with the Pandavas. Those heroes are possessed of godly power. Bhima alone has already slain Hidimba, Baka and Kirmira, Rakshasas of immeasurable strength, as well as the mighty Jarasandha. Who is there who can face him and his brothers, especially when they have Krishna as their friend and relation? Pay heed prince, make peace with them. Do not place yourself in unnecessary danger."

Duryodhana made no reply, still not looking at Maitreya. Stretching out his leg, he slapped his thigh and scratched the floor with his foot, showing complete disinterest and offering insult to the rishi.

Maitreya's eyes turned red with anger. As if impelled by fate he immediately uttered a curse, his angry voice resounding through the hall. "Hear my words, insolent one. You shall soon reap the consequences of your acts. In the great war which will arise due to your sinful deeds,, Bhima will smash your thigh with his mace."

Dhritarastra became alarmed. He tried to pacify the rishi, asking him to be merciful, but Maitreya said, "This will surely come to pass unless your son makes peace with the Pandavas."

Hearing the curse mitigated, Dhritarastra felt some relief and he said, "Great sage, please tell us more about how Bhima killed Kirmira. We have only heard about the other two Rakshasas."

Maitreya shook his head and rose to leave. "I shall not say anything more in the presence of your son. Vidura here also knows about this; ask him to describe the incident."

The sage strode out of the hall and Dhritarastra then asked Vidura to tell him about Kirmira. Vidura replied that he had heard the story from Yudhisthira when he visited him in the forest. "He told me how they had encountered the Rakshasa one night as they were travelling through the forest. The demon came before the brothers, holding a blazing torch and obstructing their way like a mountain. By his roars alone he made birds and other forest animals drop down in terror. Draupadi practically fainted in fear and had to be held up by the twins."

Vidura then described how Bhima had attacked and killed the demon, smashing him on the ground and breaking his back in two. "I saw for myself the Rakshasa's colossal and bloodied corpse as I came back to Hastinapura."

As Vidura finished his account Duryodhana rose up and walked out of the hall. He tried to appear unconcerned, but his mind was alarmed. Dhritarastra sat absorbed in thought, remembering again his omission during the gambling match.

CHAPTER FIFTEEN

MORAL INSTRUCTIONS IN THE FOREST

When news reached Dwaraka of the Pandavas' exile, Krishna went with Balarama and other leading Yadus to visit them in the forest. Seeing the Pandavas attired in deerskins and seated on the bare ground he cried out in anger. "The earth will drink the blood of Duryodhana, Karna, Shakuni and Dushasana. Slaying them and all their followers we shall install the virtuous Yudhisthira on the throne. This is eternal morality."

Krishna seemed as if he were on fire. His eyes glowed red. Knowing him to be capable of consuming all created things, Arjuna quickly sought to placate him. He praised Krishna's inconceivable power and recounted his many incarnations in former ages, describing the wonderful feats they had all achieved. "Rishi Vyasadeva has told me that you are the cause of creation and the beginning and end of all things. O Krishna, whatever you desire is immediately brought into being."

Arjuna spoke at length about Krishna, finally becoming overwhelmed with spiritual emotion. Struck dumb, he simply gazed at Krishna with tear-filled eyes.

Krishna smiled at Arjuna and replied to him in an affectionate voice. "Arjuna, you are mine and I am yours. What is mine is also yours. Whoever hates you, hates me, and whoever follows you is also my follower. O hero, you are Nara and I am Narayana. We are born in this world of men for a special purpose. None can understand us."

Draupadi was sitting amid her husbands. Folding her palms, she also began to praise Krishna as the Lord of all the worlds. She then said, "Lord, I am the wife of the Pandavas, Dhristyadyumna's sister, and above all your friend. How is it then that I was so grievously insulted?"

Draupadi buried her face in her hands and wept. She had taken a vow not to dress her hair again until Dushasana was slain, and it hung loosely around her shoulders, which shook as she softly cried. She lifted her tearstreaked face and said in a trembling voice, "It seems I have none to protect me. Not husbands, brothers, friends or anyone, for you all sit here and do nothing. Who will assuage my grief arising from Karna's insult and ridicule in the assembly? Krishna, I seek your shelter."

Krishna gently consoled her. "Fair lady, the wives of those who insulted you will soon weep even as you do now. They will see their husbands lying dead on the ground, pierced with arrows and weltering in blood. Do not grieve. I will do everything in my power to help the Pandavas. Your husbands will be kings and you will be queen. Know that the heavens may fall or the Himalayas split, but my words will never prove false."

Draupadi felt reassured. She glanced across at Arjuna, seeking his confirmation of Krishna's words. Catching her glance, Arjuna said, "Do not weep, beautiful lady. What Krishna has said will come to pass. It cannot be otherwise."

Krishna turned to Yudhisthira and said, "When the gambling match was announced I was indisposed and could not attend. Otherwise, even if not invited, I would have gone there and saved you from this calamity. By pointing out the many evils inherent in gambling I would have stopped the game."

Still appearing angry, Krishna declared that if Dhritarastra had not accepted his advice he would have compelled him by force. "If anyone, passing as Dhritarastra's friend, had tried to prevent me and offer contrary advice, they would have been destroyed."

Yudhisthira asked Krishna where he had been when the match took place. Krishna replied that he had been engaged in combat with a demonic king named Shalva, who had attacked Dwaraka during Krishna's absence. "When I returned from the Rajasuya I saw the damage he had caused, and I learned that my son Pradyumna had pursued him with a number of Yadu fighters. I thus went to give them assistance."

At Yudhisthira's request Krishna described in detail his battle with Shalva, which culminated in that king's death. He described how the evil-minded monarch had obtained a wonderful airship from Shiva. He had used it to oppress Dwaraka and when Krishna found him, he smashed the ship to pieces. He then slew Shalva with the Sudarshan *chakra*.

The Pandavas applauded Krishna who concluded, "It was for this reason I could not attend the gambling match. Otherwise I think Duryodhana would not be alive today; but what can be done now? It is difficult to stem the tide once the dam has been broken."

Krishna knew that Yudhisthira would certainly remain in the forest until the full thirteen years had expired. Only then would it be possible to assist him to recover his kingdom, should it be necessary. After spending some hours with the brothers, Krishna finally mounted his splendid chariot again.

When Krishna and his party had departed Yudhisthira decided to move more deeply into the forest. Still accompanied by numerous brahmins, the brothers set off into the thick woods, travelling until they arrived at a great lake known as Dwaitavana. It was decorated with swans and surrounded by rishis who sat rapt in meditation. Yudhisthira decided to stay there. The region around the lake resembled heaven, with countless blossoming trees that filled the air with a sweet fragrance. Golden fruits hung from those trees, and peacocks, cuckoos and many other birds played in their foliage, singing delightful songs.

Dhaumya performed various rituals to sanctify the area where the brothers constructed their residences. They began to live there peacefully, serving the rishis by offering them food gleaned from the forest. During the day they practiced their martial skills by hunting. According to scriptural direction, they culled the population of wild beasts in the forest, protecting the rishis from attack and disturbance. The rishis reciprocated by reciting to them Vedic histories replete with spiritual instructions.

Finding forest life a welcome interlude from the onerous and often harsh duties of a king, Yudhisthira did not lament for the loss of his wealth or kingdom. The gentle son of Dharma enjoyed the association of the rishis. However, he knew that his God-given duty was to rule over the people, and he remained always conscious of the time when his period of exile would end.

Draupadi, though, was not enjoying her time in the forest. Her heart burned with the memory of the dice game. It seemed to her that Yudhisthira had taken everything far too easily. The Kauravas had clearly acted abominably. Surely any virtuous monarch should see it as his duty to immediately punish them. Why had Yudhisthira simply gone meekly into exile?

One evening when the Pandavas were seated together, Draupadi began to question Yudhisthira. "My lord, when I think of Duryodhana living happily in Hastinapura while we reside in this lonely forest, I am seized with anger. Does it not anger you? Does the fact that you have been consigned to obscurity by sinful men through a sinful act not move you? Look at you now, clad in barks and deerskins when formerly you wore the finest silk robes. You sit on a grass mat instead of your jewelled throne. Your body is daubed with mud from the riverbank, when before it would be smeared with the costliest unguents. How do you tolerate all this in silent acquiesence?"

Draupadi found herself crying again. It was so frustrating. Yudhisthira seemed gentle to a fault, but his grasp of the laws of morality was without equal. Still, his present mood was hard to understand. Looking across at Bhima she continued to speak. "Just see your powerful brother Bhima, glancing at you again and again. It is only his love for you that prevents him from rising up at once and annihilating the Kauravas. Arjuna, griefstricken himself by your plight, is always trying to pacify him. The twins are similarly afflicted. Why then do you do nothing? There is a time for forgiveness and a time for anger, especially for powerful rulers. I feel you have got these two confused. Surely now is the appropriate time for you to display fierce anger and punish Duryodhana."

Yudhisthira looked compassionately at Draupadi. She had suffered much and was still feeling great pain. The Pandava king shed tears. Draupadi's suffering was his own. The moment when she had been dragged into the hall was still vivid. He would never forget that. Why had he not checked himself? Due only to his fault had poor Draupadi and his brothers been put through such misery. Still, anger was not the proper response—not yet.

Yudhisthira's golden features reflected the light of the fire around which they sat. Lifting a hand, he calmly replied, "Most intelligent lady, you advocate anger as the right course for me now, but I am doubtful. Although through anger one may sometimes achieve immediate gains, ultimately it leads to destruction. Anger clouds one's discrimination and impels one to act in ways he would never otherwise consider. For this reason the wise keep anger at a distance."

Yudhisthira went on to praise the virtue of forgiveness. "In my view forgiveness is best. It always behooves a man of character to exercise forgiveness, for if there were no forgiving men then chaos would soon prevail throughout the world. If kings give way to anger the people will soon meet with destruction. If inferiors do not tolerate their superiors' admonishments sin will quickly take root and destroy mankind. In ancient times the great rishi Kashyapa said, 'Forgiveness is virtue, sacrifice, purity, penance, truth, piety and religion. By practicing forgiveness, a man can achieve regions of everlasting happiness.'"

Yudhisthira made it clear that he would not renounce forgiveness. Any other course would certainly lead to conflict. "Bhishma, Drona, Vidura and Kripa will all counsel Dhritarastra to peacefully resolve this matter. If he does not take their advice and give back our kingdom, he will be destroyed but let me not be the cause. Forgiveness and humility, both unknown to Duryodhana, are attributes of the self-controlled and they lead always to victory. I shall therefore adopt them, gentle lady."

Draupadi seemed confused. "How can pacific virtue lead to success when we see you in such adversity? Who is more virtuous than you? Who more self-controlled and indeed more humble? Even when you assumed control of the earth, we did not see in you even the slightest pride. You could abandon me and your brothers before giving up virtue. Yet destiny caused your mind to become confused and you gambled away everything. It is quite incredible."

Draupadi went on revealing her mind. It seemed to her that the only explanation for Yudhisthira's having acted so out of character was that he was moved by the supreme will. After all, God was the ultimate ordainer of everything. How though could he have ordained something so contrary to virtue? How had he allowed the sinful Duryodhana to prosper and Yudhisthira to suffer? It made no sense.

Yudhisthira could see that his wife was bewildered by her grief and anger. He replied to her in a gentle voice. "Surely you are afflicted by atheistic doubts. Virtuous acts should never be performed with a desire for their fruits. Such a sinful mentality deprives one of the results, as does doubting the efficacy of virtue. There is no question that true virtue always has a glorious result. You have seen for yourself the limitless powers of great rishis like Narada and Vyasadeva, which have been acquired through virtue. These rishis declare piety and virtue to be the foremost duty."

Yudhisthira instructed Draupadi at length. He explained that although it sometimes appears that sinful men flourish, in the end they are always destroyed. Becoming degraded, they descend into lower and lower states of life. "The fruits of both sin and virtue are not immediately seen, gentle lady, but they manifest in due course. This is a highly mysterious subject, bewildering to even the gods. The results of work, known as karma, are controlled by Supreme Providence and he alone understands its mysteries. Never speak ill of him, Draupadi, for he is never partial or vicious toward anyone."

Night fell as Yudhisthira spoke and the rishis began to light fires which illuminated the lakeshore where they sat. The crackling of the fires mingled with the chirping of crickets and the murmur of rishis chanting their evening prayers. Many of them sat around the Pandavas, listening to Yudhisthira. They nodded in agreement as he concluded his speech.

Draupadi, however, was still doubtful. "I accept all you have said, O foremost of the Bharatas. God is certainly giving us the results of our own acts, but we are still free to take further action. We must still endeavour to achieve virtue, as you have said. Why then do you not act now to recover your kingdom. Is this not the right thing to do?"

Bhima had been listening carefully. Draupadi's words resonated with him and when she stopped speaking, he said, "O king, this acetic life is not meant for you. How can you acquire virtue in this lonely wood? You are a king; meant to possess wealth, give charity and protect the people, not live like a yogi. What trifling virtue will you gain by keeping a promise made to sinful men?"

Bhima spoke with passion. Like Draupadi, he could not bear the thought of the Kauravas living in opulence, while Yudhisthira languished in the forest. His angry voice echoed across the lake as he went on. "Lord of the Bharatas, have you lost sight of your duty? Has despair deprived you of your manliness? How can you allow

Duryodhana to enjoy your wealth? He is exactly like an offal-eating jackal stealing a lion's prey. To him your forgiveness and virtue is nothing more than weakness. It was folly alone that made us desist from killing him when we had the chance. Let us no longer fall victim to that folly. We should rise up at once and kill the Kauravas to a man."

Yudhisthira summoned patience as he listened to Bhima venting his long pent-up anger. The Pandava king felt chastised by his brother but made no attempt to defend himself. When Bhima had at last finished speaking Yudhisthira sat silent for some moments, then finally said, "I cannot reproach you for lancing me with your sharp words, Bhima, for it was truly my mistake that has brought about our present condition. I should have exercised more self-control during the dice game. It was always clear that Shakuni could not be defeated. Yet, even though my mind was overcome by pride and foolishness, I still believe that everything was preordained."

Yudhisthira fell silent again, thinking back to the day of the match. What had come over him? He had felt that he was acting only for virtue, but the result had been misery for everyone he loved. Something must have moved him to act so averse to his nature, but what could he do now? An agreement had been made. It could not be broken, especially when it would almost surely lead to a wholesale carnage.

"I cannot falsify my word, Bhima. Truth is certainly the highest virtue and duty of all. We shall remain here for thirteen years, in pursuance of truth. Without doubt better times will come, for virtue always has its rewards."

Seeing that Bhima was still seething with frustration, Yudhisthira continued, his tone becoming more grave. "Listen to me, mighty-armed hero. We should not be rash. Acts performed out of pride or passion will end in grief. Let me tell you what I feel will be the result of your suggestion, born as it is from mental agitation."

Yudhisthira listed the many kings and warriors who would support the Kauravas. As well as all the mighty Kurus themselves, which included Bhishma, Drona, Kripa and dozens of other fighters who could all contend single-handed with great divisions of warriors, there were also numerous monarchs who had been subjugated by the Pandavas prior to the Rajasuya. Those kings would take Duryodhana's side without doubt.

"Since our departure you can be sure that Duryodhana's main business will have been to build his military strength. He now has control of tremendous wealth and can amass an immense and unassailable army. We, however, are without anything, alone in the forest, and unable to put together even a small force."

Yudhisthira spoke about Karna, whom he especially feared. He reminded his brothers how Karna had matched every martial feat displayed by Arjuna during the exhibition. "I consider the impetuous and ever-angry Karna our greatest danger. Encased in his natural armour and accomplished in the use of every weapon, he will be difficult to overcome. Therefore I feel that victory is far from assured should we join battle now with the Kurus."

Bhima became pensive and said nothing, sqeezing his hands together. Thinking on Yudhisthira's words, all his brothers began to feel almost hopeless about recovering their kingdom. How could men like Bhishma, Drona, Kripa and Karna ever be overpowered, even by the celestials?

As the brothers sat in thought, Vyasadeva came into their midst. He took his seat by their side and told them that he had understood their anxiety. "O Yudhisthira, I saw what was in your mind, thus did I speedily come here. Listen now as I tell you how you will be able to defeat your foes."

Vyasadeva said that he would impart to Yudhisthira the knowledge of a mystic power called *pratismriti*, which enabled its user to achieve success in any endeavour. "Give this power to Arjuna. With it he will be able to approach the gods and learn from them the secrets of their celestial weapons. In due course of time he will achieve great feats with these mighty missiles."

After teaching Yudhisthira the *pratismriti* mantras Vyasadeva then left. Yudhisthira consulted with the rishis and on a day made auspicious by favourable constellations, he passed the knowledge on to Arjuna, instructing him to begin his quest for the celestial weapons. Arjuna then clad himself from head to toe in armour and took up his Gandiva bow and inexhaustible quivers. Blessed by the brahmins and bid a loving farewell by his brothers and Draupadi, he set off toward the north. His aim was to reach the celestial Mandara Mountain, the gateway to the gods' abode, that lay amid the Himalayas.

CHAPTER SIXTEEN

Arjuna Meets the Gods

Arjuna moved swiftly along the forest paths. He chanted the *pratismriti* mantras and found himself travelling at tremendous speeds. The forest creatures ran away in all directions as he raced by, his bow held at the ready. At the end of one day he reached the Mandara and began to ascend its heights. As he climbed toward the bluish peak, he saw brightly coloured flowers and trees, as well as sparkling waterfalls falling onto gem-studded rocks. Siddhas, Charanas, Gandharvas and other celestial beings sported in delightful wooded groves. The air was heavy with fragrance and resonant with the sound of countless exotic birds.

Reaching a broad plateau halfway up the mountain, Arjuna stopped and looked around, considering that he might remain there and practice asceticism. He knew he would only be able to see the gods if they revealed themselves to him, and for that he would need to perform yoga and meditation. As he continued across the heavenly landscape, he heard a voice that seemed to come from the sky. "Wait!" it commanded.

Startled, Arjuna stopped and looked around. He saw a brahmin seated at the foot of a tree, ablaze with spiritual effulgence. Matted locks hung around his powerful shoulders and he was clad in simple tree bark garments. He said, "Who are you who has come here bearing weapons and wearing armour? This is the abode of peaceful brahmins. There is no need for any aggression here. Throw away your bow."

Arjuna bowed to the brahmin and introduced himself, but he made it clear he would not part with his weapons. The brahmin then smiled and revealed himself to be his own father Indra. "My child, I am pleased to see you," he said. "Ask from me some boon."

Arjuna was overjoyed. If the great Indra had come to him then surely his mission would soon be successful. He folded his palms and replied,

"My lord, I desire that you impart to me all the knowledge of the gods' divine weapons."

Indra continued to smile. "Why do you want weapons? You are virtually in heaven now. What do you have to achieve by fighting? Only ask me and I shall raise you to regions of bliss."

Arjuna was respectful but firm. "My lord, I have no desire for celestial pleasures. My brothers await me in a lonely forest. They are depending upon me. How can I desert them for my own happiness?"

Seeing Arjuna's distress as he remembered his brothers, Indra consoled him and said, "Dear child, try to see the great god Shiva. By gaining his audience all your desires will be fulfilled."

Indra then disappeared, leaving Arjuna standing under the tree where he had been seated. Arjuna began at once to practice asceticism. He leaned his bow against the tree and removed his armour. After bathing in a nearby mountain stream, he fashioned himself a crude garment from the long grasses growing all around. Tying it around his waist he spread blades of *kusha* grass on the ground and sat down to meditate. He focused his mind on Shiva and began to intone the sacred syllable Om. Days became weeks as he remained in that place, eating sparsely and keeping his mind and passions in check. After a full month he assumed a standing posture with his arms raised above his head. He bathed three times daily and ate once in a week. After another month he began to stand on one leg. Eating only dry leaves, he controlled his breathing to the point where he inhaled and exhaled once every hour. Eventually he suspended his breathing entirely by the technique known as *kumbhaka.*

The great rishis living in that region soon noticed Arjuna's austerities. By the force of his fierce asceticism he generated such power that the very order of the universe appeared threatened. Understanding Arjuna's desire, the rishis went in a body to Shiva and said, "Almighty one, see how Arjuna is engaged in rigid asceticism on the breast of Mount Mandara. If he is not soon stopped, we fear he will destroy the world. Please check him."

Shiva raised a hand in blessing and replied, "Fear not, I will fulfill Arjuna's desire this very day."

The relieved sages then left and Shiva immediately assumed the form of a hunter. Tall and golden-hued, he seemed like a shining mountain.

He descended to earth accompanied by his consort Uma as well as many of his female goblin followers, who all assumed attractive forms. As they came to the region where Arjuna stood, it seemed aglow with radiant beauty. A strange quiet fell over the whole area; the birds stopped singing and even the flowing streams ran silently.

At that moment a powerful demon was passing that region. Seeing Arjuna meditating he decided to attack him. He assumed the form of a huge boar and charged at Arjuna with a blood-curdling roar. Arjuna fully opened his half-closed eyes and glared at the fast approaching beast. Within seconds he took up his bow and drew back an arrow. He shouted out, "Wicked one, I do not know who you are, but as you seek to injure me who has done you no harm, I shall send you to Death's abode."

Just as he was about to fire his arrow Arjuna heard a voice behind him. "Stop! Leave this one to me. I saw him first and have already aimed my arrow."

Ignoring that request, Arjuna released his shaft. At the same time Shiva also fired an arrow. Both shafts thudded into the charging demon simultaneously with a crack like thunder. Screaming in pain, the demon fell dead and resumed his natural form.

Arjuna wheeled around and saw the hunter. He smiled but spoke strongly. "Who are you? Why do you wander here surrounded by women? Tell me why you shot this Rakshasa who was first targeted by me? I cannot brook such an insult. You will pay with your life."

Shiva took a few steps closer and replied, "Do not worry about us. We are hunters and the forest is our residence. Who are you? You look like royalty and hardly belong in such a place."

Arjuna kept his bow at the ready. "Depending upon my Gandiva, I live here without any fear. See how I slew this mighty demon."

Shiva laughed. "This one was killed by me, not you. I saw him first and it was my arrow that struck him down. You should not boast so much. Indeed, it is I who has received insult here. Stand ready, for I shall shoot my thunder-like arrows at you. Resist them if you can."

Before Shiva could even raise his bow Arjuna shot a volley of arrows at him that whistled through the air. All of those shafts seemed to disappear into Shiva's body. The god replied with his own arrows and Arjuna expertly countered the attack. The Pandava fired countless arrows at his adversary but they had no effect on the unusual hunter. Arjuna gazed at him in surprise and awe. "Well done! Excellent!" he called out in admiration. There were few men who could withstand arrows shot from the Gandiva with such impunity.

Arjuna began to wonder who his foe might be. He was surely a celestial, perhaps even Shiva himself. Maybe that god had come to him in disguise; but whoever this hunter was he had come as an aggressor. Arjuna concluded that if he was anyone other than the invincible Shiva then he would soon be killed. He raised his bow and fired another cluster of deadly arrows at him. Again they were swallowed up by the hunter. Arjuna fired hundreds and thousands of shafts but they had no effect whatsoever on his opponent. Then, to his amazement, Arjuna saw that his previously inexhaustible quivers were empty.

Filled with wonder, Arjuna surveyed his imperturbable foe. The hunter stood smiling at him with no sign of any wounds. Arjuna rushed at him and began smashing him with the Gandiva. Still the hunter was unmoved. He snatched Arjuna's bow and drew it into his body. Arjuna quickly took up his sword and brought it down on Shiva's head but it simply smashed to pieces.

Arjuna tried everything to overcome the hunter. He tore up trees to strike him and hurled great rocks at him. When this failed, he pummeled him with his bare fists. The hunter fought back, catching Arjuna with blows that felt like thunderbolts. Arjuna seized him in his powerful arms and tried to crush the life out of him. Shiva in turn grasped hold of Arjuna and the two fighters stood locked together, their bodies emitting smoke and sparks as they exerted immense pressure on each other.

Pressed with such force by the god of gods, Arjuna became practically senseless. He turned blue and fell to his knees in a swoon. Observing the rules of combat Shiva stood back. Arjuna soon came around and he looked up at the still unharmed hunter. There was no doubt that he must be the exalted Shiva.

Covered in blood and exhausted, Arjuna bowed before his opponent. He fashioned an image of Shiva from the earth and worshipped it with flower petals. He saw that the hunter was covered with flowers. Arjuna was filled with joy. This was indeed the great deity.

Shiva then spoke to Arjuna in a powerful voice that filled the plateau where they stood. "I am pleased with you, Arjuna. No other warrior has your courage or determination. Your strength is practically equal to mine. Soon you shall acquire all the weapons you need to vanquish your enemies. Now behold me as I am."

Arjuna folded his palms and bowed in respect as Shiva exhibited his actual form. Seeing the effulgent god, with his three eyes and great trident, a divine serpent draped around his bluish neck, Arjuna offered prayers. He begged forgiveness for attacking him. Shiva replied that he had already pardoned him. He gave back to Arjuna the Gandiva bow and said that his quivers would again be inexhaustible. "Now ask from me a boon," said Shiva, holding up his hand which was adorned with every auspicious mark.

Arjuna said, "Please give to me the knowledge of your personal weapon, the Pashupata."

Shiva agreed and he taught Arjuna the mantras for summoning the weapon. As he chanted them the Pashupata appeared in his personal form and stood by Arjuna's side, saying he would be at the Pandava's service. Shiva then said, "Go to heaven now and receive the other divine weapons. I shall depart."

Before Arjuna's astonished eyes Shiva rose up to the skies along with all his followers. He stood gazing up at the sky for some minutes, wondering at his good fortune. As he looked up, he saw a blazing circle of light appearing in the heavens. Gradually it assumed a form and Arjuna saw that it was Indra, seated on the back of his celestial elephant Airavata. He descended onto a nearby mountain ledge. Arjuna saw that all the other principal gods had also come there. They shone like so many suns and lit up the whole region.

In a voice that rang out like thunderclaps, Indra said, "Arjuna, sinless one, you shall soon accomplish a great service for the gods. All the deities will bestow upon you their own weapons. You should now come to the heavens where I shall teach you all of my martial skills."

At Indra's command the gods approached Arjuna one by one and gave him their weapons. They then went away with Indra, leaving Arjuna standing alone on the plateau. Suddenly he heard a tremendous sound in the sky. Looking up he saw a huge chariot coming down, pulled by many hundreds of golden-hued steeds. It seemed to divide the heavens as it raced toward him. Furnished with canon, swords, missiles, thunderbolts, maces and other celestial weapons, it came to a halt by Arjuna's side. The charioteer got down and said, "I am Matali, Indra's driver sent here to fetch you to his abode."

After paying his respects to the Mandara Mountain, Arjuna climbed aboard the wonderful chariot and it rose up into the sky. It soon reached the heavenly paths that led to the higher worlds. Arjuna saw thousands of other celestial vehicles coursing in all directions. He saw countless brilliant planets, shining rishis, and warriors who had been slain in battle, thereby attaining heavenly forms. Matali told him that they were visible as stars from the earth.

Gradually the chariot approached Indra's planet which shone like a second sun. Fanned by fragrant breezes, it was covered with celestial trees and flowers. Siddhas and other perfected beings moved gracefully across the beautiful landscape as the chariot passed overhead.

Seeing Arjuna's amazement at the planet's spectacular opulence, Matali said, "This region cannot be reached by any of atheistic temperament. Only those who have practiced sacrifice and penance can come here. Heroes who never turn their backs in battle and rishis of rigid vows ascend to this planet, O pure minded one. The sinful can never see it even in their dreams. Behold now Amaravati, Indra's capital."

The chariot passed through a golden gate studded with brilliant, many-hued celestial gems. It entered the famed Nandana pleasure-gardens, filled with charming groves where the gods sported with beautiful Apsaras. Passing mansions of diverse and exquisite design, they came at last to Indra's immense palace. Arjuna was greeted by Gandharvas who eulogised him with captivating songs. While brahmins and bards chanted Vedic hymns, he was led to Indra, who immediately got down from his throne and tightly embraced him. The king of the gods then brought Arjuna up onto his expansive gold seat and sat next to him. Indra spoke consoling words to his son, telling him that he and his brothers would soon be restored to their rightful position.

After he had been refreshed with varieties of ambrosial food and drink and entertained with song and dance by the Gandharvas and Apsaras, Arjuna was taken to his residence in Indra's palace.

Arjuna began to live amid the splendid affluence of Indra's abode. Indra taught him the science of arms known only to the gods, instructing him in the use of his own weapon, the Vajra thunderbolt. At Indra's command he also studied under Chitrasena, king of the Gandharvas, who taught him the skills of celestial music and dance. Indra told him that these abilities would prove useful in the future.

Five years passed, during which time Arjuna thought always of his brothers in the forest, and of the dice game and the insulting of Draupadi. Although surrounded by every conceivable kind of enjoyment, his mind could not be peaceful, and he longed to rejoin his brothers. As the time for his departure drew close, he received a visit one evening from Urvashi, one of Indra's Apsara consorts. Seeing the bewilderingly beautiful maiden at his door, Arjuna bowed and closed his eyes out of modesty. "Please come in and take a seat," he said, nervously. "Pray tell me why you have come here at this late hour."

Urvashi had been asked by Indra to go to Arjuna. The god had seen him casting glances at her in his assembly. Smiling demurely, she explained this to Arjuna and said, "I am thus here to wait upon you. O hero, seeing you and knowing of your many virtues, I am held under Cupid's sway. Give yourself to me and satisfy my desire."

Arjuna felt almost intoxicated by her heady fragrance, but he controlled his mind and averted her gaze. Covering his ears as she spoke, he replied, "Blessed lady, I could never accept you as a wife. Indeed, you are exactly like my mother."

Arjuna explained that he had only been looking at her out of wonder, thinking of how, thousands of years previously, she had married one of his great ancestors. She was the mother of a famous forefather of Arjuna's dynasty. "How then could I possibly enter into a conjugal relationship with you?" he asked.

Urvashi's smile seemed to light up Arjuna's room. She replied in a voice that resembled the tinkling of golden bells. "You need not fear incurring any sin. Apsaras are not bound by wordly morality. We are free to consort with all who reside here. Indeed, other descendants of your dynasty have sported with us and you may also do so."

Urvashi implored Arjuna to accept her, but he could not agree. He made it clear that he was unable to see her as anything but a mother. Urvashi felt insulted by his refusal. She began to tremble in anger.

Contracting her delicate eyebrows, she said, "As you refuse a woman who has come here on the order of your father, a woman pierced by love's arrows, so you shall have to lose your manhood and live among women."

The indignant Apsara then rose up and left the room, leaving Arjuna in a state of consternation. He went at once to Indra and told him what had happened. Laughing, Indra said, "My child, your patience and self-control is surely without comparison. Do not worry about this curse. It will serve you well during the thirteenth year of your exile. After passing one year as a eunuch, you will regain your power."

Indra then informed Arjuna that he would arrange for his return to earth the next day. Greatly relieved, Arjuna thanked Indra and went back to his room, his mind eager for the company of his brothers and Draupadi.

CHAPTER SEVENTEEN

HEAVEN ON EARTH

After Arjuna had departed for the Himalayas, the other Pandavas continued to live in the Kamyaka forest. They missed their brother and prayed for his swift return. Spending their time hunting, gathering food and hearing from the brahmins, they fell into a routine that made the days pass quickly. Among the many rishis who visited them, one named Vrihadashwa came one evening to their ashram. He was fully acquainted with the mystical science of dice playing. After Bhima revealed to the rishi his anxiety that Yudhisthira may again be challenged by Shakuni, even after the Pandavas had left the forest, Vrihadashwa taught Yudhisthira the science. When he saw the king was fully proficient, he told him, "Not even Shakuni will now be able to defeat you at dice."

Soon after Vrihadashwa left the Pandavas were visited by Narada. He suggested that while they waited for Arjuna's return they should visit the many *tirthas*, pilgrimage sites situated in that Himalayan region. He described the merits that accrued from going to each of dozens of holy places. When he had finished, he told the brothers that Lomasha Rishi would soon arrive. "He will lead you to these *tirthas*," said Narada, as he departed from their ashram.

A few days later, as Narada had predicted, the famous rishi Lomasha came to the Pandavas. He told them that he had been travelling in the higher planets and had seen Arjuna. "Your brother is sharing Indra's throne. He has already received Shiva's mighty weapon and is now being instructed by Indra."

Lomasha said that Indra had sent a message confirming Narada's suggestion that Yudhisthira and his brothers visit the many sacred pilgrimage sites in the Himalayas. "By going to these *tirthas* you will see many highly exalted sages and gain great spiritual power," Lomasha said. "I have already travelled to them all and can lead you to them."

Overjoyed to hear of Arjuna's success, Yudhisthira replied, "What great good fortune is ours that the king of the gods thinks of our welfare. That fortune is made complete by your presence, great sage. Pray take us to the *tirthas*."

Yudhisthira then addressed the many brahmins who were living with them. The journey into the high Himalayas, where many of the *tirthas* lay, would be difficult. He did not want to expose the brahmins to unnecessary suffering and he warned them that food and drink may be hard to obtain. "The climate will be severe and the ways fraught with danger. If you wish you may now go to Hastinapura where king Dhritarastra will provide your maintenance."

Most of the brahmins decided to go to Hastinapura and they sorrowfully took their leave from the Pandavas. Accompanied by only a few brahmins and servants, the brothers set off, with Lomasha and Dhaumya leading the way. As they began their journey Yudhisthira, asked Lomasha, "O foremost of rishis, I do not think I am without virtue and yet I am afflicted with so much sorrow. On the other hand, I feel my enemies have very few morals. Why then do they prosper?"

Lomasha said, "It seems contradictory, dear child, but you should not grieve. Any success obtained as a result of sin is soon lost. It may be seen that wicked men prosper for a while, but eventually they are destroyed to their roots."

The party walked single file along a narrow forest path. Bhima carried Draupadi, and all four brothers kept their weapons at the ready. The twins went ahead with the rishis, alertly watching all sides with their swords drawn. Rakshasas were known to frequent the mountain passes and the Pandavas did not want to take any chances.

Lomasha went on speaking. "In a previous age I saw how the Daityas and Danavas, the powerful demon races, once gained ascendancy over the gods by virtue of penance. They took possession of great wealth and became filled with pride. Shunning all virtuous acts, they engaged in nothing but licentious and sinful behavior. The goddess of prosperity, Lakshmi, soon forsook them and they were afflicted by adversity. Anger then overtook them, and they were quickly ruined."

Lomasha described how on the other hand the gods had practiced asceticism and virtue. Visiting holy places and serving the brahmins, they entirely eschewed sin. Thus, Lakshmi sought them and they again flourished. "In the same way, Yudhisthira, you brothers should adhere to virtue and you will soon see your good fortune returning. Dhritarastra's sons are exactly like the demons and will surely meet with the same end."

Reassured by Lomasha's words, the Pandavas made their way through the forest. Gradually they visited the many *tirthas,* bathing in the sacred lakes and hearing spiritual instruction from the rishis. The sages recited to them the fascinating histories of their forefathers and other great kings, which they heard with rapt attention. They offered oblations to their ancestors and worshipped the ascetics. Dhritarastra had sent wealth to the forest and Yudhisthira had his servants carry this with them to give in charity to those sages.

After travelling for a long time, they came to Mount Mandara. As they gazed at the splendid mountain with its peak shrouded in clouds, Lomasha said, "Behold the holy abode of Kuvera and his hordes of Yaksha followers. It rises fifty miles into the heavens and cannot be accessed by the sinful. Concentrate your minds and proceed with caution. On account of your virtue and asceticism you will be able to enter this region and mix with the celestials."

Lomasha said that Arjuna would soon be descending from heaven onto the summit of Mandara. "Let us therefore ascend the mountain and wait for him. We shall meet with Kuvera and receive his blessings also."

Close to the foot of the mountain was the kingdom of Suvaka. The party rested there for a night before beginning their ascent. They were well received by the king who offered them all hospitality. Leaving their servants and possessions with him, they left in the morning and headed for Mandara Mountain. Lomasha began offering prayers to the Goddess Ganga, who had her source somewhere in its heights. He spent some time praying that she protect them before they proceeded up the mountainside.

Yudhisthira said to his brothers, "Keep your thoughts pure and guard Draupadi carefully. Lomasha's apprehension is astonishing. The way ahead must surely be precarious."

Bhima placed Draupadi on his shoulder as they began their climb. The terrain was rugged and virtually inaccessible. Thick with trees and creepers, there were no paths and the ground was strewn with rocks. They could hear the roars of fierce beasts and a strong wind blew in their faces. After climbing throughout the day they reached a plateau where they rested, exhausted from their toil. As they looked around them it seemed they had arrived in heaven. The ground was carpeted with soft bluish grasses and expanses of wildflowers. Trees filled with brightly coloured blossoms stood around lakes of clear water that were covered with lotuses and crowded with swans, cranes and storks. The whole region seemed to be illuminated by its own effulgence.

In the distance they saw what appeared to be a number of massive white rocks. Lomasha told them they were the bones of Naraka, a great demon slain in ancient times by Vishnu. He related the story to them as they continued on their way.

Leaving behind the heavenly region they began climbing snow-bound and treacherous paths. As the brothers slowly made their arduous ascent toward the distant summit of the mountain they thought only of Arjuna. Gradually the climb became so perilous and the wind so fierce that they felt they could not continue. Their limbs were frozen, and, with the exception of Bhima, they were utterly exhausted.

Bhima placed Draupadi on the ground and she lay there barely conscious. Yudhisthira slumped onto a rock and said, "Alas for our lot. We have become rangers of the wilderness. The beautiful Draupadi is close to fainting. Her lotus-like hands and feet are blue with cold. Oh, I am the most wretched man. My addiction to dice has caused immense suffering for this innocent princess. Her noble father has vainly bestowed her upon the Pandavas in the hope of her happiness. Now she lies here on the bare ground, overcome by hardship and sorrow."

Lomasha and Dhaumya consoled Yudhisthira with gentle words. They uttered mantras which gave strength to Draupadi. The twins laid out a deerskin and the princess lay on it to rest as they massaged her feet.

Yudhisthira looked up at the great mountain. It seemed impossible to go any further. He turned to Bhima and said, "How shall we carry on?"

Bhima suggested that they summon his son Ghatotkacha. "Surely he will be able to carry us up this steep mountain pass."

Yudhisthira agreed and Bhima concentrated his mind upon his son. Within moments Ghatotkacha appeared. He prostrated himself before the Pandavas and the rishis, touching their feet and saying, "I am your servant. Command me what I should do."

Bhima embraced his son and Yudhisthira said, "O Bhima, let your heroic and powerful son carry Draupadi, who is like his own mother. With his help I think we shall be able to reach our destination."

Ghatotkacha smiled, his huge mouth opening to reveal rows of sharp fangs. "I will carry the queen. My Rakshasa followers will also carry the others. Tell us where we should go."

Several powerful-looking Rakshasas appeared in the sky and on Ghatotkacha's order they came before the Pandavas with folded palms. They took the brothers up onto their shoulders, while Ghatotkacha respectfully carried Draupadi. Lomasha, by virtue of his own mystic power, rose unaided into the sky alongside the Rakshasas, blazing like the sun. Travelling swiftly, they coursed over the mountain, seeing beneath them a myriad of wondrous regions inhabited by the celestials. Passing over the celestial land known as Harivarsha with its great northern mountains, they came at last to the immense Gandhamadana. On Lomasha's order the Rakshasas alighted close to a huge *badari* tree.

"Here is Badarika Ashram," said the sage. "This is the ancient hermitage of Nara and Narayana Rishis."

The brothers gazed around in awe. The *badari* tree spread out its limbs like a vast green umbrella of lush foliage. It exuded freshness and calm, inviting shelter beneath its boughs. Ripe fruits hung down and all kinds of birds, maddened by the honey falling from the fruits, played in its branches. Nearby they saw the crystal waters of the Ganges where she descended from the heavens onto the earth. Crowded with sages' hermitages, the entire region resounded with the sacred chanting of those rishis. It was lit by its own mystical effulgence and seemed to exist in a separate and transcendent dimension of space. As soon as they arrived there the Pandavas felt all their bodily and mental pains assuaged. Even hunger and thirst left them, and their minds became profoundly peaceful.

Some of the rishis, who by their own inner vision had already understood their visitors' identities, came forward to greet them. The Pandavas lay flat on the ground in obeisance and were blessed by the sages. After being honoured with offerings of celestial fruits and flowers, the brothers took up their residence in a spacious cottage near the river. Yudhisthira asked Ghatotkacha to remain with them until after Arjuna's arrival, when they would return to the Kamyaka. They then began to spend their time in hearing discourses and instructions from the rishis.

* * *

In Hastinapura, Dhritarastra had learned from Vyasadeva of Arjuna's ascent to heaven. He heard how the Pandava had performed severe austerities and gained the favour of the gods. Dhritarastra was already experiencing acute anxiety and when he heard this news it grew even more intense. The period of exile was fast passing and the Pandavas would be back before he realised it. What would be their mood? Yudhisthira was peacefully inclined, but Bhima would never renounce his fury. Nor would Draupadi let her husbands forget the events in the assembly; and now Arjuna was acquiring the gods' own weapons. There could only be one reason for that. Dhritarastra recoiled at the thought. He called for Sanjaya to seek solace.

When his secretary was present, the king said, "O Sanjaya, have you heard about Arjuna's activities? That foe-slaying hero has gone to heaven in his mortal body. Gifted with the Pashupata by Shiva, he has also received all the other celestial weapons of the gods. How can there be any hope for my wicked sons? Soon they and all who follow them will lie prostrate on the battlefield."

Tears fell from Dhritarastra's blind eyes. He foresaw disaster. Duryodhana's intractable attitude toward the Pandavas made war seem inevitable.

Tapping his fingers against his forehead, the blind king continued, "Reflecting day and night I do not see a single warrior who can stand against Arjuna. He is wrathful, unretreating, proud and greatly powerful. Even the thunderbolt falling on a mountain peak may leave some portion unburnt, but Arjuna's arrows leave absolutely nothing standing. It seems to me that our armies have already fled in all directions, terrified by the clatter of his chariot wheels."

Sanjaya listened in silence. Many times since the Pandavas' departure his master had bewailed along similar lines. Yet he was still not making any move to control Duryodhana. There had been no chastisement for his heinous behavior during the gambling match. Nor had Karna received any punishment for ordering Draupadi to be stripped. With Karna's assistance Duryodhana was now ruling the kingdom. Dhritarastra was given to extended periods of depression, sitting alone for hours on end, his mind overcome by fear of the future.

Sanjaya looked up at the king, "Your words are true, great monarch. The immeasurably powerful Pandavas were consumed by anger when they saw their chaste wife insulted. I do not think they will forgive the Kauravas. Your sons have brought upon themselves a fearful calamity. The Pandavas will surely annihilate them."

Dhritarastra winced at his secretary's strong words. He replied in doleful tones. "O charioteer, seeing me blind and inactive Duryodhana considers me a fool. He does whatever he likes. Counselled by avaricious wretches he fails to properly understand anything. Even the arrows shot by Arjuna in sport can consume all my sons, what to speak of those fired in anger. He has already defeated the gods at Khandava, now he has also gratified the immortal Shiva. United with his brothers and Krishna he will obliterate our armies to a man."

Sanjaya spoke consolingly to his old master. The king seemed to understand the situation well enough. It now remained for him to take the right action when the Pandavas returned from the forest, but there was little cause for optimism. Despite his censures of Duryodhana, he seemed as attached to him as ever.

* * *

The Pandavas lived peacefully on Gandhamadana Mountain for some time, enjoying their heavenly surroundings, but they thought continuously of Arjuna. Then one day soon after their morning prayers, they saw a brilliant light in the sky. As they gazed upward it expanded and as it approached the mountain the brothers saw that it was a celestial chariot. To their overwhelming joy they saw Arjuna seated on that chariot, dressed in radiant silk robes and adorned with jewels, a brilliant coronet on his head. As the chariot reached the ground Arjuna dismounted and bowed before Dhaumya and Yudhisthira. He touched Bhima's feet and received his embrace, and the twins offered him their obeisance. Arjuna then affectionately greeted Draupadi, who appeared like a lotus flower opening to greet the morning sun. He presented her with many splendourous celestial gems which Indra had given him.

Yudhisthira greeted and worshipped Indra's charioteer Matali as if he were Indra himself. He enquired after the gods and Matali spoke to him in gentle words, conveying Indra's good wishes. He then ascended the chariot and drove it away back to the heavens.

The brothers all crowded around Arjuna, eager to hear of his adventures. Arjuna told them everything, from his arrival at the Gandhamadana and meeting there with Indra and Shiva, right up to the moment of his departure from heaven. He described how, just before it was time to leave, Indra had asked him to do something for him, by way of *dakshine*, the preceptor's traditional fee, in return for the weapons he had received. Indra had requested him to fight with a race of fierce demons known as the Nivata-kavachas, who had been disturbing the gods for a long time. "Indra gave me a suit of impenetrable armour and placed this coronet on my head, saying, 'Go out and win victory over all your enemies.' I then proceeded for battle on his chariot."

As his brothers listened in awestruck silence, Arjuna described in detail the cosmic battle that had ensued. Using all the celestial weapons he had acquired, Arjuna had eventually overpowered the demons after a terrible fight.

When Arjuna finished his narration, his brothers cheered him. Yudhisthira said, "We are fortunate indeed to have you back. Great too is our fortune that you have received these incredible weapons. I consider the earth conquered and the Kauravas already subdued."

Yudhisthira asked Arjuna to display the weapons. Arjuna stood up and began to concentrate in order to invoke them. Suddenly, however, the brothers began to see all kinds of natural disturbances. The ground trembled and the sky became covered with dark clouds. The brahmins found themselves unable to recite the Vedas and all creatures felt oppressed. As the Pandavas looked around in surprise they saw the sage Narada coming toward them. He said, "I have been sent by the gods. Do not invoke the weapons without good reason, Arjuna, or their divine power may destroy the world."

The sage turned to Yudhisthira. "O king, you will see Arjuna's prowess with the weapons in the war with the Kauravas."

The Pandavas bowed to Narada and he disappeared, leaving them to discuss their plans now that Arjuna had returned. Consulting with Dhaumya and Lomasha, they decided to stay at Badarika Ashram. Five years of their exile remained before they needed to enter some inhabited region. That time would be best spent in the association of the great rishis in Badarika.

Four years passed and the brothers increased their spiritual knowledge by hearing from the sages, as well as their personal power born of asceticism. At the end of this period Arjuna and Bhima approached Yudhisthira to suggest that they begin their descent back to the Kamyaka forest. Bhima said, "Eleven years have now gone by with us living in the forest. Out of our love for you, and restrained by morality, we have not killed Dhritarastra's sons, but the time for our return is coming close. Let us therefore leave this heavenly region and think about finding some place to spend our final year."

Yudhisthira agreed and after discussing with the rishis he concluded they should leave at once. As it was summer, he decided to go on foot and he dismissed Ghatotkacha and his followers, asking that he come again to assist them if a war with the Kauravas ensued. Then they slowly made their way back to Kamyaka, arriving just before the start of the monsoon season. They set up camp on high ground near the Dwaitavana lake and watched as the rains fell, flooding the earth and sending bubbling streams surging through the forest.

CHAPTER EIGHTEEN

DEMONIC INFLUENCES

As the Pandavas' exile wore on, Duryodhana grew increasingly confident. For eleven years he had enjoyed his position as a virtual emperor. His father had left the affairs of state to him and he had steadily increased his strength and influence by forming alliances all around the world. If and when the Pandavas ever came back he would be more than ready for them. The impoverished brothers would no doubt have become emaciated and weak from their long sojourn in the wild. It should not prove too difficult to deal with them. As the Kaurava prince sat on his splendid throne looking supremely satisfied, Shakuni began to address him.

"O king, you now have no rivals on earth. The Pandavas are gone and no longer pose any threat. Their wealth, which formerly gave you grief, is now the source of your pleasure. The world's kings are subservient to you and you are adored by countless brahmins. All this has been achieved by the force of intellect alone."

Duryodhana folded his hands together and smiled, looking around the great hall where the gambling match had taken place. Now it was frequently visited by state leaders bringing him tribute, which they had previously given to Yudhisthira.

Shakuni went on, "Now your position is secure why not pay a visit to the Pandavas? The wise say that wealth which is seen by both friends and foes alike is truly wealth. Let Yudhisthira and his brothers suffer as you once suffered, seeing you possessed of all grandeur and surrounded by the Kurus while they rot in the forest."

Duryodhana looked at his uncle's sinisterly smiling face. His idea was appealing, but Duryodhana was not sure. "I think my father would object to this suggestion," he said, remembering how Dhritarastra was always consumed by anxiety about the Pandavas. "He would immediately understand my motives and would be fearful of the consequences. The old man seems to imagine they have grown more powerful during their exile."

"Do not worry about the king," said Karna. He found Shakuni's proposal attractive. It would be good to see the Pandavas and their haughty wife clad in barks. "I am sure we can find a good pretext for our excursion."

Duryodhana did not take much convincing. He got up from his throne and put an arm round Karna's massive shoulders. "Yes, let us think of a reason that will convince the king. What greater delight could there be for us than to see Yudhisthira, Arjuna and especially Bhima sunk in misery? If those proud men see me graced with all wealth then the goal of my life is attained."

The three men then conferred together for some time. Finally they hit upon an idea which they felt sure would work. They had heard that the Pandavas were living in the Dwaitavana region, which was exactly where the Kurus were presently grazing their cattle herds. It was not uncommon for members of the royal order to personally go and check on the cattle.

After hatching their plan, they went as usual the next morning to see Dhritarastra. While they were talking with him a cowherd arrived. As previously instructed by Duryodhana, he began to speak about the cows at Dwaitavana, saying that it was time to mark the calves. Karna at once took the opportunity and said, "Why not let us go to Dwaitavana and take care of the cows, king? It would be a pleasant break. We can also enjoy some hunting in that charming region."

"I am not sure about this suggestion," said Dhritarastra. "I have heard that the Pandavas are there. Who knows what may happen if they see you? Arjuna has been to heaven and acquired the gods' divine weapons. Why then will he not kill you all? Remembering your insults to Draupadi and their own abuse, both he and Bhima will instantly scorch you with their fury should you appear before them."

Shakuni dismissed the king's doubts. "There is no possibility that Yudhisthira will not fulfill his vow. He will not permit his brothers to fight the Kauravas now. Anyway, we will keep clear of them, have no fear."

Dhritarastra still looked uncertain but seeing his son's eagerness he finally relented. Duryodhana immediately assembled a large force of troops. Taking all his brothers and their wives he soon set off for the forest. Thousands of chariots, elephants, horses and infantry made up the procession as it left the city. Dressed in their most elegant clothes and richly ornamented, the women travelled in fine carriages drawn by tall white steeds.

When he arrived at the Dwaitavana Lake, Duryodhana learned that Yudhisthira was engaged in performing a sacrifice on its opposite shore. He decided to set up camp nearby so the Pandavas could see him in all his opulence. His men went ahead to search out a suitable site, but when they came near the lake they were accosted by a voice from the waters. "Stop! Who goes there? Know me to be Chitrasena, king of the Gandharvas. This lake and its surrounding woodlands are mine. Leave at once if you value your lives."

Duryodhana's soldiers looked down into the lake and saw the radiant Gandharva surrounded by Apsaras and other celestials. They quickly returned to Duryodhana and informed him, but the Kaurava prince was not inclined to submit to Chitrasena. He ordered his men to confront the Gandharvas and they returned to the lake in force. They rushed forward, roaring and sending up a huge clatter with their chariot wheels. Thousands of Gandharvas rose from the waters and stood on the lakeside to meet the attack.

A fierce battle ensued. The Gandharvas quickly killed hundreds of Duryodhana's soldiers. With a mighty roar Karna entered the fray. He began displaying his dazzling prowess with a bow. Hundreds of Gandharvas fell as his mantra-charged arrows flashed toward them in thousands. Duryodhana also joined battle and the two friends fought side by side. They soon put the Gandharvas to flight. Seeing this Chitrasena himself came to the fight. He appeared to be dancing on the battlefield as he released countless deadly arrows. Conversant with all mystical forms of warfare he bewildered his opponents. It seemed as if a hundred Chitrasenas were assailing them from all sides. Arrows flew at them from every direction. Huge maces and battleaxes fell from the sky.

Encouraged by their leader, the other Gandharvas rallied and fought with renewed energy. They surrounded Karna, raining down showers of weapons. Slaying his horses and charioteer, they smashed his chariot apart. Karna felt hopelessly outnumbered. He leapt from his broken chariot and fled. Jumping aboard another chariot he raced away into the forest.

As the Gandharvas gained the upper hand only Duryodhana and his brothers remained facing them. Gradually they were overpowered by the many thousands of celestial fighters bearing down on them. Chitrasena personally targeted Duryodhana. He smashed his chariot and struck him with a hundred blazing arrows. Duryodhana fell stunned to the ground and Chitrasena raced forward and seized him by the hair. While other Gandharvas took hold of his brothers, Duryodhana was bound and taken prisoner. The Gandharvas then ran to the Kaurava camp and captured their wives as well.

Some of the fleeing Kuru soldiers ran around the lake and fell before Yudhisthira, begging him to help. Yudhisthira felt compassion toward the wretched looking soldiers, but Bhima laughed when he heard their pleas. "It seems the Gandharvas have already achieved our ends for us, saving us so much effort. Obviously, he came here to gloat over us. Why should we save him? This is all he deserves."

Yudhisthira held up a hand to silence Bhima. "Where is your honour, dear brother? These men are afraid and have sought our protection. Furthermore, we are Kurus and it is our own family who are being assailed. Among ourselves we may be five and they a hundred, but when an enemy of the Kurus comes we are a hundred and five brothers. We must act. As well as capturing our cousins, the wicked Gandharvas have insulted the Kuru ladies in our presence."

Yudhisthira instructed his brothers to go at once to rescue the Kauravas. He smiled at Bhima. "Your sworn enemy now depends on you. What could give you more happiness than this opportunity to protect him?"

Arjuna rose up at once and took hold of his weapons. "Either the Gandharvas release the Kauravas or the earth shall drink their blood."

Accepting Yudhisthira's words, Bhima also leapt up and began to prepare for battle. The twins followed, leaving Yudhisthira to continue with the sacrifice. All four brothers mounted chariots provided by the Kuru soldiers and they pursued the Gandharvas. Seeing them rushing forward with raised weapons, looking like four blazing fires, the Kuru soldiers shouted for joy.

The Gandharvas quickly assumed their battle formation again, preparing to face the Pandavas. Arjuna tried to reason with them before fighting. He called out, "O celestials, it is not right for you to fight with ordinary men, nor indeed to seize their wives. We are here on Yudhisthira's order to ask for their release. Please comply and we shall avoid any unnecessary bloodshed."

The Gandharvas only laughed and said they would not release their prisoners. "Chitrasena is our leader and it is his command alone which we obey."

Angered, Arjuna immediately fired a volley of gold-winged arrows at them. The Gandharvas responded with their own shafts. They surrounded the four brothers and hurled every kind of weapon at them. Undaunted, the Pandavas expertly countered the assault and continued attacking their foes. An extraordinary battle ensued with the four humans standing against thousands of Gandharvas. Arjuna's eyes turned red with rage. He invoked mystical weapons, slaying many hundreds of Gandharva warriors.

Oppressed by the brothers' forceful attack, the Gandharvas rose into the sky, but Arjuna checked them with a network of arrows shot from the Gandiva. Chitrasena then came to the fight, but after only a brief skirmish with Arjuna, he shouted out, "Hey Partha! Behold, I am your friend Chitrasena."

Seeing the Gandharva king approaching them in peace the Pandavas withdrew their weapons. Arjuna asked him why he and his followers were persecuting the Kurus and Chitrasena replied, "They came here only to gloat over you. Indra understood this and he ordered me to capture them. Allow me to carry them away. They have grievously wronged you and your wife. Imprisonment is only right for them."

Arjuna replied that whatever their sins they were still family members and Yudhisthira had asked for their release.

"I think your brother did not know why the evil minded Kauravas came here," said Chitrasena. "Let us take them before him and hear his judgment."

Agreeing to this, the Pandavas went with Chitrasena and his followers to Yudhisthira, with Duryodhana and his brothers held in chains. Yudhisthira thanked Chitrasena for not slaying the Kauravas. "You have thus saved our family honour and it will be further saved if you release them," he said, folding his hands in respect.

Delighted to see Yudhisthira's tolerance, humility and compassion, Chitrasena at once agreed. He had the bedraggled Kauravas released in Yudhisthira's presence and their women taken back to their camp. Indra then appeared and revived the slain Gandharvas by sprinkling them with *amrita*, heavenly nectar. All the celestials then rose into the sky and vanished.

Yudhisthira turned to Duryodhana and spoke in a gentle voice. "Dear cousin, do not again be so reckless. A rash and thoughtless man never achieves happiness. Go home now in peace with all your brothers. Do not be despondent."

Duryodhana was devastated. He could make no reply nor even look at Yudhisthira. Turning away, he walked off like a wooden doll, hardly even conscious of his own movements. He and his brothers mounted their chariots and slowly made their way back to their camp, leaving the Pandavas to continue with their sacrifice.

The Kauravas decided to leave immediately for Hastinapura. They set off; a sorry looking train of travellers compared to the pompous procession that had left Hastinapura. After they had covered around ten miles Karna caught up to them. Covered with wounds, he went straight to Duryodhana and said, "O king, regretfully I had to abandon the fight for fear of my life. Hard pressed by hordes of Gandharvas I fled into the forest. Yet I see you here, safe and well. Surely you have achieved a great feat today, defeating those superhuman beings. Tell me how you did it."

Duryodhana sighed and looked at his friend. Tears fell from his eyes as he replied, "You do not know the truth. Alas, I am ruined. My friend, life has lost all its lustre for me."

Karna listened in dismay as Duryodhana described what had happened. At the end of his account the crestfallen prince said, "Having become a source of joy for my enemies and grief for my friends I cannot continue to live. How can I return to Hastinapura? What would the Kuru chiefs say? Alas, I am a wretch who deserves only to die."

In his misery Duryodhana realised his foolishness. It was madness only that had made him come to the forest. Why had he not heeded

Vidura's often given advice? Now he was receiving the bitter consequences of that mistake.

Weeping, the prince turned to Dushasana and said, "Vain and insolent men like me cannot achieve happiness for long, even when they attain prosperity. I cannot drag on my miserable existence any longer. Dear brother, here and now do I hand over the kingdom to you. Take my place and rule this earth. I shall stay on this very spot and give up my life."

Before the eyes of his aghast brothers and friends, Duryodhana cast off his armour and royal robes. Tying on a waistcloth he sat on the ground in a yogic posture and expressed his determination to fast till death. Dushasana fell at his feet and cried out, "Relent! Do not do this, brother. How can I rule without you?"

Karna also tried to dissuade Duryodhana, imploring him in many ways and reassuring him that there was no shame in his defeat at the hands of the celestials. "Do not make yourself the butt of ridicule by this act. Rise up, great hero. The Pandavas only did their duty by protecting you, their king. There is nothing to be lamented in that."

Shakuni also tried to stop Duryodhana, but the prince would not be diverted from his purpose. He had made up his mind to die. As everyone gradually stopped speaking, he began to enter a trance of meditation, intending to observe the *praya* vow of fasting until death.

In the nether regions, the demons became aware of Duryodhana's resolve. Defeated in a war with the gods, the races of Daityas and Danavas had been planning how to gain revenge. Many of them had taken birth on earth as kings and warriors with the hope of overthrowing the pious kings who made sacrifices to the gods. Fearing their party would not succeed without Duryodhana to lead them, they began a ritual to invoke a powerful demoness capable of bringing Duryodhana to their presence. By her power the Kaurava was brought to their planet in his subtle body.

As if in a dream, Duryodhana found himself standing in an assembly of Danavas. Their leader addressed him in respectful tones. "king of kings, why have you undertaken such a rash vow? Suicide always leads to hell. One who takes his own life is reviled on earth and gains no auspicious destination. Your resolve is thus contrary to your own best interests. Nor is it necessary. Listen now as I describe how all success will soon be yours."

The Danava told Duryodhana how there were many thousands of mighty demons incarnated on earth. They would join his army to fight against the Pandavas. Other celestial demons would also possess the hearts of Bhishma, Drona, Kripa and all the principal Kuru warriors. They would thus lose all restraint in battle and mercilessly slay anyone and everyone who came before them.

"You need not fear Arjuna, king, for your friend Karna is the very powerful Naraka, a demon formerly slain by Vishnu himself. He has reincarnated to assist you on earth. Even if he does not kill Arjuna then there are hundreds of thousands of Daityas who have become the Samsapatakas, an invincible army who will challenge him again and again. Your success is certain. All your enemies will be annihilated. Be in good cheer and await your time. It will soon come."

Duryodhana was then returned to his physical body, which still sat in meditation. He opened his eyes and looked around in amazement, vividly recalling his meeting. Had it been a dream? It certainly seemed real. The promise it held out was too good to pass up. The prince decided to get up and return to Hastinapura. He would not reveal his mystical experience, in case it proved to be nothing more than a hallucination, but he had a strong feeling it had been real. He got to his feet with a smile.

Seeing him abandoning his determination to die, his brothers joyfully surrounded him. Karna embraced him with tears in his eyes and said, "By good fortune you have regained your senses. My dear friend, a dead man cannot conquer his enemies. Do not die so ignominiously. Go out and attain victory and immortal fame. With me as your ally why do you grieve? As soon as the Pandavas emerge from exile I swear I shall crush them. Have no doubt."

Duryodhana returned Karna's embrace. "So be it," he replied and he gave the order to return to Hastinapura, his mind now set on amassing an army for war.

CHAPTER NINETEEN

THE GODS INTERVENE

Some time after the fight with the Gandharvas, the Pandavas went out hunting together. Dhaumya remained at the hermitage along with Draupadi. While the brothers were gone, the king of Sindhu province, Jayadratha, passed their ashram while travelling to another kingdom. Seated on a great chariot and surrounded by numerous troops, he happened to see Draupadi as she was gathering flowers. He was struck by her beauty and practically lost his senses with desire. Stopping his party, he gazed at her for some time. Draupadi saw him looking at her and she pulled her sari over her head. Picking up her basket of flowers she hurried back to the cottage.

As he stared at Draupadi's faultless body covered only by a light summer dress, Jayadratha was entranced. He had to have this woman. Along with a few of his followers he jumped down from his chariot and walked over to the cottage. He called in, "Most beautiful maiden, are you there? Who and whose are you? Are you an Apsara? Why do you live in this lonely wood? Know me to be Jayadratha, lord of the Sindhus."

Draupadi shrank back into the cottage. She could sense the king's lusty intentions, but she replied respectfully, "You are welcome here, O king. I am Draupadi, wife of the Pandavas. They will soon be back. If you wait, I am sure Yudhisthira will receive you with all hospitality."

Jayadratha, his mind overpowered by desire, stepped into the cottage. "I am surprised that you remain with the Pandavas, charming lady. You deserve better. Your husbands are fallen from their position and have lost everything. Renounce them and become my wife. Give up this wretched forest life and share with me the opulent Sindhu kingdom."

Draupadi scowled and backed away from Jayadratha. It was as she suspected. This king had no morals. Her face flushed deep red as she rebuked Jayadratha. "How dare you speak in such a way? Are you not ashamed? Only dogs would make such a suggestion. The wise never criticise men who practice devout penance, even if impoverished."

Jayadratha laughed. He was even more enchanted by the furious Draupadi, who was trying to evade him. He stood squarely between her and the door. She reproached him even more fiercely. "Fool! Your destruction is close. You are rousing a sleeping lion by plucking a hair from his face. When Arjuna and Bhima return you will not know which way to run."

Bewildered by passion, Jayadratha disregarded Draupadi's warning. Laughing loudly he stepped forward and tried to seize her arm. Draupadi cried out and swung round with her clenched hands. She caught him on the side of the head and sent him sprawling to the ground; but as she lunged toward the door, he jumped up again and grasped her in his powerful arms. He began dragging the squirming princess toward his chariot.

Dhaumya heard the commotion and ran out of his hut. Seeing Jayadratha with the weeping Draupadi he called out, "Stop! Hear me king, you cannot take this lady without first defeating the Pandavas. This is the *kshatriya* code. Truly you will soon reap the result of this wicked act."

Jayadratha ignored Dhaumya. He pulled Draupadi onto his chariot and urged on his horses. As his chariot picked up speed Dhaumya ran after him, constantly reprimanding him with strong words. Although able, the rishi did not utter a curse as he knew the Pandavas were close by. They would soon deal with the sinful monarch.

Jayadratha and his followers had not long gone when the Pandavas returned. Yudhisthira had been perceiving evil omens and he raced anxiously toward the ashram. His fears were confirmed when he saw Draupadi's servant, Dhatreyika, lying sobbing on the ground. She told Yudhisthira what had happened. "The wretched Jayadratha has snatched away Draupadi, disregarding her Indra-like husbands. O heroes, give chase and you will soon catch him. He has not long left here."

Dhatreyika pointed in the direction which Jayadratha had gone and the five brothers rushed after him. Twanging their bows and breathing hot and heavy sighs, they raced along the forest paths. Before long they saw ahead of them the dust raised by Jayadratha's party. As they came near his soldiers, they saw Dhaumya still running after him and loudly wailing. Yudhisthira consoled the rishi and told him to return to the ashram. "O sage, be assured that this low-minded sinner will soon be punished."

Bhima bellowed out his terrific war-cry and the soldiers froze with fear. They turned to face the Pandavas. Bhima began to release his deadly shafts at them, but Arjuna checked him, saying, "What will you gain by killing these poor soldiers? It is Jayadratha we want."

Bhima lowered his bow. He and Arjuna then charged through the ranks of soldiers, scattering them as they made their way toward Jayadratha. They saw that he was surrounded and protected by many hundreds of chariot warriors. Those fighters released showers of arrows at the advancing Pandavas. Raising their maces and swords, they rushed into battle.

Infuriated, Arjuna raised the Gandiva and began picking off his foes. Arrows flew from his bow in hundreds. The ground became covered with severed heads and arms. Shattered armour and gleaming helmets dropped to the earth. Chariots were smashed and their riders cut to pieces before Arjuna's relentless onslaught. Ravens, vultures and jackals cried out in delight and came to feast on the mangled bodies that littered the earth.

Seeing his men being massacred, Jayadratha became terrified. He quickly got Draupadi off his chariot and fled into the woods. Bhima grasped hold of his mace and began to give chase, but Yudhisthira called out, "Remember that this one is the husband of Gandhari's daughter Dusshala. He should not be slain."

Draupadi, who had been taken onto Sahadeva's chariot, found it hard to accept Yudhisthira's words. "Why should he be spared?" she exclaimed. "An enemy who carries off one's wife should be immediately killed."

Yudhisthira consoled Draupadi and returned with her to the hermitage. Bhima and Arjuna then pursued Jayadratha, as the twins put to flight his remaining followers. The Sindhu king had already gone some distance. Arjuna fired four arrows from his bow. Charged with mantras, those shafts flew a full two miles and slew Jayadratha's four horses. The king leapt from his chariot shaking in fear. Leaving the path, he began to stumble through the bushes. The Pandavas soon caught up with him. Arjuna called out, "Wretch, with what prowess did you dare to steal our wife? Stand and fight. How do you flee, leaving your followers to fight?"

Jayadratha did not look back. He crashed through the woods in terror. Bhima jumped down and ran after him. Seizing hold of him, the Pandava punched him repeatedly. He grasped him by the hair and dragged him about. Arjuna reminded him of Yudhisthira's command. "Do not slay him," he shouted.

Bhima restrained himself with difficulty. He kicked the half conscious king and threw him to the ground. "Yudhisthira is always merciful," he said, through clenched teeth. "I will not kill him, but according to the accepted custom he is now our slave." Bhima took out a razor headed arrow and shaved off Jayadratha's hair, indicating that he had been defeated in battle and enslaved. He said, "Let us take this sinful man to Yudhisthira for his decision."

The brothers brought Jayadratha back to their ashram. By this time Draupadi's mind was pacified and she felt compassion for the humiliated king, and especially for his wife Dusshala, with whom she was friendly. She said, "Yudhisthira is right. Let him be spared. He has already become our slave and that is punishment enough."

Yudhisthira went over to Jayadratha, who knelt trembling on the ground. "Being weak yourself, you should not provoke others. You may go now, but do not commit such a vile act again. Be blessed. May your heart grow in virtue."

Jayadratha got up and silently slunk away. Mortified, he let out deep breaths. He had to exact revenge, but how? He would never be able to overcome the Pandavas in battle. His best hope was the all-powerful Shiva, his venerable deity. Perhaps by the grace of that powerful god he would be able to defeat them. Going deep into the forest he began to practice severe asceticism, his mind bent upon destroying the Pandavas. For many months he ate sparsely and constantly prayed to Shiva. Eventually the god appeared to him and said, "What do you desire?"

The delighted king replied, "O almighty one, let me conquer the Pandavas."

Shiva laughed. "This can never be. They are protected by Krishna and cannot therefore be conquered, even by me. I will, however, grant you one thing. Except for Arjuna, who is the immortal sage Nara incarnate, you will be able hold off all the brothers once only in battle."

Shiva then vanished, leaving Jayadratha to return to his kingdom, wondering when the day would come when he could use the boon.

* * *

Filled with a new hope after his meeting with the Danavas, Duryodhana entered Hastinapura. He began to see the kings and warriors who supported him in a different light, realising that many of them must be incarnations of powerful demons. Surely when they all came together there would be little the Pandavas could do to avoid defeat.

Bhishma, however, saw the events at Dwaitavana as an opportunity to make Duryodhana see sense. Soon after Duryodhana's return from the forest, Bhishma said to him, "You have now seen for yourself the Pandavas' power, and indeed Karna's inferiority. Your hopes for defeating Arjuna rest largely on the charioteer's son, but know for certain that he is not even a fourth part of Arjuna. My dear child, make peace with the Pandavas now before it is too late."

Duryodhana only smiled and said nothing. What did old Bhishma know? Even he would soon be playing his part in crushing the Pandavas when the demons possessed him. Thinking of this Duryodhana suddenly laughed. He stood up and left the room, leaving Bhishma sadly shaking his head.

Duryodhana went straight to Karna and told him what Bhishma had said. Karna felt pained. Bhishma was always berating him with harsh words. It was hard to understand. Karna felt he had shown his loyalty to the Kurus beyond any doubt. He only wished for Duryodhana's success and was prepared to lay down his life for the Kuru prince. Why then did Bhishma always deride him?

Karna asked Duryodhana if he could do something which would prove his power. "Formerly the Pandavas conquered the earth. You are now enjoying the result, but if you permit I will go out and conquer the whole world on your behalf. The senile and crooked minded Bhishma will be consumed with regret when he sees my prowess and my allegiance to the Kurus."

Duryodhana's eyes expanded with delight. He embraced his friend and said he would arrange for a vast army to accompany him. Within a short time Karna was on his way, surrounded by the powerful Kuru forces. Ranging to all quarters of the globe, he again established the Kuru empire, just as the Pandavas had done before him. He took the opportunity to solidify existing alliances and to make new friendships through diplomatic negotiations. Any king who opposed him in battle was soon subdued by the unstoppable power of the Kuru army, with Karna himself fighting at their head. At the end of his expedition he returned victorious, offering to Duryodhana the immense amount of tribute and booty he had collected.

Seeing him marching back into Hastinapura with an almost endless line of asses, camels and elephants bearing wealth, Duryodhana beamed with joy. With the mighty Karna by his side, the world under his control, and the Danavas backing him, his position was unassailable. The prince considered the Pandavas as already defeated. Strolling in his spacious palace garden with Karna, he said, "Dear friend, my desire now is to perform the Rajasuya, even more opulently than Yudhisthira."

Duryodhana told his friend that despite his desire the brahmins had said he could only perform the Rajasuya when Yudhisthira had died. Lifting his manicured and sandaled foot the prince kicked out at a flower. "Unfortunately, that geatest of all sacrifices cannot be performed by two different kings co-existing on the earth."

Karna stopped walking and looked toward Duryodhana. He spoke solemnly. "O king here and now do I make a vow. As long as I have not slain Arjuna I will not taste meat nor accept any luxuries. When asked for anything in charity I will not refuse."

Duryodhana embraced Karna with a smile. Feeling even more confident of his ultimate success, he entered his palace for the evening.

After Karna had made his vow Indra decided to help the Pandavas. He knew that Yudhisthira's greatest fear came from Karna. Although Arjuna had so far shown greater prowess than him, Yudhisthira still felt that Karna posed a real threat due his natural bodily armour. The Pandava king knew it would be difficult to kill him. Indra therefore disguised himself as a brahmin and went one morning to see Karna.

Karna had just come out of the Ganges after performing his daily worship of the sun-god. At that time he always gave charity and on this particular day he saw an effulgent brahmin approach him. He welcomed him and asked what he would like. Indra then said, "I wish to have your bodily armour."

Karna at once realised the brahmin's identity. In a dream he had already been warned by the sun-god that Indra would try to take his armour. The sun-god had advised him not to give it, but Karna knew he could not refuse. Still, he tried to change the brahmin's mind. "I will give you anything you desire. Why take my armour? I can give you enough wealth to maintain you for your whole life."

Indra insisted that he only wanted the armour and Karna said, "Very well, it must be so. O brahmin, I know you are Indra. Surya has already informed me that you would be coming. O lord of the gods, you may take my armour, but I ask that in return you grant me something in exchange."

Indra agreed. "With the exception of my thunderbolt you may ask for anything you like."

Surya had told Karna that if were to surrender his armour to Indra then he should ask the deity for his Shakti weapon, a great dart that could not be resisted even by the gods. Karna therefore asked Indra for that missile and the god replied, "I will give this infallible weapon to you, but on one condition. You may release it only once. It will certainly slay your opponent, but it will then return to me."

Karna said, "I agree. There is only one mighty foe whose death I desire."

With a razor-edged dagger Karna then slit off his natural armour. With his mind fixed on his vow and his desire to adhere to virtue, he smiled through the pain as the golden armour came away from his body. He then handed it, wet with blood, to Indra. The god thanked him and gave him the Shakti. Then he soared into the heavens, feeling that the Pandavas' purpose had been accomplished.

* * *

In the forest the Pandavas knew they would soon have to find a town or city in which to spend their final year. They did not know where to go. How could they possibly remain incognito without separating? That was a painful prospect—especially for Draupadi. Even then there would still be no guarantee that someone would not recognise them. The brothers were world famous and it was well known that they would soon be emerging from the forest. Duryodhana would certainly have his spies everywhere. Their discovery seemed inevitable. Then there would be another thirteen years of exile. Yudhisthira would not break his word.

One day as the brothers sat discussing their situation, a brahmin in obvious distress ran up to them. Pointing in the direction of the thick forest, he said, "Great heroes, help me. It is time for my daily sacrifice, but all my paraphernalia, tied into a bundle, has been snagged on a deer's horns. The animal has gone deeply into the woods carrying the bundle."

Yudhisthira jumped up at once. It was always a warrior's duty to protect brahmins. He took hold of his bow. With his brothers right behind him, he ran into the forest. Before long they saw the deer ahead of them, but despite their best efforts, they could not capture it nor strike it with their arrows. The animal bounded away deeper and deeper into the forest with the five brothers close behind.

After some time, it seemed that the deer had disappeared. The Pandavas came together and sat down on a fallen tree branch, exhausted and perspiring. Distraught at their failure to rescue the brahmin's paraphernalia, they looked around at the dense foliage, wondering which way the deer had gone. Yudhisthira said to Nakula, "Dear brother, see if you can find us some water. Let us refresh ourselves and then resume our search.

Nakula put down his bow and quickly shinned up a tree. Not far off he saw waterfowl circling around. Realizing that there must be a lake nearby, he took an empty quiver and set off to fetch water. He soon came to a large clear lake covered with lotuses and lilies. Dropping to his knees on the shore, he was about to drink the water when he heard a stern voice. "Stop!" it commanded. "O child, this lake is mine. You must first answer my questions before you may drink."

Nakula looked around but could not see anyone. Feeling intensely thirsty he decided to drink the inviting water and then search for the source of the voice. He cupped his hands and drew the water toward his mouth. As soon as it passed his lips, he fell dead.

After some time Yudhisthira became anxious. He told Sahadeva to go after his brother. Sahadeva soon found Nakula lying on the lakeshore. Shocked, he fell by his side and cried out in anguish. Nakula's bodily lustre had not left him, although he appeared to be dead, with no sign of any heartbeat or breathing. Sahadeva was perplexed. He too was burning with thirst and he leaned over to the water's edge to take a drink. Again, the voice commanded him to stop, telling him that he must first answer some questions.

Even more perplexed at this, Sahadeva looked all around him but saw no one. His hands were already in the water. Oppressed with thirst, he brought a palmful to his mouth. Suddenly he too fell dead next to his brother.

When neither of the twins returned after almost an hour, Yudhisthira told Arjuna to follow them. Arjuna took his bow and proceeded cautiously through the forest. Before long he found the twins by the lake, apparently dead. He cried out in grief. Setting an arrow on his bowstring he looked around carefully. There was no sign of any struggle. Who could have killed the twins without a fight? Everything seemed peaceful; the broad lake was calm, and the surrounding trees swayed gently in the breeze. Only a few waterfowl disturbed the tranquil atmosphere as they flapped across the lake.

Like his brothers Arjuna desperately needed a drink. He knelt at the water's edge and reached down with cupped palms. Once more the voice rang out. "Do not drink the water. First answer my questions."

Arjuna leapt to his feet and raised his bow. Unable to see anyone, he began firing mantra-charged arrows capable of striking invisible targets. They flew in all directions. Arjuna filled the sky with shafts, but no foe became visible. The voice spoke again. "Do not waste your time Arjuna. Answer my questions or, if you drink the water, you will die."

Infuriated, Arjuna cared nothing for the warning. If he drank the water perhaps the speaker would come out. Then he would see about his questions. He began to drink, but within moments he too had fallen to the ground next to his brothers.

Back in the woods Yudhisthira felt increasing anxiety. He said to Bhima, "What can our brothers be doing? O tormentor of foes, I think you should find them and bring them back."

Bhima got up and ran through the woods. Finding his three brothers prostrate by the lake he was astonished. Were they dead? The horrified Bhima could see no signs of life. What mighty being could have slain them? It was unimaginable. Bhima considered that he would soon have to face some tremendous enemy in battle. He had best slake his thirst and overcome his fatigue. Just as he was about to drink the voice commanded him to stop.

Bhima thought the voice belonged to whoever had killed his brothers. He would soon deal with him. First he would drink, then the fight could commence. He leant down to the water. As soon as it passed his lips, however, he dropped down dead alongside his three brothers.

Left alone, Yudhisthira was filled with foreboding. As the time went by and still his brothers did not return, he decided to go after them. He pushed his way through the bushes, going quickly toward the sound of cranes in the distance. Suddenly he came into a clearing and saw the lake. Seeing his brothers lying on the shore he wailed in grief. Completely baffled at that seemingly impossible sight, he ran over to them and fell to the ground. There were no signs of life. Yudhisthira looked around with tear-filled eyes. The tranquil lake appeared as if transported from heaven. A sweet fragrance filled the air and the trees around were covered with red, blue and yellow blossoms; but surely some sinister danger must lurk behind the apparently peaceful exterior.

Yudhisthira thought carefully. Although his brothers appeared dead, their bodies were lustrous. It seemed their souls were still present but their life energy was gone. Who could have done such a thing? It did not seem as if they had been slain in any normal fight. Perhaps the god of death himself had taken their lives. Why? Yudhisthira looked down at the lake. The answer must be there. This lake was somehow the cause of their deaths. Yudhisthira plunged into the water. As he surfaced, the voice called out, "Dear child, do not drink. This lake is mine. Answer my questions first or die like your brothers."

Yudhisthira gazed around the lake. "Who are you?" he shouted.

"I am a crane who lives in these waters. Your brothers disregarded my warning and have thus been brought under death's control. Do not suffer the same fate."

Yudhisthira then saw a large crane sitting on a tree bough close to him. "Are you a god?" he asked. "Surely no mere bird could have killed my brothers."

Suddenly the crane transformed into a huge, frightening looking being. With large red eyes and tall pointed ears, he blazed with effulgence. He roared like a thundercloud and said, "Know me to be a Yaksha. Your brothers died for their own faults. I forbade them to drink but they ignored me. This water is mine. Anyone wishing to drink it must first answer my questions."

Fearful and apprehensive, Yudhisthira replied, "O Yaksha, I do not wish to take what is yours. Ask me your questions. If it is in my power, I shall answer them."

"Very well then. Tell me, how does the soul rise out of his entanglement in matter? Who keeps him company, who is his guide and on what is he established?"

"Knowledge of God makes the soul rise. Godly qualities are his companions, eternal religion is his guide, and he is established on truth."

The Yaksha smiled and began to place more questions. One after another Yudhisthira answered them all. For half an hour the questioning went on. At last the Yaksha said, "O son of Pandu, here are my final questions: What is the most wonderful thing? What are the tidings of this world, and how can one find the path of eternal religion?"

Yudhisthira, who was kneeling on the lakeshore before the Yaksha, replied, "The most wonderful thing is that although every day countless creatures go to Death's abode, still a man thinks he will not die. The tidings of this world are that all beings here are being destroyed by time, and the eternal religious path is found in the hearts of great saints."

The Yaksha appeared pleased. He congratulated Yudhisthira. "You have answered my questions correctly. Which of your brothers would you like revived?"

Yudhisthira thought for a moment, then replied, "Let Nakula be brought to life."

"I am surprised," said the Yaksha. "I expected you to choose either Bhima or Arjuna."

Yudhisthira explained that he chose Nakula because he wanted to act equally toward both his mothers. If he did not select one of the twins, then Madri would be left with no surviving sons. "I will not abandon virtue for my own sake," he said.

"Excellent!" Expressing his satisfaction, the Yaksha said, "Since you are always so virtuous, never harming any creature, I shall restore all your brothers to life."

As the Yaksha spoke Yudhisthira saw his four brothers begin to stir. Rubbing their eyes, they sat up and looked around, as if waking from a deep sleep. Yudhisthira was overjoyed. He thanked the Yaksha and then asked, "O great being, who are you? Are you a god? Perhaps you are my father, the lord of religion." Yudhisthira knew that no ordinary Yaksha could have brought about his brothers' deaths—and then revived them again.

The Yakska replied, "I am indeed your father, O best of the Bharatas. Know me to be Dharma. I came here to meet you and to test you. My dear son, every godly quality rests in you and your great fame has been expanded today. Ask me for a boon."

Bowing low before the god, Yudhisthira asked that the brahmin's paraphernalia be restored to him. Dharma then told him that it was he who had assumed the form of a deer to take away the paraphernalia. "It is here. Take it but ask from me some other boon."

"O mighty deity, we shall soon commence our final year of exile and must remain incognito. Please grant that wherever we stay, even if we are our actual selves, no one will recognise us."

"It shall be so. Through my favour you shall remain unrecognised for the whole year. Dear Yudhisthira, you are a part of me. So too is your friend and well-wisher Vidura. Let me grant you one further boon before I depart."

"My lord, I am satisfied simply by seeing you, but as you wish to benedict me, I ask only that my mind always be inclined to charity, asceticism and truth."

In a voice that resembled rolling thunder, Dharma said, "You are the very embodiment of virtue already. It shall surely be as you desire."

The god then vanished. Yudhisthira and his brothers got to their feet and collected the brahmin's paraphernalia that lay nearby. In complete wonder, they returned to their hermitage.

CHAPTER TWENTY

A LESSON NOT LEARNED

It was the end of the rainy season. According to Dhaumya's astrological calculations the time for the Pandavas to enter a city had arrived. After some discussion they decided to go to Virata. It was not far away and the king, also named Virata, was a friend of the Pandavas. Feeling assured by Dharma's boon, the brothers decided it would be safe for them to remain together. Still, they did not want to take any unnecessary chances and they thought carefully about the guises they should assume. Knowing of Virata's affinity for dice, Yudhisthira said he would present himself to the king as an expert at the game. "I shall say that I was formerly Yudhisthira's personal servant. Entertaining Virata with my skills, I shall become his friend and minister."

Bhima decided that he would offer his services as a cook, at which he was highly skilled. Nakula, a past master at handling horses, said he would find engagement in the king's stables. For his part, Sahadeva said he would utilize his considerable talents as a cowherd and work with the king's cattle.

Arjuna remembered Urvashi's curse and Indra's words thereafter. "It is already destined that I should become a member of the third sex. Calling myself Brihannala, I shall offer to instruct the young girls of the royal house in singing and dancing, which I have learned from the Gandharvas."

Arjuna's brothers looked at him in wonder. It was hard to imagine the mighty hero as a eunuch. The ways of destiny were certainly unfathomable.

Draupadi then said she would enter the city as a serving maid, seeking engagement in the king's palace. When everything had been decided, Yudhisthira told Dhaumya to go to Drupada's city, Kampilya, and wait there for the final year. He also sent all the servants with him.

The brothers then set off for the city of Virata, in the kingdom of the Matsyas.

When they reached the outskirts of Virata they decided to leave their weapons in a safe place outside the city. They bundled them into a cloth and then tied them high upon a tree, announcing to the local people that it was their deceased mother. One by one, on successive days, they entered the city. When the king saw each of them approaching, he was amazed. They appeared like mighty monarchs, regal in bearing, and striding with the gait of lions. The king was especially astonished at the sight of Arjuna dressed in a sari, his powerful bowstring-scarred arms completely covered with bangles and bracelets. Virata listened to the brothers introduce themselves in the way they had agreed. Accepting their stories and feeling fortunate that such obviously qualified men should have come to him, he engaged them in his service, but by the gods' arrangement did not at any time suspect them to be the Pandavas.

Draupadi caused a considerable stir when she entered the city dressed as a serving maid. Her transcendent beauty bewildered the mind of every man who saw her. She went to the queen and asked to be accepted as a maidservant. The queen, fearing that her husband would become besotted with this beautiful new arrival, was at first reluctant, but Draupadi assured her, "I have five powerful Gandharva husbands. They will always protect me, and I will never even cast a glance upon another man."

The Pandavas and Draupadi began to live peacefully in Virata. Carefully applying themselves to the duties given by the king, they kept a low profile and rarely came together. It was a difficult year, especially for Draupadi who had to remain in the servants' quarters and could not associate with her husbands. But the time passed quickly and soon only a few weeks of exile remained. No one had any inkling of their real identities and they began to think of coming out of exile and reclaiming their kingdom.

In the final weeks, however, Draupadi was again assaulted. The king had a powerful brother-in-law named Kichaka who became enchanted by the Pandavas' wife. Despite her warnings about her five husbands, he tried to forcibly win her over. In desperation she went in secret to Bhima. "Save me from this depraved beast," she pleaded. "I will give up my life before allowing him to possess me." Bhima was apprehensive, worried about giving away his identity, but Draupadi finally convinced him. She then agreed to meet Kichaka late one night, arranging for Bhima to be present. When Kichaka came for the meeting the furious Bhima pounced upon him and pounded him to death.

The king was amazed that his mighty brother had been killed, but he accepted Draupadi's story that it was her Gandharva husbands. He became highly fearful of her but hearing that she would soon be leaving the city he agreed to let her stay until that time.

News of Kichaka's death also reached Hastinapura. During the final year of the Pandavas' exile the Kauravas had despatched thousands of spies around the world to search them out. None of them had reported any sightings of the brothers and Duryodhana was growing increasingly concerned. Although confident that he could win a war with the Pandavas, he would prefer to avoid it. It would certainly be very costly and result in a wholesale loss of life; and no one could absolutely guarantee the result.

Duryodhana's anxiety was stoked by the repeated cautions of his elders. Bhishma, Drona, Kripa and Vidura were particularly worried about what would happen when the Pandavas emerged from exile. All of them warned that a war would be catastrophic for the Kurus. In their opinions the Pandavas were invincible. Realizing that Duryodhana was loath to hand them back their kingdom, the Kuru elders tried by every means to change his mind. "You will rue the day that you ever joined battle with the Pandavas," they counselled.

As usual Duryodhana cared little for his elders' advice. He had already been planning for the war by securing whatever alliances he could. It would be a brutal battle. Far better if the Pandavas could somehow be discovered. Hearing the news about Kichaka he became thoughtful. It was not bad news—Virata's mighty brother had been a constant thorn in the Kurus' side; many times they had been approached by tributary kings seeking protection from the warlike Kichaka. He had been difficult to overpower. Duryodhana had been considering for some time how to deal with him. Now it had been done—but by who? Who could possibly be powerful enough? There were only a few men who could have beaten Kichaka to death and Bhima was one of them. It was especially suspicious as Kichaka had been killed secretly in the dead of night. Bhima would have had to do it that way.

After giving the matter some thought, Duryodhana stood up in the Kuru assembly and said, "Now that Kichaka is dead the Matsyas have lost their protector. We can now exact revenge from them for Kichaka's long aggression. I propose we go there immediately and recover the wealth he has seized. We can also gain their acquiescence to our rule."

Duryodhana's suggestion met with approval and an army was assembled for the expedition. Before long they were on their way to the Matsya kingdom.

* * *

In Virata the king was considering who he could find to replace Kichaka. He thought about the new arrivals to his kingdom, each of whom appeared able to lead his entire army. It was not long before an opportunity to test this idea arrived. As he sat in his court one day a cowherd ran in exclaiming, "O king, come quickly! An army is carrying away your cattle out in the fields."

The king at once gave orders for his army to assemble. He also asked that the Pandavas, except for Arjuna, be given armour and weapons. "I do not see how men with bodies like mountains and arms like elephant trunks cannot fight."

Charging out at the head of his army, Virata led them toward the cow pastures. In his burnished gold armour, decorated with the motifs of a hundred suns and a hundred eyes, the king shone brilliantly as he stood aboard his great chariot. A force of sixty thousand warriors followed him, with the four Pandavas in their midst.

The Kurus had deployed their troops into two forces. They had sent one force, headed by the Trigarta king Susharma, to take the cattle, while the Kurus themselves attacked the city from elsewhere. Virata and his army came upon the Trigartas and shouted out their war cries, immediately launching volleys of arrows at them.

The Trigartas turned and met the Matsyas. The two armies closed and began to engage in fierce combat. A huge cloud of dust rose up as the warriors tore into each other. The clash of weapons and the screams of men and animals was deafening. Bodies began to fall in hundreds.

Severed arms and legs dropped to the ground, which was muddied with blood. Many heads, adorned with helmets and gleaming earrings, rolled about.

While this battle raged, Duryodhana and the Kurus reached the other side of the city. Finding more cattle grazing there, they began to herd them away. The cowherds ran off in terror. They raced into the city and went before Bhuminjaya, Virata's son who was left to administrate in the king's absence. They found the prince surrounded by the palace ladies, and when he heard that the Kurus were stealing Virata's cows he boldly declared, "Watch today as I exhibit my prowess in battle. The haughty Kurus will soon regret their folly. I shall put them to flight and recover the cows. They will wonder if it is Arjuna himself come to fight with them."

The prince, who knew he had no chance of single-handedly overpowering the Kuru army, then said, "Alas, though, I have no charioteer. All the best men have gone out with my father to the other side of the city. I cannot fight unless a suitable man be found to govern my horses."

The prince carried on boasting about his strength and how he was Arjuna's equal. Draupadi heard this and, finding his references to Arjuna intolerable, she said, "There is one present who can drive your chariot, prince. Brihannala was formerly Arjuna's charioteer. He is a matchless driver."

Bhuminjaya looked at her in disbelief. "Brihannala? How can I ask a eunuch to be my charioteer?" he asked with a laugh.

Draupadi reassured him that she was speaking the truth. "With Brihannala as your driver you will doubtlessly vanquish the Kurus."

Everyone looked at the bemused prince. It was time for him to make good his boasts. He swallowed. "Alright, I shall try him." He had Brihannala fetched from the ladies' quarters. Equipping him with armour, he led him to his chariot and was soon charging out of the city to confront the Kurus. When Bhuminjaya saw them in the distance his heart sank. The vast Kuru army resembled a shoreless ocean. Their many tall standards were like a forest moving through the sky.

Ordering Brihannala to stop his chariot, the prince said, "This is madness. How can I face such an army? In their midst are Bhishma,

Drona, Kripa, Karna and the heroic king Duryodhana. The very gods would find it hard to overpower them."

Throwing back his long braid of hair, Arjuna frowned at the terrified prince. "You are a warrior and it behooves you to fight. Having vaunted of your prowess, how can you turn back like a coward? As for myself, I will certainly not run from this army."

Bhuminjaya stood shaking in the chariot. He declared that even if he became the butt of jokes and ridicule he had no intention of fighting.

Arjuna looked around for the tree where his weapons lay. "Very well then, prince, if you permit, I shall fight in your place. You take the reins."

Bhuminjaya stared at the Kurus. How could anyone face them and live? Brihannala must surely have lost his mind, but he seemed extremely confident. Reassured by Brihannala's fearlessness, the prince said, "How do you propose to challenge this tremendous army?"

Arjuna pointed across to the great tree with the bundle still high in its branches. "Drive the chariot to that tree and you shall see."

Taking the reins, the prince drove the chariot to the tree and Arjuna had him bring down the weapons. When the deerskin covering was cut open the prince gasped. Seeing the array of terrific weapons, he was astonished. "Whose are these? They look like so many sighing serpents ready to leap up of their own accord."

Arjuna realised it was time to tell Bhuminjaya the truth. "These are the Pandavas' weapons. Indeed, I am Arjuna and my four brothers reside with me in Virata. The bow you see there shining like a brilliant rainbow is the famous Gandiva."

The prince's mouth fell open. He looked from Arjuna to the bow and back to Arjuna. "Is this true? How have you managed to remain concealed for so long? Can you prove that you are Arjuna? He has ten names. Tell them to me and I shall believe you."

"The gods have protected us," Arjuna replied. He then told the prince all his ten names. Bhuminjaya's eyes opened wide. Thinking of how Arjuna and four other mysterious men had entered his city a year ago, as well as a beautiful woman, the truth dawned on him. He fell prostrate before Arjuna. "I had no idea. Please forgive me if I have offended you in any way."

Arjuna reassured the prince and then said, "Let us go now and face the Kurus. I have been waiting a long time for this opportunity."

Arjuna removed his bangles and pulled on a pair of gloves. He sat on the chariot and thought of his celestial weapons. They appeared within his mind and said, "We are here, O son of Pandu, ready to do your bidding."

"Dwell within my memory," Arjuna replied. He looked across the field toward the Kurus. They would soon realise his identity, but it did not matter. The period of exile was now over. This seemed like a good way to end it. Arjuna strung the Gandiva and gave it a mighty twang. The bow produced a sound like that of two mountains colliding. The earth vibrated and trees shook.

Hearing that terrific sound the Kurus stopped taking the cows and looked around in surprise. Bhishma and Drona both knew at once that it was Arjuna with the Gandiva. They felt joy, realising that the Pandavas were well, but apprehension at the prospect of an encounter with Arjuna.

Drona said to Duryodhana, "O king, from the sound of his bow, from the way in which the earth shakes, and from numerous portents I am sure that Arjuna is approaching."

Duryodhana looked across at the solitary chariot racing across the field in the distance. Arjuna? That would certainly be fortuitous. The Pandavas' exile was not yet over. If Arjuna showed himself then another thirteen years in the wilderness awaited them.

Drona described how he was seeing evil omens which indicated great danger to the Kuru army. "The troops appear cheerless and bereft of energy. A pall of gloom hangs over them and crows swoop down upon them with harsh sounds. Make ready for battle. When Arjuna confronts us, you will have to repent for your actions."

Duryodhana scowled. It would be Arjuna who was soon repenting. The Kaurava went over to Bhishma and said, "Grandfather, it seems Arjuna approaches. Have you calculated the time? Is the exile complete?"

"This is certainly Partha coming upon us," Bhishma replied. Like Duryodhana he too had carefully considered the report about Kichaka, concluding that the Pandavas must be in Virata. He had already astronomically calculated the period they had been away. It was now more than thirteen years.

As Bhishma spoke Karna began to laugh. "Whether or not the exile is complete is of no consequence. Arjuna will meet his end today at my hands. By killing him I will repay my debt to Duryodhana. All of you may stand down. Even if all five brothers come onto the field you will see them crushed by me."

Kripa threw a contemptuous glance at the bragging Karna. "It seems you have quickly forgotten the incident with the Gandharvas. Where then was this mighty prowess of yours? Who was it who came to Duryodhana's rescue then?"

Bhishma and Drona voiced their agreement with Kripa and looked over at Karna. Fuming, he raised his bow and gazed across at Arjuna. He said nothing in reply to the Kurus. They would soon be silenced when he felled Arjuna. Karna felt he had been caught by surprise by the Gandharvas but he was ready now.

Bhishma spoke again. "The virtuous sons of Pandu have fulfilled the terms of their agreement. Their time is complete. We need not fear them, for they will never do anything sinful. They should now be received by us with affection. Give them back their kingdom, Duryodhana, and avoid an unnecessary slaughter."

Duryodhana ground his teeth. "I will never give them anything," he snarled. "Our reunion will take place on the battlefield."

Bhishma drew a deep and sorrowful breath. He recalled the time long ago when he had made his vow of celibacy, renouncing the throne. His father had then blessed him that he would only die when he willed it himself. In return Bhishma had sworn that, even though he would never occupy Hastinapura's throne, he would nevertheless always protect it. He had to stand by Dhritarastra's side—and that meant supporting Duryodhana. Duty was surely a difficult path.

Drona began issuing orders for battle. As he spoke a couple of arrows fell out of the sky at his feet. Other arrows also fell at Bhishma and Kripa's feet. "Seeing his elders after a long time, Arjuna is offering his respects," said Drona. "Stand firm. His next arrows will not be carrying respects."

Arjuna gave orders to Bhuminjaya. "Approach this army with caution. Karna should be carefully watched, for he always desires my death. So too does Duryodhana but the others, headed by Bhishma, Drona and Kripa, never wish me any harm."

The Matsya prince began to drive toward the Kurus. Arjuna held the Gandiva at the ready. He had no wish to hurt any of his elders, nor even Duryodhana and his brothers, if it could be avoided. Now the exile was over there should first be some attempt at a peaceful settlement. Yudhisthira wanted that. Perhaps, though, this encounter would help Duryodhana see sense. When he realised the power of Arjuna's weapons—which had already overcome hordes of celestial demons—he might be more inclined to peace.

"Take me straight toward Duryodhana." Arjuna fixed his gaze on the Kaurava prince. He began to release arrows in thousands. They sped toward Duryodhana like swarms of locusts. The Kurus raced to his assistance. Drona and Kripa countered Arjuna's attack by striking down his arrows with their own. Smiling, Arjuna stepped up his assault. His mantra-charged shafts filled the sky. Holding off his two teachers, who were fighting only half-heartedly, he pressed on toward Duryodhana.

Struck all over by Arjuna's steel shafts, which seemed to come from every direction, Duryodhana reeled. He was hardly able to raise his own bow to defend himself. Arrows embedded themselves in his chariot, cut down his standard, pierced his horses, and glanced off his armour. "Get away from here fast!" he yelled to his sorely oppressed charioteer. The charioteer urged on his steeds and the chariot raced away.

"Let us leave this coward for now," said Arjuna. Make your way to Karna, who stands roaring over there in his chariot marked with the emblem of an elephant rope."

Bhuminjaya veered his golden chariot around and faced Karna. As he closed on him, Karna's brother came between them. He attacked Arjuna with a fierce cluster of barbed arrows. The Pandava expertly warded off those shafts. Smiling tautly, he fired four arrows in swift succession which slew his opponent's horses. He then shot a single crescent-headed arrow that beheaded Karna's brother right before his eyes.

Screaming in fury, Karna attacked Arjuna with lightning fast shafts. Arjuna responded in kind and the two warriors traded thousands of arrows. They appeared like the sun and moon meeting for a contest in the heavens. Both invoked celestial weapons which lit up the sky. Skilfully countering each other's attack, they both fervently sought the advantage. Their chariots wheeled and zig-zagged from side to side. The other warriors on the field watched in amazement as the two mighty heroes battled together. Their hands were hardly visible as they fired their arrows with blinding speed.

Gradually Arjuna gained the edge over his foe. His arrows penetrated Karna's defences and began piercing through his armour. Karna's arms, thighs and breast were badly lacerated. Stunned by the incessant ferocity of Arjuna's attack he fell back. He shouted in pain. Ordering his charioteer to retreat, he fled from the fight.

Arjuna then turned his attention to Duryodhana's army. He rushed into their midst with the Gandiva constantly twanging and firing off countless deadly shafts. Warriors fell on all sides. Arjuna seemed hardly approachable. From whichever angle he was attacked he was ready. He created carnage among the Kuru forces.

Bhishma and the other Kuru elders watched in admiration. They had no desire for a serious fight with their beloved Arjuna. Like Yudhisthira, they too hoped for a peaceful settlement to the dispute between the Kauravas and Pandavas.

Seeing his troops being overpowered by the rampant Arjuna and realising that his elders were not fighting to their full power, Duryodhana decided to desist from fighting. It was not yet time to defeat the Pandavas. First, he needed to assemble his allies into an unassailable army. He needed to secure the commitment of Bhishma, Drona and Kripa for the fight. And when the time came, he would have the support of his celestial allies, the Danavas and Daityas. It would be a different story then.

The prince issued the order to withdraw. The Kurus turned and began pulling away from Virata. They headed back to Hastinapura, with Duryodhana thinking of how he could best prepare himself for war, while his elders considered how it could now be avoided.

* * *

On the other side of the city king Virata had watched with amazement as his four newest fighters had shown their power. Who were these men? Just one of them, his cook, had almost single-handedly routed the enemy army. Whirling around the battlefield with his mace he had sent horsemen, chariots and even elephants crashing to the ground. The other three had also exhibited unparalelled prowess.

Between the four of them they had forced the terrified Trigartas to flee in all directions. As the Matsyas made their way back to the city Virata looked in awe at the three men. With them on his side he need not fear even the gods and demons combined.

When the king reached his city, he was informed that his son had gone out to confront the Kurus, with Brihannala as his charioteer. Shocked, he turned to Yudhisthira and said, "My son is in dire danger. What chance does he stand against the Kurus?"

Yudhisthira smiled. "Have no fear, with Brihannala on his chariot he could face even the celestials."

Virata looked incredulously at his minister. Was he serious? A single eunuch against the Kuru army? The king began ordering his generals to have his army march out again. But suddenly a breathless messenger ran up to him and said, "The Kurus have been routed and are withdrawing. Your son is on his way back."

The king threw up his arms in delight. "Amazing! I never knew my son had such power. Decorate the city with festoons and garlands. This is a cause for celebration."

As the prince entered the city his father ran up to him and tightly embraced him. "Well done, my son! Well done. Tell me how you overcame the Kurus."

The prince shook his head. "No, father. It was not me who defeated them." He pointed to Arjuna. "This man here is no eunuch. Know him to be Arjuna, the famous son of Pandu. It was he who scattered the Kuru forces."

The king stared in disbelief at Brihannala. He turned toward Yudhisthira, who was now surrounded by his other three brothers. How did he know?

"Your son speaks the truth," said Arjuna, "and the man who has been your minister this past year is no mere courtier. Worthy of sharing a seat with even Indra, always engaged in sacrifice and the practice of virtue, know him to be the far-sighted, truthful and ever forgiving Yudhisthira."

Virata looked carefully at Yudhisthira. Was it true? How had he not recognised him? He looked back at Arjuna. "Then these other three must be..."

"Yes, king, you are right. That mighty-armed mountain of a man who has been preparing your dishes is none other than Bhima. By his side are the twins, Nakula and Sahadeva. And in your inner chambers lives Draupadi, spending her days in menial service to your queen. We are all in your debt. For the last year we have lived safely in your city like creatures in the womb."

Virata's eyes flooded with tears. Of course! Why had he not realised earlier? Who else could have shown such power on the battlefield?

Exclaiming, "What good fortune!" the king folded his hands and bowed to Yudhisthira. "Take my entire kingdom, O sinless man, with its lands, treasury and army."

"I am already in your debt, king," Yudhisthira replied. "By God's grace I am sure my own kingdom will soon be restored to me."

"Then let Arjuna accept my daughter's hand in marriage," Virata said. "What else can I offer?"

"It would be better if she became my daughter-in-law," answered Arjuna. "Since I have been her dancing instructor, I have dealt with her like a father with his daughter. I could not change that relationship, but she will make an excellent bride for my son Abhimanyu."

Virata happily agreed. A marriage alliance with the Pandavas was more than he might ever have hoped for. After arranging for the brothers to be accomodated in his palace, the king sent out messengers to announce that they were now out of exile and living in his kingdom. He invited their friends and allies to come to his city and before long they began to arrive. Krishna and Balarama came from Dwaraka, bringing Abhimanyu and many other members of their family. Drupada arrived accompanied by his sons and a huge army, and in the next few weeks many other kings also came to Virata.

The wedding between Abhimanyu and Virata's daughter Uttara duly took place. Arjuna's son resembled a god and with the beautiful Uttara by his side he appeared like Vishnu accompanied by the goddess of fortune. The city was filled with celebration and vast amounts of charity was distributed to brahmins and other citizens.

CHAPTER TWENTY-ONE

PREPARING FOR WAR

Soon after Abhimanyu's wedding the Pandavas discussed their next move with Krishna. No word had been received from Hastinapura. It seemed the Kauravas were not inclined to honour the agreement made at the gambling match; to return the Pandavas' kingdom. Krishna suggested that an assembly be called for a general discussion among the kings present. Virata agreed and arranged the next day for the monarchs to be brought into his hall and the conference began.

Krishna spoke first. Rising from his gem-studded seat he seemed like the moon appearing from the ocean. His voice resounded throughout the great chamber like the melodic beat of deep-toned drum. "It is well known that Yudhisthira was unfairly deprived of his wealth and kingdom by Shakuni. Nevertheless, he has fulfilled the terms of the agreement made with the Kauravas. Thirteen years have passed with the Pandavas dwelling in exile. That time is now complete, and they seek to again possess their rightful kingdom."

All five Pandavas had their eyes fixed on Krishna as he spoke. They were ready to accept whatever he decided. Pleasing him meant more to them than even possessing the entire earth, but it was clear that he wanted them to recover their kingdom. It seemed the vows they had made at the time of the gambling match would soon have to be fulfilled.

Krishna looked around the assembly as he continued. "Yudhisthira will never renounce virtue, and his brothers are always obedient to him. Despite everything that has happened he still wishes Duryodhana well. Perhaps this matter can be settled peacefully. Let us send a messenger to Hastinapura to establish the Kauravas' intentions. If they refuse to return the kingdom then I see war as the only recourse. The Kauravas will be slain with all their followers. If, O kings, war should ensue and you feel the Pandavas' cause is just, then I urge you to unite with them and march out for battle. What do you all say?"

A murmur of approval went through the hall. The kings looked at each other and nodded in agreement with Krishna's words. As they again fell silent Balarama got to his feet and raised a hand to speak. Everyone turned toward him. Krishna's brother appeared extraordinarily attractive with his pure white complexion, a jewelled helmet on his head, and a garland of white lotuses around his neck. Resting a hand on his golden plough weapon, he said, "Krishna has spoken well. The Kuru kingdom should be shared between the Pandavas and the Kauravas. Send a man to Hastinapura to address the Kauravas but ensure that due deference is shown to them. After all, it was Yudhisthira's fault that he gambled and lost the kingdom. Although unskilled, he accepted Shakuni's challenge. Therefore, we should approach the Kauravas in a conciliatory mood. War should be avoided by any means."

Yudhisthira bowed his head. Balarama was right. The whole awkward situation had come about only due to his foolishness. He looked down and said nothing, but Bhima and Arjuna looked querulously at Balarama. They knew Krishna's brother had a soft spot for Duryodhana, who was his student at mace fighting, but when he had last seen the Pandavas in the forest he had expressed anger at the Kauravas. His present mood was difficult to understand.

As Balarama stopped speaking, a powerful Yadu warrior named Satyaki stood up. He was a great friend and student of Arjuna, and he found Balarama's words hard to tolerate. His angry voice echoed through the hall. "How can anyone listen to such suggestions without objecting? How can you say that Yudhisthira was at fault? How were the Kauravas not guilty of trickery and deceit? They induced Yudhisthira to play against a man who knows every facet of dice play and gambling. Yudhisthira had no desire for the game, nor did he wish to stake his kingdom. He was drawn into it by the wicked minded Kauravas who had but one intention—to divest him of everything by whatever means possible."

Satyaki stood with his hand on the hilt of his sword. He strode into the centre of the hall and looked around at the assembled kings. "Whatever may have happened in the past, there can be no doubt that

Yudhisthira should now be given back his kingdom. It is his by birthright, and indeed by virtue of his undeniable qualifications. He is fit to rule the entire earth. If the Kauravas will not agree then I for one am ready for a fight. By means of cold steel I shall change their minds. O heroes, take up your arms and join me. After killing all of the usurpers let us install Yudhisthira as emperor."

Red-faced with fury, Satyaki glared at Balarama and marched back to his seat. Balarama smiled. He knew how much the hot-blooded Satyaki loved the Pandavas. Drupada then rose from his seat to speak. The old king was respected by all for his wisdom and maturity and everyone in the hall listened attentively. Looking directly at Krishna, he said, "In my view we need to prepare for battle. I will send my priest to Hastinapura, but I do not expect a peaceful settlement. War seems inevitable. We must therefore send out messages to all our friends and allies. We shall soon need their help. Duryodhana will certainly be doing that even now as we speak. There are many noble kings who will assist whoever first comes to them with a plea."

Drupada named over fifty monarchs who he felt they should immediately approach. When he had finished Krishna applauded him, recommending that his suggestion be taken seriously. Everyone in the assembly agreed. Krishna then said, "I shall now depart for Dwaraka. O kings, do all that you can to bring about peace. If, however, the attempt fails, then summon me again. I shall do all in my power to resolve the situation."

The assembly withdrew and Virata, after worshipping both Krishna and Balarama with all respect, sent them on their way back to Dwaraka. Then he began preparing for war. Swift messengers were despatched to all parts of the world. Soon large armies began arriving in Virata. Troops poured in from all directions and set up camp around the city. Crowded with men and animals, the earth seemed covered with dark clouds. Their clamour resembled the roar of the sea. Virata ensured that all of them had everything they needed.

When at last a huge force had assembled, Drupada requested his priest to leave for Hastinapura. He asked him to speak reasonably and gently to the Kurus, trying to convince them of the justness of Yudhisthira's claim. "Although I am sure you will not be able to change Duryodhana's mind, you may still win the hearts of the other Kuru elders. At least you may sow the seeds of dissension among them. That will give us more time to make ready for the inevitable war. And who knows, perhaps Dhritarastra may yet accept our plea and do the right thing."

The priest then left for Hastinapura, leaving Virata to continue preparing for battle.

* * *

After returning from Virata, Duryodhana had thought only of amassing his forces. Smarting from yet another humiliation at the Pandavas' hands, he simmered with anger as he went about preparing for war. There was no question of returning their kingdom. He despatched emissaries to all his allies. There was only one way to end this dispute. All advice to the contrary would be ignored.

When news of Krishna's return to Dwaraka reached Duryodhana, he decided to go personally to ask for his assistance. Krishna and his Yadu forces were unconquerable. Duryodhana knew that Krishna would hardly be able to refuse his request if he got there first. The Yadu chief had always made it clear that he was equally disposed to both the Kauravas and the Pandavas. Till now Duryodhana felt he had not had any cause to seek Krishna's assistance. It had always been the Pandavas who had turned to him for help—which he had never refused. Now it was time to redress the balance.

Mounting a swift horse, Duryodhana raced toward Dwaraka. At the same time Arjuna left Virata with the same idea in mind. Accepting the inevitability of war, Yudhisthira decided that Krishna's dear friend Arjuna should ask for his personal assistance. Arjuna reached Krishna's palace in Dwaraka just after Duryodhana. He saw him being shown into Krishna's chamber. Walking in right after Duryodhana, Arjuna saw that Krishna was asleep on his bed. Duryodhana had taken a seat by his head. He smiled smugly at Arjuna. The Pandava had arrived too late. Arjuna stood at Krishna's feet, gazing at him with tears of affection.

After some time, Krishna awoke. As he opened his eyes, he saw Arjuna, who bowed to him in love. Sitting up, he saw Duryodhana by his side. Krishna welcomed both of his visitors and ordered a servant to bring them refreshments. After politely enquiring after their welfare, he asked what had brought them there.

Arjuna raised his hand toward Duryodhana to let him speak. The prince said, "O Keshava, it is well known how you are equally disposed toward the Kauravas and Pandavas. I have thus come here to ask your assistance in the war which will soon be fought between us."

Krishna had seated his two visitors together on a large white couch. Duryodhana turned to Arjuna as he went on, "Arjuna will confirm that I arrived here before him. I therefore have first claim for your help. This is the practice of good men and you, Krishna, are the best of men."

Krishna looked thoughtful. He nodded slowly and replied, "I accept that you arrived first, king, but I first saw Arjuna. I will therefore help you both. Scripture ordains that the youngest should be helped first, which means I must give Arjuna first choice. I offer either my army, consisting of a million highly powerful warriors known as the Narayanas, or myself alone. However, I shall not fight. My weapons will be laid aside and not lifted for the whole battle."

Krishna turned his lotus-petal eyes toward Arjuna. "What then do you choose, O son of Kunti?"

Without the least hesitation Arjuna replied, "I select you, Krishna. With you by my side what more could I want?"

Duryodhana, who had been apprehensive as Krishna had spoken, smiled broadly. Arjuna had let his sentiment overcome his reason. "Fair enough, then, I shall take the army," he said, getting to his feet. "I will not take any more of your time, Krishna. Please permit me to leave."

Duryodhana went out of Krishna's room almost laughing. A million man army! The Narayanas were famous as ferocious and implacable warriors. What would the Pandavas do now? The prince then thought of Balarama, his friend and well-wisher. Surely, he would also help. Duryodhana quickly made his way to Balarama's palace and was shown into his room.

After hearing Duryodhana's request, Balarama said, "O hero, for your sake I spoke out in Virata's assembly. However, Krishna did not accept my words. You should know that I cannot exist for a moment separated from him. My decision therefore is to help neither side. I will not take part in the war. Go forth and fight to the best of your ability. May good fortune be yours."

Balarama stood up and embraced Duryodhana. Knowing that Krishna was assisting the Pandavas he considered the Kauravas as already defeated. Disappointed, Duryodhana left his palace and went to see Kritavarman, the commander of the Narayana army. The Yadu general, although unhappy to be opposing Krishna, felt duty bound and he soon gathered his army and left Dwaraka with Duryodhana.

Arjuna and Krishna travelled together to Virata. When they arrived at the great city they saw men streaming in from all directions. Satyaki had followed them from Dwaraka, bringing a large force. Drupada arrived with his two sons and another great platoon of warriors. Virata himself had provided a division and numerous other kings came with their armies. Eventually seven enormous divisions of warriors, on foot, horseback, chariots and elephants, were assembled, over two million in total.

In Hastinapura an even larger force had amassed, totalling eleven great divisions. They crowded the city and its surrounding regions so that there was hardly any free space anywhere. Bearing their polished swords and maces, as well as axes, lances, spears, mallets, and bows of every type, the armies appeared like dark clouds adorned with countless lightning flashes. The earth trembled under their weight. Their shouts, the clash of their weapons, and the cries of their animals combined to create a tremendous roar that filled the whole city.

* * *

Soon after the troops had assembled on both sides, Drupada's priest arrived at Hastinapura. He made his way through the crowded streets and was received by Dhritarastra, Bhishma and Vidura. They brought him to the royal court where an assembly had been called. After worshipping him with various respectful offerings, they asked him to address the assembly.

Standing before Dhritarastra's throne, the priest said, "I come in peace and desiring peace. As you all know, both Dhritarastra's sons and those of Pandu are equally entitled to the Kuru kingdom. Yet somehow the Kauravas have wrested away the Pandavas' share from them. They have persecuted their cousins in many ways, even trying to take their lives, but by God's grace the Pandavas have survived. Despite everything Yudhisthira bears the Kauravas no ill will. He only wishes to have his kingdom returned. Let war be avoided—this is his desire."

The priest paused. He slowly surveyed the hall. By the king's side sat Bhishma, Drona, Kripa, Vidura and other senior Kuru ministers. Duryodhana and all his brothers sat opposite, with Karna and Shakuni. Many other kings filled up the seats around the great chamber. Everyone remained silent and the priest continued. Realising that appeals to reason were likely to fail, he began describing the Pandavas' military might. "They have amassed seven great divisions of men. Besides this, they have the inconceivably powerful Krishna on their side. Many kings are with them and each of the brothers is himself a mighty *maharatha*, capable of contending single-handedly with thousands of other warriors. Arjuna alone exceeds the strength of your entire army. Therefore, give them back their kingdom. Do not ruin yourselves and the world for nothing."

Duryodhana drummed his fingers on his knee and said nothing. He knew his own army was almost twice the size of the Pandavas' forces— and he recalled the Danavas' words. This war would no doubt see their fulfilment. What was there to fear?

Bhishma then spoke, thanking the priest for coming to Hastinapura and praising him with kind words. He concurred with him, agreeing that even Arjuna alone could defeat the Kuru army. They had already seen enough evidence of that.

Galled as ever by Bhishma's speech, Karna jumped up and interrupted him. "O brahmin, do not waste your breath trying to scare us. The Kauravas have done nothing wrong. Yudhisthira was fairly defeated and went to the forest in accord with our agreement. I for one do not believe his prescribed term of exile has even ended. Why then is he demanding the kingdom? Duryodhana will not yield to any threats. He will, however, always act in accord with virtue. Let the Pandavas complete their term of exile and then come humbly before Duryodhana. He will surely afford them refuge."

Duryodhana would not accept any calculations which concluded that the Pandavas had been away for their full term. Brahmins faithful to him had told him otherwise, and that was good enough for him. In any event, whether or not their time was up did not matter. It was going to end in war without a doubt.

Bhishma rebuked Karna, reminding him again of the occasions when he had experienced Arjuna's superiority in battle. The hall became agitated, some kings agreeing with Bhishma and others supporting Duryodhana. A clamour of voices rose up and Dhritarastra raised his hand for silence. He addressed the assembly. "Bhishma has spoken well. He has only our interests in mind. I need time now to deliberate. Let us adjourn this assembly. Return to the Pandavas, my dear brahmin, and tell them that I shall soon send Sanjaya with my reply."

The brahmin left the assembly and it broke up, leaving the king sitting alone. He thought for some time before calling for Sanjaya. Bhishma's assessment of the situation was accurate. The Pandavas, and especially Arjuna, were powerful beyond measure. Wisdom therefore dictated that their demands be met, but Duryodhana would never agree. The prince had been almost peaceful these last thirteen years, with his cousins out of the way and the world under his control. He would certainly not relinquish his position without a fight.

The old king loosened his silk tunic. As usual he felt torn. He had lost many a night's sleep worrying about a fight with the Pandavas. Maybe there was some way he could persuade the ever virtuous Yudhisthira to avoid war, while at the same time keeping Duryodhana happy. Surely Pandu's pious son would not be attached to worldly wealth and opulence. Without doubt he would go a long way to avoid fighting.

Making up his mind, Dhritarastra summoned Sanjaya and said, "O wise man, I wish for you to go to the Pandavas. They are affectionate toward you and will receive you well. Those heroes are devoted to virtue and I cannot think of a single fault in any of them. It is only my weak-brained son and his wicked followers who wish them ill. Duryodhana thinks that his greater sized army will assure him of success, but he has not thought deeply enough. In my view the five brothers, with Krishna as their support, are unconquerable."

Dhritarastra had heard the rishis describe Krishna's power many times. They said he was the origin of everything, including even the immortal lord of the gods, Vishnu. It hardly mattered that he was not fighting. If he really was God, then his will alone would be sufficient to destroy any enemy.

Sanjaya murmured in agreement as the king spoke, listing the numerous demons who Krishna had already slain. The old charioteer was himself a believer in Krishna, having heard much about him from Vyasadeva.

The king went on, "I also greatly fear Yudhisthira. He has practiced long asceticism and is dedicated to virtue. His spiritual power is immense. If we incur his wrath, we will be burned to ashes like reeds falling into a fire."

The king instructed Sanjaya to leave at once. "Say whatever you can to pacify and please the Pandavas. Give them every assurance that I am their well-wisher. Here is my suggestion for Yudhisthira."

Sanjaya listened carefully as the king spoke, memorising every detail. Then he immediately left for Virata.

CHAPTER TWENTY-TWO

KRISHNA'S PEACE MISSION

When the Pandavas heard of Sanjaya's arrival they called him in and greeted him warmly. Asking after everyone's welfare, Yudhisthira said, "Although we desire peace, I do not think we will ever win Duryodhana's friendship. Alas, Sanjaya, war now seems unavoidable."

"It is as you say," the charioteer replied, standing before Yudhisthira with his hands folded in respect. "The prince is guided only by fools and seems incorrigible. The way he has treated you is unforgiveable. His father sincerely regrets it and wants to forge a lasting peace with you. He has thus sent me here with his message."

Yudhisthira asked that Sanjaya speak in the assembly where all the kings could hear. He brought the charioteer into the hall and everyone was soon assembled. Standing in their midst, Sanjaya then said, "Here are Dhritarastra's own words. Pandu's sons are all virtuous men who could never perform a vicious act. Yudhisthira himself is mild, generous and always forgiving. How then could he ever do anything which would destroy us all? Surely those men are blessed who can sacrifice their own interests for the welfare of others."

Dhritarastra's message was immediately clear. Sanjaya made it even clearer. "O king, sons of Pandu, do not begin a war which will end in the deaths of all your relatives. This is Dhritarastra's request. Even if you thus regain your kingdom, what pleasure will it give you?"

Sanjaya looked around the hall, supplicating all the kings not to engage in battle. He spoke for some time, but without making any suggestion that the Pandavas would have their kingdom returned.

When Sanjaya finished, Yudhisthira glanced over at the smiling Krishna and calmly replied, "What have I ever said which indicated that I desire war, Sanjaya? Only a cursed man would seek through war that which can be had by peaceful means; but peace can only be had when we control our senses. One who acts only for the pleasure of his senses soon encounters misery. Dhritarastra and his sons plainly do not see this truth. Therefore, they act in ways which can never bring about peace and happiness."

The Pandava monarch rose from his seat. In his fine robes and ornaments he looked like a jewel studded banner raised in honour of Indra. He continued to address Sanjaya. "It seems the king will not check his avaricious and lustful son. He has had ample opportunity and enough advice from the wise Vidura, but he does nothing. He and his son desire to rule the earth undisputed, enjoying another's property which they have gained through deceit. Obviously, they have not carefully considered the consequences of such a sinful desire."

Yudhisthira looked around at the many kings in the hall. They sat in silence, listening as the Pandava spoke. "All of these kings here know well the actual situation. They are ready for battle. Make no mistake, Sanjaya, if Indraprastha is not given back then war will ensue. However, it need not happen. The Kauravas can keep Hastinapura and be happy with that prosperous realm. We only ask that they give us what is rightfully ours."

Yudhisthira looked at Krishna and said, "Here is Krishna. He knows every facet of morality and religion. Let him say what is right. I will do whatever he decides. Indeed, he is everyone's greatest well-wisher and we should follow his advice without hesitation."

Krishna rose from his seat. He seemed to illuminate the hall with his bodily lustre. Dressed in brilliant yellow silks and decorated with many jewelled ornaments, he appeared like a blackish cloud framed by sunlight and adorned with lightning flashes. Raising a graceful hand, he said, "No fault can be found in Yudhisthira. He desires to do his God-given duty as a king. Indraprastha should be given back. If it is not, then Yudhisthira will perform his duty by fighting."

Krishna spoke firmly. In his view the Kauravas were acting sinfully. He reminded Sanjaya of the awful incidents which ocurred thirteen years ago in the Kuru assembly. By tolerating those acts of aggression Yudhisthira had already demonstrated his great commitment to peace. Now it was Dhritarastra's turn. "Everything depends upon the Kuru monarch. Let him do what is right and war will be averted. Otherwise a great destruction is imminent. I shall personally go to Hastinapura to negotiate with him. Either he peacefully restores to the Pandavas their property, or he loses everything on the battlefield."

The assembly voiced its approval of Krishna's speech. Arjuna, knowing that the Kauravas would not honour their agreement, had already requested him to go to Hastinapura and try to persuade them. Out of his love for Arjuna and his brothers, Krishna had readily agreed.

Yudhisthira had nothing further to add. He told Sanjaya to deliver his and Krishna's words to Dhritarastra. After asking each of his brothers to also add their own personal messages, he bade Sanjaya farewell and sent him back to Hastinapura.

Sanjaya arrived back in his city · to find Dhritarastra waiting anxiously. The blind king had sought Vidura's counsel and been told in no uncertain terms that he faced ruin. Vidura had tried to make his brother see sense, warning him that he had no chance of denying the Pandavas their rights. Now that Krishna had taken their side Dhritarastra should give up any hope that they might be overpowered in battle.

Dhritarastra was still not sure. His mind went one way, and then the other. Would Krishna really make such a big difference? He had not done anything to prevent the Pandavas from losing everything and being exiled. Now he had promised that he would not even fight. He had given his personal army to Duryodhana. He was certainly an enigma. But no matter what Krishna decided to do, it still appeared that the Kauravas' position was the stronger. Their army far outnumbered the Pandavas, and on their side they had an array of invincible heroes like Bhishma, Drona, Kripa and so many others. For that reason alone, Yudhisthira might finally decide that war was not a wise choice.

Dhritarastra's hopes that war might be avoided were soon dashed when Sanjaya delivered the messages of Yudhisthira, his brothers and Krishna. Standing before the Kuru assembly he said, "The Pandavas desire their ancestral lands. If these are not returned, then battle will be joined without delay."

Sanjaya spoke word for word Arjuna's message, which was full of heroic assertion and deadly threats. Arjuna restated the vows he and his brothers had made during the gambling match. Summoning the full fury with which Arjuna had spoken, Sanjaya said, "The Kauravas will pay for their many sins. They will be consumed like a field of dry grass in a fire. With Krishna as my charioteer none will be able to stand before me. Anyone desiring to overcome Krishna wishes to extinguish a blazing fire with his bare hands, or to swim the ocean with a stone slab secured to his neck."

Sanjaya delivered similar messages from the other Pandavas. There was no question of peace without them getting back their kingdom. Duryodhana simply sneered and said nothing. He looked toward Karna and smiled. Seeing his indifference, Bhishma stood up and said, "There is no doubt it will be as Arjuna has said. He and Krishna are the two immortal sages Nara and Narayana—indeed they are much more. None can know them, and none can overpower them at any time. Duryodhana's hope that Karna will overcome him is vain and useless. Karna does not possess even a fraction of Arjuna's power."

Karna leapt to his feet. "Again you criticise me! Why? You will soon see my power when I slay the Pandavas."

Bhishma looked at Karna with a mixture of sadness and annoyance. "Do not waste your breath, foolish man. You give Duryodhana false hopes. It is largely your fault that we face such a calamity now. We have already seen your power. Should I remind you? The incidents at Dwaitavana and Virata. Surely you have not forgotten already?"

Karna snorted. Things would be different next time. He would make no mistake. Indra's Shakti weapon would take care of Arjuna. It was a shame he had not thought to bring it when he went to Virata.

Understanding Karna's mind, Bhishma said, "You will see your cherished Shakti missile smashed and rendered useless when you direct it at Arjuna and Krishna. Cursed by your own guru and by the brahmins, your position is hopeless."

Karna winced. He recalled how he had offended a brahmin by accidently slaying his cow when out hunting one day. In grief and anger the brahmin had said, "When you face your deadliest enemy in battle the earth will swallow your chariot wheel." Still reeling from that curse, Karna had not long after upset his martial teacher, the sage Parasurama. Karna had lied to him, saying that he was a brahmin in order to receive the sage's instructions. Discovering the deceit, Parasurama had cursed Karna, saying, "When you most need it, you will forget how to invoke the most powerful Brahma weapon."

Karna writhed as Bhishma rebuked him. He felt he could take no more. When the Kuru grandfather stopped speaking, he jumped up and said, "Since, O Bhishma, you deride me and consider me without prowess, I will not fight while you are commander-in-chief. As you will lead the Kuru army I will only come out for the fight when you are laid low. Then the world will see my actual power."

Karna stormed out of the hall and Bhishma laughed. "The *suta's* son is rash and given to passion. He says whatever comes to his mind without ever weighing its worth or truth. At the very moment he cheated the holy sage Parasurama he lost all virtue and merit."

The discord between two of his most powerful warriors made Dhritarastra even more anxious. He spoke out in apprehension. "Surely our party now faces a dire danger. I do not see how we will ever overcome those divinely born sons of Kunti. Hearing about Arjuna and Krishna's actual identities convinces me of this fact. Duryodhana, be peaceful. Give up all thought of war. Live happily with your cousins. Even half of this wide and prosperous kingdom is more than enough for anybody."

Duryodhana sat scowling. He had heard enough. He stood up from his great gilded throne and gazed around the hall. Karna's sudden exit had disturbed him and he spoke out angrily. "All I ever hear is how the Pandavas are so powerful. Are they not mortals like us? They can be defeated, without doubt. Just see how we have already obliged them to go like hermits into the forest. What use then was Arjuna's much vaunted prowess? Where was Krishna's help then? We have nothing to fear. You have yet to see *my* prowess. Why, with my mystic powers I can hold back blazing fire, break apart mountains and solidify great lakes so that armies can march over them."

Becoming enlivened, Duryodhana went on praising himself for some time. He asserted that, if necessary, he alone would crush the Pandavas. When he was finished his brothers applauded him, but Bhishma, Vidura and Drona sadly shook their heads. They looked toward the blind king. His admonitions of Duryodhana were empty words if he did not back them up with stern action. But there was no sign of that. It was plain that Dhritarastra had abdicated his power to the prince.

Once again Dhritarastra asked for time to think and he dismissed the assembly. Days passed, during which time the king was visited by

Vidura and Sanjaya, who both tried hard to sway his mind. Sanjaya even called for Vyasadeva to speak with him, and the sage clearly described how events were being arranged by Krishna. "He desires to lift the earth's burden," the rishi solemnly said. "Many demonic elements will be destroyed, among them your sons."

Dhritarastra said nothing. The sage's words were worrying, but it was far from certain that his sons would lose, supported as they were by invincible fighters like Bhishma, Drona and Kripa. The king sighed. Ultimately, everything depended upon destiny. If it was God's will that the Kurus be destroyed, then what could anyone do?

* * *

In Virata the Pandavas consulted with Krishna. After hearing Sanjaya's message there seemed little doubt that Dhritarastra would not give them back their kingdom. It had been over a month since Sanjaya had gone back with their reply, but they had heard nothing more. All that remained now was for Krishna to go to Hastinapura, as he had promised. Sitting with him in Virata's palace, Yudhisthira said, "O Krishna, we have no better friend than you. Your willingness to carry our petition to the Kauravas proves it beyond doubt. But I fear they will not receive you well. They will surely laugh away your respectful submissions. Duryodhana especially will never respond to sweet speech. He will see it as a sign of our weakness. All he understands is the language of force."

Krishna was seated amid the Pandavas on a golden throne. Curling black hair fell around his face and a brilliant diamond-encrusted crown shone from his head. His shark-shaped earrings flashed as he turned toward Yudhisthira and said, "You are right, O Pandava, but still I must go. Every chance must be given to the Kauravas before war begins."

The prospect of a war with his relatives depressed Yudhisthira. He was tempted to forget the whole thing, but he knew it was not Krishna's desire. Nor was it his prescribed duty as a *kshatriya*. Sighing, he said, "I cannot see any way of recovering our kingdom other than war. When the times comes, fighting even with loved ones is the hard duty of kings, but how can I challenge respectable elders like Bhishma and Drona?

Would it not be more virtuous to humbly stand down and let them keep the kingdom? Please guide me, dear Krishna."

"You are not challenging anyone," Krishna replied. "The choice of whether or not to fight lies with Dhritarastra. If he will not act virtuously then he must face the consequences, along with all those who side with him. An elder, teacher or superior is fit to be rejected when he abandons virtue. No sin will attach to you for killing the Kurus under such circumstances."

Krishna said he would try his best by every diplomatic means to avoid war and thereby save the Kurus from destruction. "No one will be able to criticise you, O Yudhisthira, for you seek peace. It is the war-like Duryodhana and his small minded followers who desire to fight. I think their wish will soon be fulfilled."

Yudhisthira told Krishna that even if the Kurus will not give back the kingdom then he should ask them for just five villages. "I and my brothers will each rule one. Thus, we will do our duty as *kshatriyas*. We are not greedy for vast provinces."

Krishna smiled and stood up to leave. Accompanied by Satyaki he went out and mounted his shining chariot. The Pandavas followed him and walked around the chariot in respect before bidding him farewell. Urged on by Krishna's charioteer Daruka, the four tall steeds moved off and soon the chariot was speeding toward Hastinapura. Travelling throughout the day they reached the outskirts of the city by evening. As they came onto the main road that led into Hastinapura they saw thousands of citizens lining it to greet them. Cheered by those people, who threw flower petals and rice grains onto the road, they entered the city where they were met by the Kuru elders.

After formal greetings had been exchanged Krishna went to visit Kunti, who was living in Vidura's house. The noble Kuru queen wept with joy when she saw Krishna and he spent some time giving her news of her sons and consoling her. Kunti then gave a message to him for Yudhisthira, exhorting him not to be hesitant about fighting. "The time for which a *kshatriya* woman bears sons has arrived," she exclaimed, expressing her anger against the Kauravas. Kunti had been distraught when she heard what had happened to Draupadi in the Kuru assembly. Now at last the Kauravas would receive justice.

"Dear Krishna, I understand your actual position," Kunti said, as he stood up to leave. "You are the all powerful Supreme Person. Your will is truth. Please bless me that I always act only for your pleasure. This is my deepest desire."

Assuring Kunti that she was dear to him and that all her desires would be fulfilled, Krishna returned to Dhritarastra's palace. The king had called for a full assembly and it rose in respect as Krishna entered the hall. He was led to a fine seat close to the king. As he walked toward it a stream of effulgent rishis entered the hall, headed by Narada. They appeared like a line of glowing planets descended from the heavens. All of them took their seats at the front of the hall, and the assembly then settled down to hear Krishna speak.

When the hall became silent, Krishna looked at Dhritarastra and said, "O Bharata chief, let there be peace between Kauravas and Pandavas. May no heroes be slain on either side. For this reason, I have come. That is the sum and substance of my message."

Krishna praised the Kuru line, pointing out how it was famous for its virtue, its good behavior, kindness, compassion and truthfulness. He told Dhritarastra that as the incumbent Kuru monarch he had a great responsibility to maintain the noble Kuru traditions. All it required was for him to order that the Pandavas be given back their lands. Then war would be averted.

"However," Krishna continued, "if you do not pursue this line, disaster is certain. All the kings present here and those in Virata will slay one another mercilessly. Your sons or those of Pandu will also die. Consider how you will feel, O king, when news of either of their deaths reaches you."

When Krishna stopped speaking several of the rishis stood up one by one and gave their opinions. All of them warned Dhritarastra that war against the Pandavas would be calamitous.

Duryodhana looked defiantly around the hall. Who cared for the advice of Krishna or these old brahmins? He exclaimed, "I am whatever God has made me! How can I change my nature? Whatever is destined to happen will happen. That too lies in God's hands."

Duryodhana looked at the rishis and smiled. They were always saying how God controlled everything. The Kaurava prince had no argument with that.

Hearing his son's outburst Dhritarastra appeared uncomfortable. He called for water and after sipping a little he said, "O Krishna, O rishis, greatly wise men all of you, I too desire peace. However, my hands are tied. My son will not obey me, nor any of his elders. Try to change his mind, for that is the Kurus' only hope."

Krishna looked toward Duryodhana, who leaned back nonchalantly on his seat. He looked back at Krishna with a half smile. In a gentle voice Krishna said, "Dear Duryodhana, best of the Bharatas, I wish only for your good. Your obstinacy is vicious, frightful and destructive to all. It will not lead even to your happiness. Make peace with your cousins. This is desired by your father, your elders, the rishis, myself, and indeed the Pandavas. Such a peace will lead to your lasting fame, and all your desires will be fulfilled. However, if you choose to follow the advice of inferior and foolish men—such as Karna, Shakuni and Dushasana—then how can you expect any good fortune?"

Karna frowned. He respected Krishna, and his berating words toward him were painful. Why was he pleading on behalf of the Pandavas? Duryodhana was the son of the ruling Kuru king. Why then should he not have first claim to the whole kingdom? The Pandavas should themselves come humbly to him and ask for some territory. The magnanimous Duryodhana would surely accord them land if they dealt with him nicely. Why should he accede to their demands made through messengers, accompanied by threats of force?

Noting Duryodhana's indifference, Krishna's tone became sterner. "How can anyone face the enraged Bhima and live? Could anyone return home after coming out to fight with Arjuna? He has already vanquished the gods, Gandharvas, Daityas and Danavas. Do not seek war with him and his brothers unless you desire yours and your dynasty's eradication."

Duryodhana said nothing. Krishna's advice was intensely annoying. The prince glared around the hall. He resembled a heap of burning coals. One by one Bhishma, Drona and Vidura stood up and concurred with Krishna. Then Dhritarastra himself again spoke, telling his son to make peace. "Dear son, go with Krishna and bring back the Pandavas. Be blessed by the ever virtuous Yudhisthira and embrace Bhima to your bosom. Offer your blessings to Arjuna and the twins and live happily as cousin brothers. Do not disobey me. The time has come to cease all hostilities."

Duryodhana's face contorted. Embrace Bhima? The thought made him shudder. He leapt to his feet and declared, "Everyone criticises me and praises the Pandavas. What is my fault? I have done no wrong. Yudhisthira lost at dice fair and square. In any event, he should never have been given half of this kingdom. That mistake was made when I was younger and had little influence. It has now been rectified. The kingdom belongs to Dhritarastra—and I, his humble servant, aim to keep it that way. I will not be moved by any threats or attempts at coercion. If the Pandavas want any part of the kingdom then they will have to fight for it. As a *kshatriya* fighting is my duty and I will not abandon that duty out of fear or anything else."

Duryodhana looked around the hall and spoke in measured tones as he concluded his speech. "Krishna, know that as long as I rule the kingdom on my father's behalf, I will not give the Pandavas even as much land as can be pierced by the point of a needle."

Krishna rebuked Duryodhana, reminding him of his many acts of antagonism against the Pandavas, and especially Draupadi. "O Kurus, I am recalling my debt to Draupadi. That chaste lady purchased me for all time when she cried out to me in this assembly. Her honour will soon be avenged."

Duryodhana snorted. He stormed out of the hall, followed by his ministers and brothers. Krishna then said, "Hear me, O Kurus, your only hope is to bind and imprison Duryodhana. Otherwise destruction faces you all."

All eyes turned toward Dhritarastra, but the blind king remained silent. He could only remonstrate with his son, but he could not follow it up with any action. Unless he gave the order to implement Krishna's suggestion there would be war.

Outside the hall Duryodhana began to confer with his close associates. Between them they had made a plan to capture Krishna, upon whom their enemies depended. Now was surely the moment to act. If left much longer then Krishna may convince his father to do something foolish. He gave the order for his men to enter the hall and surround Krishna. As the soldiers began entering through the hall's broad entrances, he went back in himself.

Seeing what was about to happen, Krishna called out to Duryodhana, "Foolish man! Out of ignorance you think me alone and vulnerable. See now the truth."

Krishna laughed and as he did his body flashed like lightning. He grew to a huge size, seeming to fill the hall. Many gods emanated from him; Brahma from his head, Shiva from his chest and Agni from his mouth. Indra and numerous other celestials also appeared. All five Pandavas were also visible, standing by Krishna's side. Sparks, brilliant light and clouds of smoke issued from his terrific form.

The warriors closing on Krishna with drawn swords fell back in astonishment, shielding their eyes. Almost everyone in the assembly looked away. Only the rishis, along with Bhishma, Drona, Vidura, Sanjaya and Satyaki were able to look upon Krishna as he displayed his universal form. He also gave Dhritarastra the vision to see him and the old king was able to witness numerous celestial rishis and brilliantly shining gods standing before Krishna and offering prayers.

Outside the hall a fierce wind suddenly blew up and the sky became dark. Thunderclaps reverberated and the earth shook. With the hall in a tumult Krishna withdrew his mystical form and signalled for Satyaki to join him. Taking Satyaki's hand, he walked out of the hall and mounted his chariot, and as he did so the various disturbances all stopped. The sky cleared and the wind died down to a gentle breeze. All the leading Kurus followed Krishna outside, folding their palms in respect. Vidura led the king out of the hall and he stood before Krishna's chariot and said, "O Janardana, protector of the people, you have seen the influence I wield over my sons. I have tried my best. Do not blame me if war should ensue. I desire only peace."

Seated on the back of his great chariot, which was covered with white tiger skins and decorated with hundreds of golden moons, Krishna smiled down on Dhritarastra. Looking around at the other Kurus, he said, "O descendants of Bharata, you have witnessed everything; how the uncultured Duryodhana walked out and how the great lord of the earth has declared his powerlessness in the matter. Now, with your permission, I must return to Yudhisthira."

The chariot moved off and soon picked up speed as it went down the broad highway. Sending up a cloud of dust and with a great rumbling sound, it went out of the city's southern gate and in a short time was out of sight. Slowly the Kurus went back into their palace. Krishna's peace mission had failed. War was certain.

CHAPTER TWENTY-THREE

WISDOM ON THE BATTLEFIELD

After Krishna had left Hastinapura, Kunti began thinking about Karna. It seemed that either he or Arjuna would soon die. Or perhaps one of her other sons would perish at Karna's hands. The mighty son of Surya had no idea that the Pandavas were his brothers. He would show them no quarter in the upcoming war. Most probably though he would die himself. By opposing Krishna, he had little chance of survival. She had to do something to help her first-born child.

The next morning Kunti slipped out of the palace just before sunrise. It was time Karna learned the truth. It had never been possible to tell anyone before now. Nor had it been necessary. From the day she first saw him it was clear he was doing well. Duryodhana had given him a great kingdom and he had been accepted as one of the Kauravas. Now it looked like his allegiance to Duryodhana would soon prove his undoing. Kunti made her way to the Ganges where Karna was performing his devotions to the sun-god. As he came out of the river he was surprised to see the Kuru queen waiting for him. He greeted her with folded palms. "Noble lady, to what do I owe this honour? How can I serve you today?"

Kunti looked at her son who stood with the sacred river water running from his powerful body. She recalled again how she had placed him in that same river many years ago. Tears came to her eyes as she spoke. "My child, there is something you must know. I am your mother. You were conceived on me by Surya, your venerable deity."

Kunti's voice trembled as she described how, as a maiden, she had feared she would tarnish her family's reputation if she kept her child. "I thus cast you away into this river. Dearest child, my heart was breaking. I prayed to the all-pervading Vishnu that you would be safe. By his grace you were found and adopted by Adhiratha and his good wife."

Karna stared speechless at Kunti. There was no possibility that she was lying. Her adherence to virtue and truth was famed throughout the world. Karna dropped to his knees and held his head. He already knew that Adhiratha had found him on the bank of the Ganges. Seeing Karna's natural bodily armour, the charioteer had thought he must have been abandoned by the gods themselves. Karna had often wondered about his natural parents but had never thought for a moment that Kunti might be his mother. He looked up at her, shaking his head.

"It is true, my son. You are the Pandavas' brother, indeed the eldest of them. You should go to them. Do not follow avaricious and deceitful men. You will be ruined. Follow instead the path of virtue and join with your brothers."

Karna could still make no reply. It was bewildering. Kunti seemed genuinely distressed out of affection for him and fear for his welfare. Why had she never said anything sooner? It was too late now. How could he abandon Duryodhana after all the prince had done for him? Whether or not the Pandavas were his brothers, he now had no choice but to fight them. Tears welled in his eyes. He had finally found his mother who obviously loved him, but he could not let his rising natural affection for her cloud his judgment.

Taking a deep breath, he said, "I believe your words, good lady, but I cannot take your advice. It is hard for me to accept that you are my well wisher. By abandoning me at birth you have done me a great harm. I have been denied the rites of a *kshatriya* and labelled a *suta*, a charioteer's son. Now when danger threatens your other sons you finally come to me."

Karna got to his feet and glanced up at the sun. No wonder he had always felt such a strong attraction to worship that deity. He looked back at Kunti, who stood with tears streaming down her face. Steeling himself, he said, "I will not leave Duryodhana. He is the lord of my life. Still, mother, your visit to me will not prove fruitless. In the upcoming war I will not kill any of your sons other than Arjuna, even if I overpower them. If I can, I will slay Arjuna and thereby win lasting fame. Or, dying at his hand, I will attain the celestial regions. There can be no other way."

Shaking with emotion, Kunti reached out to embrace Karna. He stepped forward uneasily and she hugged him, saying, "The Kurus will soon be destroyed in a fierce fight. Remember then your promise to me, dear son. Be blessed. I shall now go."

As Karna bowed to her, the sorrowful Kunti walked quickly back toward the city. It was plain that at least one of her sons would soon be dead.

* * *

The Pandavas were hardly surprised when Krishna returned unsuccessful from Hastinapura. It had never seemed likely that Duryodhana would have a sudden change of heart. Urged on by Krishna, Yudhisthira began at once to arrange for war. After some consultation with his brothers and Krishna, he selected Dhristyadyumna to become the overall commander of his forces. As the huge army mobilised itself, the city of Virata was filled with a great clamour. The cheers and shouts of men, the blasts of conchshells, the cries of elephants and the beating of drums was tumultuous. Along with his fighting forces, Yudhisthira arranged for another virtual army of cooks, doctors, engineers and all kinds of other skilled workers to support his troops. The whole assembly marched out of Virata in a line extending for many miles and resembling a sea moving across the face of the earth. At their head was Bhima and the twins, with Dhristyadyumna right behind. Yudhisthira rode in their midst on a splendid war chariot, and Arjuna rode next to him, with Krishna driving his chariot.

Many brahmins accompanied the procession, continually reciting Vedic hymns extolling the virtues of righteous battle. The warriors shouted in joy. Either a glorious victory or death and ascent to the higher planets now awaited them.

The army gradually made its way to the Kurukshetra plain where the battle would take place. They arrived there after six days and set up camp around Lake Hiranvati. Soon a city of tents had been erected and the Pandavas waited for the Kuru leaders to come and discuss with them the rules of engagement. Then the war would commence.

In Hastinapura, Duryodhana's forces were also on the move. Personally marshalled by him they stacked their weapons onto thousands of chariots. Bows, arrows, axes, lances, spears, spiked clubs, maces and heavy darts were loaded, as well as bombs, bullets and many other types of explosive missiles, along with the machines for launching them. There were large baskets full of poisonous snakes, and vats filled with molasses and sand which would be heated and hurled at the enemy.

Moving up and down his almost unending line of chariots, horsemen, infantry and elephants, Duryodhana was elated. How could the Pandavas even look at such an army? It resembled the surging ocean during a full moon. With its countless heroes clad in brilliant armours and bearing gleaming weapons, it was dazzling to behold. The Kaurava leader sat aboard his own immaculate war-chariot, emblazoned with golden images of suns and many kinds of fierce beasts, and equipped with every conceivable weapon.

When all the arrangements were underway, Duryodhana went to Bhishma and said, "Grandfather, none can equal you in either virtue or prowess. You are always the Kurus' best protector. Please become our leader in this war. March at our head like Kartikkeya leading the celestials."

Bhishma looked across at Duryodhana, who stood before him with folded palms. The day he had long feared had finally arrived. War among the Kurus. From the moment Draupadi was insulted it had been certain. At that moment he realised he would have to oppose the Pandavas. As well as his vow to protect Hastinapura's throne, after years of living under Dhritarastra's keep he was now obliged to fight for him, even though it meant fighting alongside Duryodhana. Raising his gloved hand, he said, "I shall command your army, but you should know one thing. The Pandavas are as dear to me as the Kauravas. I will not slay any of them."

Duryodhana nodded. This was expected but it hardly mattered. Provided the Kuru grandfather wrought havoc among the Pandavas' troops, as he undoubtedly would, other warriors could deal with the them directly. Karna would settle his score with Arjuna. As for Bhima... Duryodhana fingered the golden mace by his side. His time would soon come.

"There is another thing you should know," Bhishma continued. "There is no warrior, not even me, who can match Arjuna's power. With Krishna by his side he cannot be conquered by the combined armies of the gods and demons."

"We shall see," Duryodhana replied with a smile. Krishna was not even fighting, and his display of mystic power had not been very impressive. Any magician or yogi could have done the same thing. So far Krishna had not done much to save the Pandavas from losing their kingdom. Without wielding weapons there would be little he could do in the war.

"To Kurukshetra, then! Victory will be ours!" Duryodhana's shout filled his troops with joy. They roared and clashed their weapons, and the immense army began to move off, slowly heading out of Hastinapura with the prince at their head. The earth trembled as they marched out, eager for the fight to commence.

Arriving after some days at Kurukshetra they set up camp a few miles away from the Pandavas. Duryodhana immediately called for a war council and the leading members of his army assembled in his great tent. He said to Bhishma, "Great hero, with yourself and Drona as our leaders I do not fear even the gods. It is time to make our strategy. Tell me of the strengths and weaknesses of both ourselves and the enemy."

Bhishma rested a hand on his ivory hilted sword. "Listen as I describe to you the power of all the warriors assembled here for battle. There are *rathas* who are capable of contending with a thousand other fighters, *maharathas* who can contend with ten thousand, and then there are *atirathas*, who can fight with sixty thousand or even an unlimited number at once."

Bhishma named many fighters on both sides, grading them in terms of their power. On Duryodhana's side he named Drona, Kripa, Kritavarma, Ashvatthama and the prince himself as *atirathas*. He also described the Pandavas as invincible fighters, stressing again Arjuna's power. "With his Gandiva bow, knowledge of mystical weapons, celestial chariot, impenetrable armour and inexhaustible quivers, and especially with Krishna by his side, he is unapproachable in battle by any other than Drona or myself. However, he is young while we are old and worn out. He will range through your army causing a tremendous devastation."

The kings in Duryodhana's tent who heard Bhishma describing Arjuna felt their arms shorn of power and hanging down uselessly by their sides. Bhishma then went on to speak about Shikhandhi. "This one is actually the reincarnation of a princess formerly kidnapped by me for the sake of my brother Vichitravirya. Filled with an intense hatred for me, she died thinking only of my death and has taken birth as Drupada's son."

Bhishma told the whole story. Many years ago, he had kidnapped the three daughters of king Kashi intending to bring them to Hastinapura as wives for his brother. One of them, however, named Amba, had already given her heart to another king. Bhishma had therefore sent her away, but that king had then rejected her. "You have been sullied by another man's touch."

The distraught Amba had gone into the forest and practised severe austerity to gain Shiva's favour. The god had finally appeared and blessed her that in her next life she would become a man who could kill Bhishma. The Kuru grandfather explained how he had heard the story from Vyasadeva. "It seems that Amba was first born as Drupada's daughter and only in her youth, by Shiva's grace, did she become a man. For this reason, I will not face him in battle, even if he comes before me desiring my death. This is my vow. I will not attack women, those with women's names, or even those who appear like women. Shikhandhi is actually a woman, but she has somehow taken a man's form."

The kings looked with respect at the noble Bhishma. He would certainly not break his vow. They would need to work hard to ensure that Shikhandhi did not get any opportunity to face him alone. As night gradually fell, they sat discussing their strategy. Battle would commence the next morning.

* * *

Early in the morning the commanders of the two armies met to agree on the rules of engagement. Warriors should only fight with equals and with equal weapons. No blow should be struck without warning, and one fleeing from the fight should not be assailed. The many servants and physicians on the battlefield should not be harmed. The generals spoke for some time and then stood up to leave for their positions at the head of their armies. Doubting that the deceitful Kauravas would follow the rules they had made, Dhristyadyumna said, "O Kurus, we will not be the first to break these codes, but if we see that you do not observe them then we too shall disregard them."

Shining like fire in his gold armour, Dhristyadyumna then mounted his chariot and headed out into the field. He began to arrange his forces into a needle formation, with himself, Bhima and the twins at its point. Yudhisthira was positioned in its centre, surrounded by many powerful chariot fighters. Near him was Arjuna, with Shikhandhi by his side. The Pandavas knew that their success depended upon overpowering Bhishma as soon as possible. As Arjuna advanced, Hanuman let out tremendous shouts from his banner, causing the horses and elephants to pass urine and dung in fear.

Seeing the Pandavas' formation, the Kauravas arranged themselves in a counter-array with Bhishma at their head. Seated on a huge chariot, with white head-dress, white banner and a white umbrella over his head, he looked like a white mountain. Behind him came Duryodhana, riding on the back of a great elephant the colour of a blue lotus. Bards and singers surrounded him chanting eulogies and he was protected by thousands of highly trained fighters.

Looking across at the Kuru forces, which resembled the ocean rolling toward him with the banners of countless warriors for its sharks, Yudhisthira's heart sank. He turned to Arjuna and said, "O mighty-armed one, how shall we ever overcome this army? The grandfather cannot be slain by anyone at any time, and he is supported by numerous other fiercely powerful fighters. This battle seems hopeless."

Arjuna encouraged his brother. "Battles are not won by prowess alone, sinless one. Virtue also plays a part. Wherever there is righteousness and truth, and wherever Krishna is found, there will be victory."

Yudhisthira sighed. Was his cause righteous? Had it not been his foolishness which ignited the conflict? And was it not his desire for kingdom and wealth which now impelled him to fight? But Krishna's presence was reassuring. He was the very personification of truth, so the fact that he was behind the war was surely the conclusive argument. Yudhisthira nodded in agreement with his brother, who then moved off toward the front of the army.

As Arjuna came alongside Dhristyadyumna at the head of the Pandava forces, he gave the order for the conchshells to be blown to signify the start of battle. Arjuna and Krishna blew long and mighty blasts on their celestial conches. Bhima and the twins also blew to their full power and the combined sound of all those conches carried over to the Kauravas, making their hearts tremble. They responded with blasts of their own. Drums were beaten and trumpets blown creating a tumultuous sound across the battlefield.

Arjuna then said to Krishna, "My Lord, infallible one, please drive my chariot closer to the Kauravas. Let me see the enemy positions and who has come out today, wishing to please the evil-minded Duryodhana."

Krishna urged on the horses and the fine chariot rumbled out into the middle of the field. Krishna raised his hand toward the Kauravas and said, "Behold all the Kurus assembled here, Partha."

Arjuna gazed across the field. The entire Kuru army was indeed present, but he too was a Kuru. How could he bear arms in a fierce conflict with his own kinsmen? Suddenly the grim finality of the situation struck him. He began to feel overwhelmed with apprehension. Here were Bhishma, Drona, Kripa and so many others whom he had loved since childhood, and who had loved him in return. For Yudhisthira to be victorious all of them would have to be killed. The thought was too much for Arjuna. It seemed as if his limbs were dissolving. His mouth was dry and he said to Krishna in a wavering voice, "O Keshava, I do not think I can fight. What good can come from killing one's relatives? It seems that only sin and misfortune will result from this war."

Arjuna's bow slipped from his hand and he sat down in his chariot. He had no heart for the fight. Virata had been different. He had not had any intention of killing his kinsmen there, nor had the Kuru elders fought to their full power anyway. Now there would be no mercy. Only one side would return from this war.

Tears streamed from Arjuna's eyes as he spoke. "I cannot fight for a kingdom bereft of all those I love, Krishna. What happiness will it bring?"

Arjuna was overwhelmed by compassion. Bhishma was exactly like his father, and Drona was equally dear. So many other kind and gentle elders were also present. Even Duryodhana and his brothers were pitiable because they were so foolish. Sweat broke out on Arjuna's brow as he implored Krishna. "If we kill learned elders, men who are our gurus, will not sin overcome us? The whole of society will go to hell as it depends upon the elders for the perpetuation of religious practices."

Arjuna argued passionately, his various arguments based on his understanding of morality. Finally, he slumped in his chariot and said, "I do not care if the Kauravas slay me unarmed and unresisting. I cannot fight."

Krishna smiled as he looked down at the weeping Arjuna. This was certainly an uncharacteristic display from the ferocious warrior. Still holding the chariot reins, he said, "How have you given way to such weakness, Arjuna? It does not befit one who understands life's true values. Rise up, great hero. Do not yield to this impotence. It leads only to degradation."

Arjuna was bewildered by Krishna's unequivocal dismissal of all his arguments. He voiced his doubts. "My dear Krishna, I can understand the necessity of killing sinful enemies, but some of these men are highly respectable. They are superiors and should not even be offered a verbal fight, never mind slain."

Arjuna gazed into Krishna's implacable face. He was obviously not impressed with Arjuna's arguments. Ultimately, he would have to follow Krishna's direction, but he had so many doubts. He needed to open his heart to his dear friend.

Folding his palms, Arjuna said, "O Krishna, it is plain that I cannot determine right from wrong. I am completely confused. You are my only hope. Please instruct me; tell me why I must fight. I surrender to you as a disciple."

Krishna smiled broadly. As the two armies stood off, waiting to see what Arjuna was going to do, Krishna began to instruct him. He started by explaining that Arjuna's arguments were based on a misconception. The Pandava warrior was not recognising that the body is only a temporary covering for the soul. Ultimately, the soul's welfare is more important than the material body's. Arjuna needed to understand how to act for the soul's benefit and that would be in everyone's best interests.

"The immortal soul is a part of the Supreme Spirit," said Krishna. "He belongs in the eternal spiritual world, a place of unlimited happiness, not here in this temporary and miserable material world." Krishna had put down the reins and was standing before Arjuna with his hand raised as he spoke. "You must therefore act in ways which take you, and indeed everyone else, toward that spiritual world."

Krishna explained that everyone's ultimate welfare lay in pleasing the Supreme Person. "And, my dearest friend, I am that Supreme. Everything, both material and spiritual, emanates from me. All things rest on me like pearls on a thread. I am the beginning, middle and end of everything. All beings owe their existence to me and depend upon me for their life. Therefore, try to act only for my pleasure."

Arjuna listened attentively as Krishna described how he is everyone's greatest well-wisher. He alone knows how the souls came into the material world, and how they can get out again. Through Krishna's grace the veil of ignorance covering the living beings can be gradually removed, and they can realise their true nature as his eternal loving servants.

"In illusion or *maya* people think their happiness will come from serving their own senses, from pursuing their mental fantasies," Krishna told Arjuna, "but this always leads to suffering. Permanent happiness can only be found when one gives up this illusion and turns to me."

Krishna instructed Arjuna for almost an hour. Arjuna put forward many questions which Krishna answered with profound and timeless wisdom. For Arjuna's benefit Krishna again displayed his majestic universal form, giving the Pandava the ability to see it in all its splendour. Arjuna felt his misgivings being dispelled. There could be no doubting Krishna's supremacy. Understanding that if Krishna wanted him to fight then it must be the best thing not only for him, but even for those who might die at his hands, Arjuna felt assured. Krishna would not misdirect him, he felt certain. It was his duty to fight, but it would not be an easy duty.

Looking across at Bhishma's chariot, Arjuna said, "Dear Krishna, my illusion is gone. I shall do exactly as you have instructed." He picked up his bow and asked Krishna to take the chariot back to the front of the army. The war was about to begin.

CHAPTER TWENTY-FOUR

THE SLAUGHTER BEGINS

As the armies were heading out to Kurukshetra, Dhritarastra sat anxiously in his palace. He cursed his blindness. As the king he should be going out at the Kurus' head. After all, he had brought about the war. Perhaps if he had been able to see the Pandavas arrayed for battle against his sons, he might have ceased hostilities and peacefully returned their kingdom. Now he could only sit and wait. The king called for Sanjaya and asked him what was happening. "Have the armies reached Kurukshetra? Destiny is all-powerful, Sanjaya. Although I could see Duryodhana's folly I could not restrain him. Surely this war has been divinely ordained. Can it therefore be so terrible? What greater honour is there for a warrior than to die in battle?"

Sanjaya sighed. The king's tendency to avoid responsibility was frustrating. They had been through it so many times. Maybe now though, as he faced imminent ruin, he might realise the truth. "Well king, it is said that man proposes and God disposes. The Lord gives us the results of our own acts, good or bad, but he also has his own desires. It is only when we understand and surrender to those desires that we can be truly happy. Otherwise we act sinfully and suffer."

As Sanjaya spoke the sage Vyasadeva entered the chamber. He came up to Dhritarastra and said, "O great king, your sons and most of the other warriors are at the end of their lives. All this has been arranged by time. It is inevitable."

Vyasadeva then told the king that he could bestow upon him divine vision which would enable him to see the battle, but Dhritarastra replied, "I have no wish to see my sons die, great sage. Let me just hear of the battle."

"So be it. I shall give the vision to Sanjaya. He will see every part of the war. O king, know one thing, victory follows righteousness. In Hastinapura the omens are bad."

Vyasadeva described the portents he had seen and Dhritarastra became alarmed. He pleaded with the sage not to blame him for what had happened. "I tried my best to bring my sons to the path of virtue."

Vyasadeva snorted. "The great slaughter of men about to occur has its root in you, king. You could still prevent it. Give the order now for the Pandavas' kingdom to be returned and the war will end before it begins."

Dhritarastra hung his head. He could make no reply. In his heart he still hoped beyond hope that his sons might somehow be victorious. Knowing this, Vyasadeva said, "Do not think that a superior sized army will necessarily win a battle. Even fifty well trained men who do not retreat and who work well as a team can defeat an entire army. Victory in any battle is uncertain. Ultimately, as you have heard so many times, virtue is the decisive factor."

Leaving the king silent, the sage walked out of the chamber, his wooden sandals clacking on the marble floor. Sanjaya closed his eyes and began to see within himself the scene unfolding on the battlefield. He described it to the king, relating to him the conversation that took place between Krishna and Arjuna. Hearing Krishna describe himself as the supreme power and hearing also how he again manifested his universal form, Dhritarastra felt his hopes of victory fading. Even with the assistance of the great Kuru fighters what chance did they stand of overcoming such a power?

"What did my sons and the Pandavas do after Krishna had spoken?" Dhritarastra asked. Fearing the worst, but still hanging on to a slender hope of success, the king sat rapt in attention as Sanjaya began to describe in full detail all the events as they occurred on the battlefield.

* * *

As Arjuna's chariot made its way back to his army the men sent up a great cheer. They had watched with apprehension as he remained stationary between the two armies, obviously overcome by uncertainty. Now though it seemed he had regained his resolve. His bow was raised, and he was moving into position. Horns, bugles drums and conchshells were sounded in a continuous uproar.

Just as the battle was about to begin Yudhisthira put off his armour and climbed down from his chariot. As his brothers and the other warriors looked on in amazement, he walked across the field toward the Kauravas. Unarmed and unprotected he made his way straight to Bhishma's chariot. The Kauravas started laughing. "It seems this wretch has been overcome with terror. He has come to beg Bhishma for mercy."

Paying no heed to those jeers, Yudhisthira approached Bhishma with folded palms. The old Kuru chief got down to greet him and Yudhisthira immediately clasped his feet and said, "O invincible hero, grant us permission to fight with you. Please bless us."

Bhishma smiled. Yudhisthira was properly observing the ancient code which required that before fighting with an elder one should offer respects and seek his permission. "Son of Kunti, fight and obtain victory," he replied. "Alas, child, although I know your cause is just, I must oppose you. Surely men are slaves to wealth. Thus do I stand here helplessly, but still I wish to do you good. Ask from me something and it will be granted."

Tears came to Yudhisthira's eyes. In a choked voice he said, "O grandfather, tell us how you may be slain."

Standing before Yudhisthira in his polished silver and gold armour, Bhishma was a formidable figure. Although over a hundred years old he had lost none of his power. His gilded bow stood by his side, almost as tall as him. Placing a hand on Yudhisthira's shoulder he said, "There is no man present here who can slay me, even if he be aided by the king of the gods. The time for my death has not yet come. Approach me again later and I will answer your question."

Yudhisthira bowed again and then walked toward Drona, who got down to greet him. Offering respects to his martial teacher in the same way, he asked his permission to fight.

Like Bhishma, Drona blessed Yudhisthira. "O king, how can you be opposed?" he said. "With Krishna as your guide your victory is assured. Alas, I am a slave to Kuru wealth and cannot fight for you but ask from me some boon."

Moved by affection, Yudhisthira falteringly replied, "O preceptor, please tell me how you may be defeated."

"As long as I stand with upraised weapons you will never obtain victory," Drona answered. "Neither man nor celestial can stand before me as I scatter arrows in all directions. Only when my weapons are lowered can I be overcome. O king, I will lay down my arms when I hear some terrible news from a credible source."

Drona held up a hand in blessing then remounted his chariot. Yudhisthira went over to Kripa to seek his permission and blessings. As he came near Kripa's chariot a surge of grief overwhelmed him. Clasping his hands, he stood before his old teacher with head bowed. Tears streamed down his face. First Bhishma, then Drona, and now Kripa. Three men who were all like fathers, and who all had to be killed. Yudhisthira could not recall a single harsh word or deed from any of them.

Seeing Yudhisthira's plight, Kripa gently said to him, "Great king, go forth and obtain victory. Waste no time trying to kill me, for I am unslayable. My father, Gautama Rishi, has blessed me so; but every day I will rise from sleep and pray for your victory."

Yudhisthira went finally to Shalya, who was Madri's brother. Duryodhana had reached him first with his plea for assistance and the noble-minded Shalya had felt unable to refuse. After giving his permission for the fight, he looked sadly down at his nephew and said, "I have become obliged to the Kauravas. Dear child, may you win everlasting fame and glory. I wish only for your success."

Yudhisthira walked slowly away and made his way back to his own forces. After again donning his armour and mounting his chariot, he called across to the Kauravas. "If any of you wish to join us before the battle begins then you are welcome. Step forward."

As well as his hundred sons from Gandhari, Dhritarastra had one other son born from a servant maid. This prince, Yuyutsu, had never shared Duryodhana's evil mentality. When he heard Yudhisthira's offer he called back, "I will join with you, sinless one. Will you accept me?"

"Come, come," Yudhisthira replied. "Fight against your foolish brothers. It seems their line will soon rest on you."

Duryodhana glared at his half-brother as he made his way across to the Pandavas. Drums were beaten and trumpets blown. The moment for the battle to start had arrived. All the warriors sent up a great cheer. Now it was either victory or a glorious death. There was no third possibility. The two armies closed on each other like two great oceans colliding. Bhima raced ahead of the Pandava forces, sending up tremendous cries which struck terror into the Kauravas' hearts. Whirling his mace above his head he resembled a violent tornado as he tore into his horrified foes. At last the time to vent his long pent-up wrath had arrived.

Taking heart, the Kauravas responded with their own battle cries and rushed toward Bhima with raised weapons. Other Pandava warriors came up alongside him and a fierce general conflict was soon raging. Neither side side flinched nor turned back. The twang of bowstrings and the slap of the strings against leather arm-protectors sounded everywhere like continuous gun shots. The air was full of long-shafted arrows that glanced off the warriors' case armour. Spears, darts, clubs, and iron balls rained down on both armies. The fighters roared and blew their conches, weapons clashed, animals screamed, infantry thudded across the field with heavy steps, chariot wheels clattered and drums were beaten to create a deafening cacophony of sound. Reckless of their lives the warriors rushed at each other in a frenzy.

Many omens were seen as the battle commenced. Thunderclaps sounded and the sky flashed red and blue. A shower of putrid matter dropped from the heavens and a terrible wind blew. Bolts of lightning struck the earth. Undeterred, the warriors fought on with full force. Powerful chariot fighters met together, discharging volleys of deadly arrows. Infantry fought together, smashing and hacking at one another with their maces and swords. Elephant riders came against other elephants, their great beasts trumpeting in fury, while horsemen charged each other with their long spears held out.

The great heroes on both sides engaged with their chosen foes. Bhima singled out Duryodhana, Dhristyadyumna assailed Drona, Sahadeva attacked Shakuni, while Arjuna engaged with Bhishma. Many other mighty heroes clashed as the first exchanges of the war took place. Men fell in thousands, their heads and limbs severed. The ground quickly became muddy with blood. The warriors' jewels and gold ornaments sparkled from the mire like stars shining in the firmament.

Divisions of Rakshasas marched out on both sides. Ghatotkacha led a huge force for the Pandavas, while a mighty Rakshasa named Alambusha led them for the Kauravas. These awful beings tore their human opponents to pieces and created a terrible carnage. The battlefield assumed the appearance of Yamaloka, Death's grim abode. Men screamed in pain, like souls condemned to the tortures of hell. They fought as if possessed by demons. No quarter was shown. In that confused melee the soldiers slew even their own relatives as their shouts of identification were lost in the general din.

Bhishma broke free from Arjuna's attack and ploughed into the Pandava army. His chariot, marked with an ensign bearing a palm tree, carved through the enemy troops leaving a trail of slaughter in its wake. His arrows sped in all directions. Anyone who came before him was immediately slain. The old Kuru warrior seemed possessed of a new life. He appeared to be dancing in his chariot as he fought. His arrows were fired with such power that they sent even great elephants tumbling to the earth.

After the first day's fighting tens of thousands of men lay dead. Due mainly to Bhishma's exertions the battle went the Kauravas' way. When Sanjaya informed him, Dhritarastra felt cheered, but then he felt guilt. Was it not sinful to revel in the death of so many men? How could he relish the hope that his own nephews may be crushed? Either way, victory or defeat, he would suffer. Sitting with head bowed he lamented. "What good will come of this, Sanjaya? Alas, Vidura was right. The noble Bhishma and Drona spoke well. I should have heeded Krishna's words."

The second day of the battle began like the first, with Bhishma wreaking havoc. As the powerful Kuru hero ploughed through the Pandava forces, Arjuna became infuriated. How could he be so committed to Duryodhana's evil cause? Arjuna said to Krishna, "O Janardana, go quickly to where Bhishma stands. It seems he is bent on massacring our entire army. I shall kill him without delay."

"Be on your guard," said Krishna. "I shall now take you to him."

Arjuna began to fight his way past the contingent of chariot fighters assigned to protect Bhishma. The Pandava fired arrows in an endless line. The twang of his bow, the slap of the string on his leather fences, and the whistling of arrows leaving his bow made one continuous sound. He whirled about in his chariot striking down the warriors who assailed him from all sides.

Bhishma saw Arjuna's standard coming toward him. Hanuman's frightful cries were distinctly audible, even from a great distance. Soon Arjuna's chariot, with its four cream-coloured steeds, broke through the troops surrounding Bhishma. Arjuna blew his conch in a challenge to the Kuru warrior. Bhishma looked across at Arjuna, tears springing to his eyes. He faced a harsh duty in having to fight his beloved grandson. The old fighter bowed his head in respect to Krishna. How wondrous that he had become a chariot-driver for his friend. Bhishma was almost overcome by surges of divine love as he gazed at Krishna expertly driving Arjuna's steeds. He took a deep breath and composed himself. It was a cruel destiny, but duty had to be done. Lifting his great bow, he continued to fire off his deadly arrows at the Pandava forces assailing him.

Drona, Kripa and Duryodhana were fighting alongside Bhishma and they attacked Arjuna. Many other powerful warriors supporting Bhishma also trained their weapons on the Pandava. "Stay! Stay! Fight with me! Be on your guard!" came the shouts from all quarters.

Unperturbed by that multiple attack, Arjuna smiled. Within seconds he sent arrows at every one of his assailants. They reeled about in their chariots as the shafts loosed from the Gandiva thudded into them. Rallying themselves, they fought back with fury. Arrows flew everywhere as the one Pandava contended with dozens of other warriors. Other Pandava heroes came to Arjuna's aid and engaged the great Kuru fighters. At the same time hundreds and thousands of Kaurava warriors advanced toward Arjuna. Encountering Arjuna's furious assault they resembled the ocean lashed by a storm. Their armours were torn off and their bows shattered. Standards were sent crashing to the ground and chariots were smashed to pieces. Bodies pierced through with dozens of arrows lay everywhere. Viewing Arjuna as Death incarnate, many warriors jumped from their chariots and ran desperately away from him.

Duryodhana went up to Bhishma and called out, "Grandfather! Do something quickly. Arjuna is slaying our men like a farmer reaping wheat. For your sake Karna has laid down his arms, otherwise he would surely check the enraged Pandava."

Bhishma looked over at Arjuna. He really did not want to fight him. In any event, with Krishna on his side Arjuna could never be overcome. Bhishma turned back to Duryodhana who was begging him to immediately engage with Arjuna. "We depend fully on you, great hero," he pleaded. Bhishma sighed. Ordering his charioteer to face Arjuna, he cursed. "Fie on a warrior's duty!"

Seeing Bhishma turn toward him Arjuna focused his attention on the Kuru chief. Still enraged, he shot ten, then a hundred, and then a thousand arrows at him. Bhishma countered all those arrows with his own. Arjuna fired so many shafts at him that Bhishma appeared covered by a network of arrows. He expertly dispelled those arrows and quickly counter-attacked Arjuna. The two heroes cheered one another as they fought. Neither could gain any advantage over the other.

Struck on the breast by several fast-coursing arrows, Krishna bled and appeared like a red-blossoming kimshuka tree. He dexterously drove Arjuna's chariot, confounding Bhishma's aim by describing swift circular motions. Bhishma also wheeled rapidly about the field and the two fighters resembled a pair of angry lions circling one another. The chariot wheels sent up clouds of dust from the earth which seemed about to split open. Many other warriors stood by and watched in amazement. They could not detect the slightest flaw in the techniques of either combatant. Much of the time both were invisible beneath clouds of arrows. In the sky the celestials looked on and said, "These two cannot be defeated by any earthly or heavenly foe. This fight will surely never end."

As Bhishma and Arjuna fought, many other fierce encounters took place elsewhere on the battlefield. Drona and Dhristyadyumna contended in a fight that was no less spectacular. Each pierced the other with steel-tipped shafts and roared in fury. Conscious of his destiny to kill Drona, Dhristyadyumna constantly sought an opening but the preceptor repeatedly thwarted his attacks.

Bhima had entered deeply within the Kalinga army. Laughing all the while, he unleashed thousands of arrows that cut down his foes on all sides. Those shafts released from Bhima's huge bow passed clean through the bodies of men and horses. The Nishadas fought him fearlessly but were slaughtered like so many deer encountering a lion. In a terrible battle Bhima met the Kalinga king who was mounted on a heavily armoured elephant. The beast screamed and tried to gore Bhima with its sharpened tusks. Finally, Bhima leaped from his chariot with his blue-bladed sword held high. He brought it down on the king's head with all his power. The king was sliced cleanly into two pieces which fell on either side of his mount. Bhima then severed the elephant's trunk and the blood-soaked beast toppled over and died.

Jumping clear of the falling elephant, Bhima rushed at the remaining Kalingas. He moved with the speed of a hawk. His gleaming sword flashed as severed heads and limbs flew everywhere. The Kaurava troops were terrified. Bhima jumped forward and backwards, spinning and somersaulting through the air. Thrusting and parrying, he resembled a frenzied dancer and left a trail of carnage in his wake. His enemies shook with fear. Before long thousands of Kaurava warriors lay slain, hacked to pieces by Bhima. Amid the blood and gore were pieces of armour and shattered chariots, as well as golden housings and shining bells from the backs of elephants.

The Kaurava forces fled away in panic from Bhima. "This one is not human. Run for your lives!" they screamed. Bhima roared triumphantly and blew repeated blasts on his conch. The terrific sound reverberated around the field and made the hair on the Kauravas' bodies stand erect. As they dashed away in all directions, twilight fell and the battle ended for the day. The two armies disengaged and withdrew from the field. Jackals and vultures, screeching in glee, began to gather around the slain and mutilated warriors. Fatigued from the fight, the soldiers slowly made their way back to their camps.

CHAPTER TWENTY-FIVE

THE OLD WARRIOR

The battle raged on for over a week with a great slaughter of men on both sides. Goaded on by Duryodhana, Bhishma created mayhem among the Pandavas' forces. So too did Drona and other principal Kuru warriors. On the other side the Pandava heroes headed by Bhima and Arjuna cut down the Kauravas in the tens of thousands. Remembering his vow to slay all Dhritarastra's sons, Bhima targeted them at every opportunity. Duryodhana wept tears of frustration and anger as he saw his brothers hacked down by the remorseless Bhima. The Kaurava prince longed to check him but found himself hardly able to approach the raging Pandava warrior. Even when backed up by other mighty Kuru fighters, Duryodhana was still repulsed by Bhima whenever they met.

Dhritarastra lamented pitiably when he heard of his sons' deaths. He tossed about on his throne and let out great sobs. "Destiny is chastising me. Surely Bhima will slay every one of them. Alas I am sinking into an ocean of distress."

After eight days of fighting, Duryodhana began to feel disheartened. He had hoped that by now his army would be well on top, but things were not going well. Perhaps the Danavas were assisting him, it was hard to say. A great number of the Pandava forces had been slain, but the Kauravas had also sustained huge losses, even more than their foes. His eleven great divisions were now no more than six. The Pandavas had to be stopped or his whole army would soon be destroyed. Bhishma and Drona were his best hopes, but they were too soft on Pandu's sons.

Thinking in this way, Duryodhana went to Bhishma on the evening of the eighth day and said, "O grandsire, it seems we can do nothing to prevent the Pandavas from annihilating us. They continuously smash apart our formations and grind down our forces. I think the gods are favouring them."

241

Bhishma shook his head. It was bad enough that he was forced to fight the Pandavas, but to also constantly face Duryodhana's accusatory remarks made it much worse. He raised his two powerful arms which were covered with lacerations and scars. "See here the evidence of my endeavour, king. I have exerted myself to the best of my ability and the limit of my strength. Tens of thousands of warriors lie slain by me. However, neither I nor any other man can kill the Pandavas. They are protected by virtue and by the very Lord of virtue himself. What can mere exertion achieve?"

Bhishma looked with compassion at Duryodhana. His foolishness was pitiable, and now he was perhaps starting to become a little humble. At least he was being humbled by the Pandavas' might in battle. Maybe he would see sense and make peace with his cousins before everything was lost. That, though, seemed unlikely. More probably he would fight to the very last man—and still not surrender anything.

Duryodhana could guess Bhishma's thoughts. "I do not believe the Pandavas are invincible," he said. "However, I know that you certainly are. You cannot be killed until you desire death yourself. With your assistance we could vanquish the gods and demons combined. How then can five mortal men survive against you?"

With folded palms Duryodhana beseeched Bhishma. Tears flowed from his eyes. Dropping down and holding Bhishma's feet he said, "My lord, be merciful to me. Slay the Pandavas even as Indra slays the demons. Make good your promise to always protect the Kurus."

Bhishma looked away from the prince. Protect the Kurus? Duryodhana seemed prone to forget that the Pandavas were also Kurus. Indeed, they might soon be the only surviving Kurus.

Duryodhana's imploring voice went on, "If out of hatred for me or love for the Pandavas you feel unable to slay them, then please stand down from this fight. Let Karna come out. He has vowed to kill at least Arjuna."

Bhishma was stung by Duryodhana's words. What did the prince think Karna could achieve that he could not? Had Duryodhana already forgotten Karna's previous encounters with Arjuna? What would it take to convince him that his hopes were futile? Perhaps if he saw for certain that even the so-called invincible Bhishma could not kill the Pandavas then he might relent.

Bhishma reached down for his beautiful gem-encrusted quiver. It was filled with long golden shafts fletched with buzzard feathers. Bhishma took out five arrows fitted with barbed heads. Spreading out a cloth on the ground he carefully placed the arrows on it. He then closed his eyes and began muttering Vedic mantras. After a few minutes he again opened his eyes and looked at Duryodhana. "I have imbued these five arrows with all my ascetic power. Tomorrow I shall fight a battle such as has never been witnessed before. I will attack the Pandavas and seek to kill them all, each with one of these shafts. Only Krishna can save them, but he has vowed not to fight. Let us see what happens now."

Bhishma picked up the five arrows. It was a vain hope that they could ever kill the Pandavas. Krishna would certainly find a way of saving the brothers. He would need to. The Kuru chief would give it his all. Surely then, when he failed, Duryodhana would realise the futility of his cause.

Duryodhana jumped to his feet beaming. This was what he wanted to hear. He clapped his hands and repeatedly praised Bhishma but thinking of Krishna he became pensive. The Yadu prince was tricky. He said, "Let me keep these arrows tonight. I will guard them carefully and give them to you tomorrow at the start of battle."

Still joyful, Duryodhana took the arrows and retired to his own quarters for the night. Now the Pandavas were doomed. Bhishma was famed for keeping his word. He would certainly try his best to kill all five brothers with his infallible arrows, and Krishna was only with Arjuna. Even if he broke his word and started to fight how would he save the others? Smiling to himself, Duryodhana lay down to rest.

* * *

Yudhisthira sat in his tent surrounded by his brothers. After eight days of fighting the battle seemed to be going his way. The Kauravas had sustained huge losses and were down to half their original number. His losses had not been so great and now the two sides were almost equal. Still, the Pandava king felt little joy. So many men were dying so that he might regain his kingdom. Soon the world would be full of widows and orphans. It was a tragedy of immense proportions but what choice was there? He had tried everything to bring about peace. Now he was only doing his duty by fighting; a duty endorsed by Krishna.

Doubtlessly some divine plan was being enacted. Yudhisthira often needed to remind himself of that. He looked over to Krishna, who sat amid his brothers like the full moon surrounded by glowing planets.

Appearing thoughtful, Krishna began to address Yudhisthira. "Great hero, you are becoming successful in this fight. The Kauravas are being crushed by your army. We can expect them to resort to every desperate means to reverse the situation. Even now I sense that they are devising some deadly scheme."

Krishna looked over at Arjuna. That day's battle had seen the death of Iravan, Arjuna's son by a Naga princess whom he had married during his one year pilgrimage. Iravan had brought a division of powerful Naga warriors to the fight, but he had been killed after a terrific contest with Alambusha. The only consolation had been that Ghatotkacha had then killed Alambusha, throwing his severed head into Duryodhana's chariot. Seeing Arjuna was seized with grief for his slain son Krishna comforted him. "Shake off this sorrow, O hero. Iravan has ascended to regions of uninterrupted bliss. What greater end is there for heroes than to die in battle?"

Arjuna wiped his eyes. He had been far away from Iravan when he had been killed and could do nothing to help him. Duryodhana's tactic each day had been to detail a vast division of warriors—the fierce Samshaptakas and Narayanas—to engage with Arjuna and keep him away from the prinicipal Kuru fighters. It was only when he returned from the battle that he heard the awful news, but Krishna was right. No one should lament the death of a hero in battle. It was an end that all *kshatriyas* longed to achieve.

"Take heart, Arjuna, for there is something you must now do," Krishna continued. "You must go to Duryodhana and call in the favour he owes you."

Arjuna widened his eyes in surprise. Go to Duryodhana? He remembered well enough the time when the Kaurava had promised him a boon, after Arjuna had rescued him from the Gandharvas. Dishevelled and humiliated, Duryodhana had tried to salvage his pride by saying he would later return the favour when Arjuna was himself in need. Krishna must have decided the time had come. Arjuna was curious. "I will do whatever you say, Krishna. Tell me what I should ask from him."

Krishna told Arjuna about the five arrows. "Go at once and ask Duryodhana to give them to you."

Arjuna stood up and left immediately. Alone and unarmed, without any fear that he would be assailed, Arjuna entered the Kaurava camp. By night the warriors would often come together as friends and the guards greeted Arjuna respectfully, taking him through the rows of torchlit tents straight to Duryodhana's quarters in their midst.

The Kaurava prince sat up in surprise as Arjuna entered. "Welcome, O hero. What brings you here at such a late hour?"

Arjuna reminded him about the favour he was owed. "I have come for that now. Please give to me the five arrows you received from Bhishma today."

Shocked but unable to refuse, Duryodhana reached down and lifted the arrows. Placing them across his outstretched palms, he offered them to Arjuna. "How did you know?" he asked.

"The all-knowing Krishna informed me," Arjuna replied, taking the arrows. He then took his leave from the bemused Duryodhana and made his way back to his own camp. The Kaurava was left sitting on his bed and shaking his head. Krishna was a cunning opponent. Was he really the Supreme? How else could he have known about the arrows? Yet he seemed so human. If he was God then he could surely end the war in a moment, having the earth split open and swallow all the Kauravas. It did not make any sense. Duryodhana lay down again and stared at the now empty cloth where the arrows had lain. How would Bhishma keep his promise now?

* * *

When Bhishma heard the next morning how Arjuna had taken the arrows after being sent by Krishna, he smiled wryly. It was not a surprise. Krishna would always find some way to save his followers. Gazing across at the Pandavas' array, Bhishma pulled on his leather finger protectors. "Krishna has made my promise false, for I cannot imbue another five arrows with the same power. However, I will still fight to my utter limit. I will target Arjuna alone. If Krishna does not give up his own promise not to fight, then he will see his beloved friend slain today."

Seeing Bhishma's grim determination as he rode out for battle, Duryodhana's hopes rose. Even if Arjuna alone was killed the Pandavas would be finished, but Bhishma would need to overcome his affection for the Pandava. Duryodhana thought again of the Danavas. Let them possess Bhishma now. Let them charge him with all their demonic fury. Shouting out his battle cry, Duryodhana began ordering the leading Kuru warriors into positions where they could guard Bhishma as he fought.

The two armies closed again for the ninth day of battle. Shrieking birds of prey flew above the armies as they charged. The sky seemed ablaze and a strong wind blew. A shower of stones rained down. The horses and other animals shed tears and stumbled as they ran. Everything portended a terrible massacre, but the warriors rushed unflinching into the fight. They fell upon one another with shouts and roars, thrusting and hacking remorselessly with their swords and daggers. The sky was filled with wave after wave of arrows. Countless spears hissed through the air like silver and gold-winged serpents.

True to his word, Bhishma began a great slaughter of men. He resembled personified Death bent upon destroying all beings. Arrows flew from his bow in unending lines. Bearing down upon Arjuna, he swept aside the warriors in his path. Before the sun had reached the meridian he had slain ten thousand chariot fighters. They lay strewn about the field with their armours, standards and chariots lying shattered around them.

Seeing the carnage caused by Bhishma, Krishna said to Arjuna, "The time has come to face Bhishma. Remembering your duties do not hesitate. Slay him now before he destroys your army."

Arjuna, who himself had been smashing apart the Kaurava forces, felt heavy with sorrow. He looked across at Bhishma. "A warrior's duty is a burden indeed, Krishna. Killing even those who should not be killed, he relentlessly seeks wealth and honour. Still, my highest duty is to please you, Lord. Take me then to the grandfather. I will slay him."

Krishna urged on Arjuna's celestial steeds and the chariot wheeled round to face Bhishma. Seeing him heading for an encounter with the Kuru commander the afflicted Pandava troops sent up a cheer. Bhishma yelled out his battle cry and immediately shot a hundred shafts at Arjuna. Krishna dexterously maneuvered the chariot away from the arrows. Arjuna shot a crescent-headed shaft that cut Bhishma's bow in two. He immediately strung another, but in an instant Arjuna had sundered that also. Bhishma called out to him in admiration, "Excellent! Well done."

Bhishma's charioteer swung his chariot around and the Kuru hero strung a third bow and began to assail Arjuna with countless shafts. Arjuna appeared covered by a blanket of arrows. He was struck all over and he reeled under the force of Bhishma's attack. Krishna was pierced by many arrows and he bled from his wounds, seeming like a dark mountain sending forth a stream of red oxides.

At the same time as attacking Arjuna, Bhishma maintained a steady assault on the Pandava army. His long steel shafts sped in all directions. They passed clean through the bodies of warriors, horses and elephants. Laughing loudly, Bhishma span in his chariot with his bow constantly bent into a circle. He resembled the Destroyer himself. Wailing soldiers fled in all directions, terrified for their lives.

Arjuna found himself unable to exert himself to his full power. He countered Bhishma's attack only half-heartedly. Noting this, Krishna felt anxious. If Bhishma was not checked he would slaughter everyone on the field. He was seized by a demonic rage. By employing celestial weapons, he released a countless number of death-dealing arrows. They flew indiscriminately across the field mowing down everyone in their path. A constant stream of them shot toward Arjuna. Krishna looked back at the Pandava. It was obvious that he was unable to overcome his affection and respect for Bhishma. The Kuru warrior was thus sorely afflicting him. Arjuna lamely resisted and was threatened with imminent death. Krishna decided he had to act himself to stop Bhishma.

He threw down the reins of Arjuna's chariot and leapt down. Taking up a nearby chariot wheel, he raised it above his head as if it were his favourite weapon, the Sudarshan *chakra*. He began to run toward Bhishma as a lion might run at an elephant. His yellow silk garment fluttered in the dusty air like lightning dancing in a thundercloud. Krishna's bodily effulgence lent luster to the wheel and it glowed like the primeval lotus which gave birth to Brahma. His dark arm was like the lotus stalk and his beautiful face, shining with beads of perspiration, was like its filament covered with dew.

Struck with transcendent emotion on seeing this wondrous sight Bhishma lowered his weapons. His limbs trembled and tears flowed from his eyes. The Lord of all the worlds was breaking his promise to protect his beloved friend. Bhishma called out to him, "O Supreme One, I bow to you. Strike me down at once. Killed by you I will obtain the greatest good fortune. My fame will be celebrated forever."

Arjuna was aghast. It was his fault that Krishna was apparently forsaking his vow. He had not taken up any weapon, but he had nevertheless entered the fray. Foolish men would no doubt condemn him for his seeming falsity. Arjuna could not have that on his conscience. He had to rectify his omission in not fighting to his full power with Bhishma. Jumping from his chariot he ran after Krishna.

Coming close to Bhishma, Krishna furiously shouted out, "You are the root of this great slaughter. A wise minister should check a wicked king by any means. If words fail, then force should be used."

As Krishna addressed Bhishma, Arjuna caught up to him. He hurled himself forward and caught hold of Krishna's legs. Krishna continued running with Arjuna clinging onto him.

Still seized with wonder and love for Krishna, Bhishma answered, "You always speak the truth, Lord. What can I say? Surely destiny is all-powerful."

Dragged by Krishna, Arjuna dug his feet into the earth. Krishna gradually slowed and finally came to a stop after taking ten steps with Arjuna in tow. The Pandava implored him. "Lord, stop! Do not break your promise. I swear by my sons and brothers that I shall fight to my full strength. You will see me do battle as never before."

Krishna lowered the chariot wheel, still glaring at Bhishma. Throwing the wheel aside he turned and walked back to his chariot with Arjuna. At that moment the sun reached the western horizon and hostilities were ended for the day. The warriors on both sides withdrew, marvelling at the wonderful incident between Krishna and Bhishma. The Kuru warrior slowly returned to his camp, his mind absorbed in thought of Krishna. The image of Krishna running in anger with the upheld wheel would be forever imprinted on his heart.

* * *

As the Pandavas reached their camp Yudhisthira wrung his hands in anxiety. Bhishma was exterminating his forces. He would have slain even Arjuna if Krishna had not intervened. The terrible Kuru fighter had clearly discarded all affectionate feelings for the Pandavas. If he was not soon checked then their defeat seemed certain.

After the five brothers and their allies had taken their seats in Yudhisthira's tent, he consulted with Krishna. "My dear Keshava, what can we do about Bhishma? We can hardly even look at him as he stands with upraised weapons. Not even the most powerful gods could face him. By confronting him we are like so many moths flying into a blazing fire."

Yudhisthira hung down his head. He had no heart to carry on with the war. Krishna said, "Throw off this grief, king. You have on your side warriors even greater than the gods. If Bhishma worries you then fear not, I shall personally kill him. Riding out on a single chariot I will end his life myself."

Krishna declared his love for Yudhisthira and his brothers. Gazing at them with affection he said, "Whoever is inimical to you may consider me an enemy. Arjuna is my friend, relative and disciple. For his sake I would cut off and give away my own flesh. He too would give up his life for my sake."

Yudhisthira was moved by Krishna's words, but he could not allow him to fight. He said, "It cannot be you that slays him, dear Krishna. Your promise should not be falsified as it almost was today."

Yudhisthira recalled Bhishma's advice to him at the start of the battle. "I think Bhishma himself will tell us how he can be defeated. Let us go to him and ask."

As he contemplated Bhishma's death Yudhisthira felt a wave of grief. He let out a sob. "Alas, how vile is a warrior's duty. We must now seek to slay he who became our father when we were fatherless children. He who has always sought our good—even he must be killed by us now."

Krishna gently consoled the distraught Yudhisthira. Becoming firmer, he said, "Take heart, king. Bhishma has chosen to follow Duryodhana, thereby ensuring his death in this war. You are right. We must go to him and ask him how he can be killed. That noble hero will certainly tell us."

Krishna suggested that all five brothers go along with himself. They all put off their armours and went at once to the Kauravas' camp.

Bhishma's face lit up with joy as they entered his tent. He waved toward the ornate seats arranged around him on fine silk rugs. "Welcome, all of you. Please be seated. What do wish from me? Consider it done, even if it be extremely hard to accomplish.

Yudhisthira stood before him with folded palms. Gazing on Bhishma's weathered face, which smiled back at him with obvious affection, the Pandava felt his throat choke up. He was unable to speak for some moments. Krishna placed a hand on his shoulder to encourage him. Taking a deep breath Yudhisthira knelt before Bhishma and said, "O mighty hero, how can we vanquish you? I asked you this before and you told me to come again. Please tell me then the means to defeat you in battle. It seems to us that you are invincible."

Bhishma nodded slowly. As he looked down at Yudhisthira he felt his heart move. Pandu's virtuous sons were surely undeserving of any suffering. It could only be by some supreme arrangement of God himself that they were being subjected to so much misery. The old Kuru felt it to be a cruel twist of fate that he had to be an instrument in that suffering. Glancing across at Krishna, who had seated himself nearby, he replied to Yudhisthira, "You are correct, king. While I stand with weapons raised you will never achieve victory. Only when I lower my weapons am I approachable. Listen then to my vow. I will never raise my weapons against the weaponless, the helpless, the frightened, the surrendered, or a female."

Bhishma then specifically referred to Shikandhi, saying that he would cause his downfall. "This one was formerly a woman and bears undying hatred for me. I will not strike him, even if he attacks me. Therefore, place him in the forefront of battle, assisted by Arjuna, and assail me with all your power. This is your only chance."

Yudhisthira thanked Bhishma and got to his feet. The others also rose and Bhishma rose with them. Bidding each other fond farewells, they parted company and the Pandavas headed back to their camp. They rode silently through the darkness, dreading in their hearts the next day when Bhishma would be slain.

CHAPTER TWENTY-SIX

TWO GENERALS FALL

As the sun rose on the tenth day the clamour of countless conchshells, drums and trumpets again filled the air. The two armies arrayed themselves for battle and then rushed at each other with loud shouts. Duryodhana, aware that the Pandavas would target Bhishma, had ordered many of the foremost Kauravas to protect him. Bhishma realised that this might be his final day in battle, and he began to exert himself for one last supreme effort. He again began a great slaughter. His arrows flew out in great showers. Defying his advanced age, he fought as if he were a youth. He wheeled about on the terrace of his chariot with his bow constantly twanging. The beleagured Pandava forces felt there were dozens of Bhishmas fighting them. They scattered in fear.

Seeing the destruction of his forces, Dhristyadyumna detailed a number of Pandava heroes to engage with Bhishma's escort. Arjuna then began to advance toward him, accompanied by Shikhandhi. As they came within range of the Kuru grandfather, the powerful Shikhandhi, remembering his former life and enmity with Bhishma, roared out an angry challenge and fired a dozen fierce shafts at him. They struck Bhishma on his arms and chest, piercing through his armour. Bhishma, although angered, only smiled and called out, "I will not fight you, Shikhandhi. The great creator made you a woman and even now I accept you as such."

Shikhandhi roared in fury. Determined to make Bhishma retaliate he released another volley of arrows and called back, "I care not for your words. They simply hide your cowardice. Stay and fight with me now. You will not escape with your life."

Bhishma turned away from him and attacked the warriors surrounding him. Invoking celestial missiles, he continued to massacre them by the thousand. Numerous Kauravas came forward to protect him from attack. Arjuna met them and began cutting them down with arrows shot from the Gandiva. Many of the principal warriors from both sides entered the fray. Ferocious duels took place on different parts of the field. At the same time Bhishma and Arjuna maintained a huge slaughter of troops. Keeping Shikhandhi close by, Arjuna relentlessly bore down on Bhishma. Great Kaurava heroes came before him one after another, but Arjuna beat them back.

A vast horde of barbarian fighters, clad in animal skins and clutching bludgeons and spears, rushed at Arjuna. Mounted on wild horses they came at him from all sides. Their spears and spiked arrows rained down in thousands. Krishna wheeled the chariot round and pulled it clear of the attack. Arjuna then invoked a mystical weapon that sent sheets of razor-headed shafts at his assailants. Cut to pieces they dropped down with terrible cries, covering the field with their bloodied corpses.

Arjuna rode around his slain foes and kept driving toward Bhishma. The Kuru grandfather was protected by Duryodhana, Kripa, Shalya and a dozen of Dhritarastra's other sons. Arjuna's four brothers came up to engage them, leaving the way clear for Arjuna to attack Bhishma. The two great heroes then met like a pair of enraged lions. They covered each other with clouds of arrows. Each invoked celestial weapons, which the other neutralised with his own. Both warriors put aside all feelings of affection and fought to their full power. They praised each other's prowess as they contended remorselessly, looking for even the slightest weakness in the other. But neither could find any gaps in his opponent's defenses.

Thousands of warriors closed on Shikhandhi, trying to keep him away from Bhishma. Drupada's valiant son pressed on without the least fear. He carved a path through the Kauravas, his gaze fixed on Bhishma.

Bhishma seemed as if sporting as he battled Arjuna. At the same time, he trained his arrows on the surrounding Pandava forces. They fell in hundreds and thousands as the Kuru warrior let go his unstoppable shafts, but thousands more warriors kept coming at him. Like clouds covering the sun they surrounded his chariot. They rained down arrows, spears, battle-axes, spiked maces, darts, bludgeons and steel javelins.

Hard-pressed under the assault, Bhishma smiled. He wished only for a hero's end. His armour was shattered and blood flowed from numerous wounds. Oblivious to the pain he fought on, slaying hundreds of his attackers. Arjuna marveled how even under such a fierce attack the Kuru chief was still a formidable foe. He continuously spun round in his chariot, covering himself from every side. Arjuna fired numberless shafts, but Bhishma cut them down again and again.

As Shikhandhi came up to his side Arjuna sensed that Bhishma's end was near. Placing Shikhandhi in his front he closed on him. With a perfectly aimed arrow he cut Bhishma's bow in two. Both Arjuna and Shikhandhi released barbed shafts that deeply pierced the Kuru hero. They killed his charioteer and horses, bringing him to a halt on the battlefield. With a crescent-headed arrow Arjuna cut down his tall standard.

Bhishma immediately took up another bow worked with gold, but Arjuna shattered it again. Bhishma hurled a great lance at Arjuna but the Pandava cut it to pieces with five swift arrows. Seeing Arjuna thwarting all his weapons Bhishma became resigned to his fate. It was the end. He looked with love at Krishna, who was dexterously guiding Arjuna's horses. What use was there in trying to overcome such a power? That was something Duryodhana should have realised a long time ago.

Resolving to go down fighting, Bhishma launched himself into one last effort. He spun round in his chariot, lifting and stringing another bow in a matter of seconds. He shot a volley of arrows at both Arjuna and Shikhandhi. Both of them replied with dozens of short-range shafts that pierced Bhishma's powerful frame, like snakes entering their holes in a mountain. Bhishma was stunned and he reeled back on the terrace of his chariot. Although struck by the arrows of both his assailants, he considered that only Arjuna's shafts could bring him down. He rallied himself and stood to face the attack with his bow drawn to a full circle, but seeing that Shikhandhi had come directly in front of him he lowered his bow.

Arjuna immediately took his opportunity. He fired arrows twenty at a time which left the Gandiva in a continuous line. Bhishma was pierced in every part of his body. Finally overcome by Arjuna's unrelenting assault he toppled from his chariot. Before the Kauravas' shocked eyes he dropped to the earth like a mountain cleft by a thunderbolt. He lay on the ground fully supported by the arrows protruding from his body.

Staying alive by his own will, he determined to wait till the sun reached its auspicious northern course before leaving his body.

The Kauravas were utterly confounded. They dropped their weapons and ran about in confusion. As the sun set, they fell to the ground and wailed. Some of them swooned and others stood as if frozen to the spot. Hearing the terrible news from Duryodhana, Drona dropped from his chariot in a faint. When he came around, he ordered the Kauravas to withdraw and they made their sorrowful way back to their camp.

The Pandava forces blew conches and danced on the field in delight. At last their scourge had been brought down. But Arjuna was deeply saddened. Along with his brothers he went over to Bhishma and asked if there was anything he desired. Bhishma told them not to grieve for him. He had achieved an end desired by all heroic warriors. By his father's boon he was able to remain alive. When the sun moved to the north, he would quit his body and attain the higher planets.

Praising him, the Pandavas walked around the fallen hero in respect and then, as Bhishma entered a state of yogic meditation, they headed back to their camp. They felt their victory could not now be far away.

* * *

Hearing of Bhishma's fall Dhritarastra was inconsolable. He wept for a long time. Consumed by remorse he fell from his throne and tossed about on the marble floor of his chamber. "Is my heart made of stone that it does not shatter upon hearing this news?" The king's loud lamentations echoed through his palace.

In the Kaurava camp there was total despair. Even Karna loudly cried when he heard of Bhishma's fall. Despite his frequent strong words toward him, Karna could not deny Bhishma's nobility and power. He knew also that the Kuru grandfather had spoken only with his interests in mind. Now he had fallen. Karna looked toward his weapons. His time had come.

As the sun rose on the eleventh day of battle the Kauravas installed Drona as their new commander. Seeing the martial preceptor leading out his forces, Duryodhana felt renewed hope. The battle raged on again with full force. The great heroes on both sides continued to cause carnage among the armies. Countless men were sent to Death's abode.

Many lay on the field, laughing as their lifeblood ebbed away and they approached the heavens. Drona, Karna, Kripa and Ashvatthama headed the Kauravas' attack and they tore into the Pandava divisions, while Bhima, Arjuna and other mighty warriors among the Pandavas smashed through the Kaurava ranks.

With the loss of Bhishma the Kuru forces were dispirited and they began to succumb to their mighty foes. Duryodhana became increasingly frantic. He begged Drona to find some means to overcome the Pandavas. "Even if all the brothers cannot be slain—and I have come to accept this—then at least capture Yudhisthira. Or slay some other great hero among his forces."

Drona then spread the Kauravas out in a great impenetrable array, hoping to surround and capture Yudhisthira. His plan was thwarted when Arjuna's son Abhimanyu broke through the formation, leaving a trail of destruction right through the heart of the Kuru army. The sixteen year old warrior was as powerful as his father and the Kauravas had no answer to his attack. At last, in sheer desperation they broke the rules of combat. Six of the Kauravas' mightiest fighters closed on Abhimanyu. Simultaneously attacking him from all sides, even when he was without his chariot and weapons, they eventually managed to bring him down. Finally, Dushasana's son slew him with a great blow from his mace.

At that time Arjuna had again been strategically removed from the main battle by Drona's arrangement. The other four Pandavas had been held back by Jayadratha, who was strengthened by virtue of the boon he had acquired from Shiva. Arjuna was devastated when he discovered that his son had been so mercilessly and unfairly killed. Wild with fury he made a terrible vow to kill Jayadratha. "It is his fault that my son now lies dead. Had my brothers reached the boy he would surely have been saved. For this mean and despicable act, the Sindhu ruler will pay with his life. Whoever tries to stop me will proceed with Jayadratha to Death's kingdom. If I do not kill him before sunset tomorrow, I will enter fire and give up my own life."

When Duryodhana heard of Arjuna's vow he arranged for Jayadratha to be protected by his whole army. There then followed an astonishing fight during which Arjuna single-handedly wiped out a quarter of the remaining Kauravas. With Krishna's divine assistance he broke through their army and reached Jayadratha. When at last Arjuna approached the Sindhu monarch Krishna created an illusion of sunset just before the sun reached the horizon. The mighty Kuru warriors surrounding Jayadratha thus lowered their weapons with great cheers, believing that Arjuna had failed. Krishna then withdrew his illusion. In the ensuing confusion Arjuna slew the Sindhu monarch, even as Duryodhana and his best fighters looked on.

At the end of the day a greatly relieved Yudhisthira embraced Krishna. Tears flowed from his eyes. "O Govinda, all things are possible for those whom you favour. Our enemies are drowned in a sea of grief and we are delivered from a fearful danger."

Among the Kauravas there was only increasing despair. After thirteen days of fighting, their army had been reduced from eleven great divisions to three. Millions of men had been killed. Still Duryodhana would not relent. He blamed Drona for Arjuna's success in killing Jayadratha. "Surely you are being soft on our enemies. It is my fault. I should have known better. Blinded by my greed for wealth I trusted you even though I knew of your love for the Pandavas."

Drona had heard such reproaches repeatedly from the desperate Kaurava prince. He sighed wearily and raised his sinewy arms, which were covered with wounds. As the physicians began tending them, he said, "What point is there in piercing me with sharp words, king? I have told you again and again that no one can kill Arjuna. After seeing even Bhishma brought down I am convinced that we are doomed. The dice that Shakuni threw against the Pandavas are returning now as blazing arrows. You were warned so many times. How did you expect your heinous sin in insulting Draupadi to go unpunished?"

Drona looked with pity at the miserable Duryodhana. Half of his brothers had been slain by Bhima. Why was he so obstinate? The old martial teacher knew the fight would only end with Duryodhana's death, even if he was the last man standing. Drona stood up to leave for his quarters. In his burnished gold armour, he shone like the sun. Encouraging the gloomy Duryodhana he said, "I cannot abandon my duty, loathsome though it may be. Tomorrow you will see me give everything to the fight. With weapons ablaze I shall head out your army one more time. Hear my vow. Until the remaining Pandava forces are slain I shall not remove my armour."

Duryodhana felt cheered. There was still hope. The Pandavas' divisions had also been decimated. The two armies were now roughly equal. If Drona was determined, then victory could surely be achieved. Especially if Karna fulfilled his vow to kill Arjuna. Duryodhana looked over at his friend. "O great hero, I think it is time for you also to display your full prowess. You still have Indra's infallible weapon. Use it to bring down Arjuna and victory will be ours."

Karna was circumspect. He had seen the incredible way that Arjuna had fought past the whole Kaurava army and he wondered if Drona's assessment of the Pandava might be right. Perhaps Arjuna really was unslayable. With Krishna by his side he was a highly formidable opponent. So far Krishna had managed to keep him clear of Karna and his deadly Shakti weapon, but sooner or later they would meet. What would Krishna do then? Indra had said that the Shakti would not fail, and the gods' words were always truth. Indeed, if Krishna really was the Supreme then it was he who made good the gods' oaths.

"I will do all that a friend can do," Karna said, looking across at Indra's glowing weapon, which he had respectfully worshipped each day since receiving it from the deity. "I shall spare no effort. In my view though, destiny is supreme. Despite our vast army, filled with invincible warriors, we have not yet been successful. We have tried everything against the Pandavas. Still those steadfast heroes stand against us, full of vigour and power. This is all due to our adverse destiny. Let us see then what fate decrees for us tomorow. I shall train the Shakti on Arjuna as soon as possible."

Throughout the fourteenth day of battle Karna, despite his best efforts, again found no opportunity to approach his mortal enemy. Many other Pandava warriors kept him engaged. Terrific duels took place between the great fighters on both sides. Bhima bore down on Dhritarastra's remaining sons like Yamaraja himself. Before Duryodhana's horrified eyes he picked them off one by one. He ranged among the Kauravas like a tempest. His mace was hardly visible as it whirled around him. Men, horses and chariots flew in all directions. Terrifed, the Kaurava soldiers ran screaming from the field. No two men were seen running together as they fled from the frenzied Pandava. "Save us from Bhima!" they cried, as he laughed almost insanely.

Elsewhere a frightening battle took place between Ghatotkacha and Ashvatthama. Both were past masters in the use of mystical weapons. Bhima's son conjured innumerable illusions on the battlefield, making hordes of terrible-looking Rakshasas appear. He fought from the sky and assumed many different forms. At one point he appeared like a towering mountain, with a fountain at its summit that incessantly showered spears, darts, swords and blazing arrows. The Kauravas were hacked to pieces. They cried out to Drona's son for protection. Ashvatthama fearlessly countered Ghatotkacha's attack. Invoking celestial weapons, he managed to beat back the huge Rakshasa and destroy much of his force.

Karna constantly sought an opportunity to encounter Arjuna. He wrought havoc among the Pandava army. With both conventional and celestial weapons he slew thousands of men. Becoming totally enraged, Bhima finally put him to flight after a mighty battle, but Karna regrouped and came again to the fray. Encountering Bhima once more he engaged in another great fight. To honour Arjuna's vow, Bhima did not wish to kill him, and he eventually decided to leave the fight. Karna pursued him but he too remembered his promise to Kunti, and thus made no attempt to kill Bhima. From his chariot he derided the Pandava, who was on foot, and hit him with the end of his bow. "Why do you flee, weak and impotent fool? Your prowess lies only in eating. The battlefield is no place for a boy like you. Run quickly to Arjuna and Krishna. Seek their protection."

Bhima seethed, but held himself back. Karna would soon meet his destined end. The Pandava wrung his hands together in fury. He watched silently as Karna moved off into the thick of battle. Arjuna was not far away. It would not be long now. Turning back to the fight, Bhima set his mind on destroying Dhritarastra's remaining sons.

In separate encounters with the twins, Karna again managed to somehow gain the upper hand, but on both occasions, he again honoured his promise to Kunti. He even managed to overpower Yudhisthira after meeting him in fierce single combat, but still did not press home his advantage. There was only one Pandava he wanted to slay. He glanced repeatedly at the Shakti missile.

The sun set but the battle raged on. Three-quarters of the warriors on both sides had been slain. It was obvious to all that the war would soon be over. Darkness fell with both sides frantically seeking victory by the light of thousands of torches. Waves of flaming arrows lit up the sky revealing ghastly scenes below. Wrecked chariots were ablaze everywhere, and they silhouetted the dark forms of countless warriors locked in deadly combat. The stench of blood filled the air along with the cries and screams of the warriors and the clash of weapons.

Seeing Karna ploughing through the Pandava forces, Krishna said to Arjuna, "It seems that Karna is intent upon destroying our whole army. Someone must stop him, but I feel you should wait. He still has the Shakti weapon. Lo, there in the distance is Ghatotkacha. Order him to face Karna. It is night now and the Rakshasa's power will be doubled. Other than you he may be the only one who can check Karna."

Arjuna looked toward Ghatotkacha's immense chariot, drawn by a hundred demon-headed beasts. Having recovered from his defeat at Ashvatthama's hands, Bhima's son was returning to the battle. He was accompanied by ten thousand huge Rakshasas whom he had summoned from the ghostly regions. When he heard Arjuna's request he smiled and turned toward Karna. Booming out his awful war-cry, he shot a hundred steel pointed shafts at him and a fearful battle ensued between the two great warriors.

The fight raged for a long time. Despite employing all his skills and power, Karna could not gain the upper hand. Ghatotkacha fought with an unrestrained fury. Remembering Karna's viciousness toward his father and uncles, the Rakshasa was intent on killing him. Karna was forced back. His horses and charioteer were slain, and he stood in his immobile chariot trying to fend off the Rakshasa's relentless assault. Observing the battle, Duryodhana began fearing for Karna's life. Ghatotkacha was impervious to all of Karna's weapons, even his most powerful celestial missiles.

When the Rakshasa at last leapt from his own chariot and rushed at Karna with his scimitar raised high, the horrified Duryodhana called out, "Use the Shakti, Karna! It is your only chance."

Karna glanced at the weapon. Duryodhana was right. The demon would almost certainly slay him if he did not stop him. What use would the Shakti be against Arjuna then? Karna snatched the missile from its golden case. Uttering the mantras, he placed it on his bow and immediately fired it at the onrushing Rakshasa. The weapon flew like a fireball at Ghatotkacha. He saw it coming and quickly expanded himself to a vast size. The missile struck him on the chest and passed through his body. With a discordant scream that reverberated around the entire battlefield Ghatotkacha died. His massive body dropped down and crushed thousands of Kauravas.

The Pandavas cried out in dismay but Krishna began to laugh and clap his hands. Arjuna looked at him in surprise. "Why this display of levity at such a terrible moment, O Keshava?"

Krishna replied, "Now that Karna has discharged the Shakti you may consider him slain and the Kauravas defeated. Ever since I heard he had received that weapon from Indra I felt anxious. Your life was in dire danger. Now my fear has gone. Karna has lost both his natural armour and his deadliest weapon. He is like an infuriated serpent, full of venom but stupefied by incantations. The weapon has returned to Indra and cannot be used again."

Arjuna remembered how it had been Krishna who had suggested that Ghatotkacha confront Karna. The Pandava realised that yet again he was still living only due to Krishna's protection. There was no doubt that without Krishna's assistance the war would have ended by now—but not with a Pandava victory.

Having fought well into the night, the warriors on both sides were grateful when Arjuna suggested they rest until sunrise the next day. They lay down on the field wherever they had been fighting. A bright moon rose in the clear sky illuminating scenes of destruction everywhere. With all the surviving men and animals sunk in sleep it appeared as if both armies had been utterly destroyed. As the sun rose on the fifteenth day they gradually stirred and took up their positions to restart the battle.

True to his word Drona ranged about the field causing complete chaos among the Pandava army. In great battles he slew both Virata and Drupada. When he saw his father killed, Dhristyadyumna was consumed by grief and anger. The Panchala prince thought only of his destiny to be Drona's slayer. He went after the Kuru preceptor, determined to take his life, but Drona resisted all of his attacks. He held off even Arjuna as the Pandava released upon him every celestial weapon in his arsenal. At the same time, he carried on slaughtering the Pandava forces in the tens of thousands.

Witnessing Drona's power Yudhisthira began to despair. He consulted with Bhima and Arjuna. "Drona will finish our whole army. How can he be checked?"

Krishna looked grave. He replied to Yudhisthira, "This is the truth, king. Drona can scorch us by his mere glance, but he has already given us the clue how he may be stopped. He must lower his weapons and this he will do after hearing some highly disagreeable news. I think if he hears that his son Ashvatthama is killed he will desist from the fight."

Arjuna turned sharply toward Krishna. "I cannot accept this, Keshava. How can we deceive the noble preceptor in such a way?"

Bhima liked the idea. He ran at once into an elephant division and slew a beast that he knew shared the same name as Drona's son. The Pandava then raced over to Drona and repeatedly called out, "Ashvatthama is slain!"

Drona lowered his bow. He stared at Bhima. Could this be true? The preceptor found it hard to accept. Ashvatthama, with his brahmin's power and vast martial knowledge learned from his father, was virtually invincible. Bhima was known to be capricious. He could easily speak a falsehood in anger or jest. Drona did not want to believe him. He lifted his bow again and continued to fight.

Seeing this, Krishna exhorted Yudhisthira to go to Drona and confirm Bhima's report. "Save us from Drona, king. In this case untruth is certainly better than truth. Speaking falsehood in order to preserve life is not sinful."

Yudhisthira was hesitant. In his entire life he had never uttered even an ambiguity. Yet here was Krishna telling him to speak a direct lie. Krishna's direction had to be followed. It was the only way to prevent Drona from destroying the entire Pandava force. Reluctantly Yudhisthira went over to Drona and called out, "Ashvatthama is dead!", adding inaudibly, "The elephant."

Hearing those words from Yudhisthira, Drona felt as if his heart had dissolved. It had to be true. Yudhisthira could never tell a lie. Drona's arms fell limply to his side. He called out to Duryodhana, "O king, I am laying down my weapons. This world and all its wealth no longer holds any attraction for me. Fight with all your power, for I shall now depart."

Distracted by grief Drona sat down in his chariot and wept. He closed his eyes and gradually calmed himself. Entering a mystical trance, he left his body by yogic power and ascended to the higher worlds.

Dhristyadyumna had been contending with Drona. When he saw him seated in meditation, Drupada's son leapt down from his chariot clasping a sword. He rushed over to Drona's chariot and lopped off his head with a sweeping blow. Roaring in joy, he picked up the head and threw it toward the Kauravas.

Duryodhana was mortified. Along with all his generals and men he fled away from the cheering Pandavas. Yudhisthira looked with mixed feelings at the body of his old teacher. With him slain the Kauravas must surely give up all hope but it had taken deceit to finally bring him down. That thought hurt Yudhisthira—especially that it had been he who had told the lie. Nevertheless, the Kauravas had been the first ones to use unfair means when they slew Abhimanyu. They could expect no less in return now, as had been agreed at the outset—and following Krishna's direction could never be sinful.

The sun had set and Yudhisthira ordered his troops to withdraw. Slowly the two armies again retired for the night.

CHAPTER TWENTY-SEVEN

A FITTING END

Duryodhana slept only fitfully on the fifteenth night. He tossed and turned; his mind wracked with anxiety. What was happening? First Bhishma and now Drona—two warriors whom even the celestials could not have brought down. Even though they fought with all their power—and perhaps also were inspired by the Danavas—still the Pandavas had overcome them. What force did those five brothers have on their side? How would they ever be defeated? Surely it had been a mistake to antagonize them but there was no way back. When so many great heroes had been slain for his sake, he could hardly abandon the fight now. Death or victory were the only choices. All was not yet lost. There was still Karna. In the morning he could take command of the remaining Kauravas. Perhaps with a last great effort he would kill Arjuna.

As the sun rose on the sixteenth day the two armies once again arrayed themselves for battle. After installing Karna as their leader, the Kauravas roared out their battle-cries and charged the Pandavas. They were met by their unflinching foes and a savage battle was soon underway again.

Fired by his position as commander, Karna fought as never before. He careered into the Pandava army sending blazing arrows in all directions. Soldiers, horsemen, charioteers and elephant fighters were ruthlessly cut to ribbons. He was supported by Ashvatthama, who burned with a desire to avenge his father's cruel death.

Arjuna engaged with the last of the Samshaptaka and Narayana armies, with whom he had been contending throughout the war. Still observing the rules of fair combat, he did not employ the terrible weapons of the gods. But that was his only restraint. The Pandava fought without mercy. Seeking to end the war he slaughtered his foes with waves of searing shafts shot off the Gandiva.

Bhima continued to pick off Dhritarastra's sons one by one. Relentlessly the two armies ground each other down. By noon on the seventeenth day less than half a million men were left from the original six million.

When Arjuna had at last overcome the immense armies the Kauravas had deployed against him, Krishna urged him to confront Karna. "Strike down this wicked-minded fool. Frustrate Duryodhana's hopes and end the war. How can Karna live after meeting you with the Gandiva in hand?"

Krishna's words stirred Arjuna. He was ready for the fight. Ahead of him he could see Karna's tall standard cutting through the Pandava army. Arjuna scowled and took a firm grasp on his bow. As Krishna urged on his steeds, he began mowing down the troops in his way.

Seeing Arjuna advancing toward their general, a cluster of Kaurava heroes rushed against him. Kripa, Kritavarman and half a dozen of Duryodhana's brothers all attacked him at once. Arjuna was in no mood to be checked and he furiously beat back his assailants. Rows of chariot fighters charged him and were struck down by volleys of straight-flying shafts. Huge elephants rocked toward him and they too were butchered by Arjuna's deadly arrows.

Karna saw his adversary from a distance. He knew the time for their final confrontation had arrived. One of them would not return from this fight. Karna gazed respectfully at his indomitable enemy. Driving Arjuna's chariot through the ranks of bejewelled warriors, Krishna resembled a dark cloud in the star-studded firmament. Behind him Arjuna looked like a second cloud sending forth streaks of lightning as he fired his arrows. Karna spoke to his charioteer, "Take me toward Partha. His time has come, as well as that of Krishna. I will soon slay those two warriors—and then the entire Pandava force."

Duryodhana saw his friend advancing toward Arjuna. He quickly detailed all the most powerful Kauravas to support Karna. They rushed in a body at Arjuna and were met with barbed arrows that struck them on every part of their bodies. Bhima came up to join his brother and he was assailed by Duryodhana's twenty remaining brothers. At their head was Dushasana. Seeing that evil-minded prince, Bhima licked his lips and smiled. Dushasana roared in anger and shot at Bhima a brilliant arrow worked with gems and gold. It hit the Pandava full on the chest with a sound like thunder. Bhima was stunned and he dropped to his knees in his chariot, clinging on to his standard pole for support.

The Kauravas rained down arrows and other weapons on the stricken Bhima. Thinking their mortal foe to be slain they cheered but Bhima soon regained his senses and stood again for battle. He glared at Dushasana and shouted, "Strike me while you still can, wretch. Soon you will lay down your life. I long to drink your blood. Feel now the force of my mace."

Bhima's chariot swung toward the prince who frantically discharged numerous arrows at him. Bhima beat down all the arrows with his whirling mace. He leapt from his chariot and charged at Dushasana. The prince hurled a blazing dart at him with all his strength, but Bhima smashed it to pieces. In moments he was upon his enemy. He struck him a terrific blow on his forehead which knocked him out of his chariot to a distance of twenty paces.

As Dushasana struggled to his feet Bhima unsheathed his sword and ran up to him. He kicked him in his face and sent him crashing back to the ground. Taking hold of his arm he wrenched it upward and with a sweep of his sword severed it and raised it high.

"Here is the arm that seized Draupadi's sanctified hair," he yelled. The Kauravas watched in horror as Bhima then tore open Dushasana's chest and with cupped hands drew his blood to his mouth. As he stood up with the blood running down his face, they ran pell mell away from him, crying out out in terror, "Save us from Bhima! Surely he is a bloodthirsty Rakshasa."

Bhima turned toward Arjuna and Krishna and called out, "I have redeemed my pledge and avenged Draupadi. Soon I will fulfill my other vow when I crush Duryodhana. Only then will peace be mine."

Ten of Dushasana's brothers rallied themselves and rushed at Bhima. The Pandava quickly remounted his chariot. Firing off razor-headed shafts decked with gold wings he slew all his assailants. Among them was Vikarna. Remembering how that prince had spoken out during the gambling match, Bhima lamented greatly at having to slay him. He jumped from his chariot and, folding his palms, he circumambulated the fallen Kaurava. "O hero, I have fulfilled my vow and my duty as a *kshatriya* by slaying you. May you attain the regions of the righteous."

Karna had been shocked to witness Dushasana's killing. He took hold of himself and prepared to fight with Arjuna, who still bore down on him. As the two great warriors came face to face the gods assembled in the sky to watch. Celestial horns were sounded, and flowers fell on both combatants.

The two heroes began a fierce exchange of arrows. Bent upon each other's death they stood like two suns risen for the destruction of all the worlds. Their bows, drawn constantly to a circle, resembled the sun's corona and their arrows blazed from their bows like sunbeams.

The battle raged for a long time with neither warrior gaining an edge. Both invoked celestial weapons which the other countered. While fighting together both maintained a ferocious assault on the other's supporting troops, killing thousands. Karna gave his utmost to the fight. Charged with the power of his illustrious heavenly father and inspired with a burning desire to defeat his lifelong foe, he fought as never before. Struck hard with hundreds of steel shafts, Arjuna reeled and he clutched hold of his chariot pole for support.

Seeing his opportunity, Karna tried to invoke the powerful Brahmastra weapon, but he could not remember the incantations. His guru's words came back to him. "When you most need your most powerful weapon you will be unable to summon it."

Crying hot tears of frustration Karna fought on with even more fury. He then saw that, true to the brahmin's imprecation uttered long ago, his chariot wheel was sinking into the earth. The chariot came to a halt and could not be moved. Confounded by this crippling disability, he leapt down and heaved desperately at the wheel. Unable to budge it even slightly, he called out to Arjuna, who was closing on him, "O hero, do not kill me like a coward. Remember virtue. No noble fighter slays a disadvantaged enemy."

Krishna smiled. He called back to the stricken Karna. "It is good that at last you think of virtue, O Karna. It is a shame, though, that you could not remember it on every occasion of cheating and abusing the Pandavas; especially when their chaste wife was so grievously insulted. Where too was this virtue when you and the other Kuru heroes ruthlessly killed the boy Abhimanyu? If all that is your idea of virtue, then do not waste your time invoking it now."

Karna hung down his head. He tried again and again to free the wheel, but it was hopeless. Krishna urged Arjuna not to hesitate. "Strike down this wicked man at once. He deserves no mercy."

Perspiration flowed freely from Karna's forehead as he grappled with his wheel. Realising that he could not free it he spun round and took up his bow. He snatched up a long steel arrow and discharged it with all his power, uttering mantras all the while. It flew at Arjuna like a thunderbolt and struck him full on the chest. Arjuna fell back. Krishna again urged him to waste no time in killing his enemy. "This one should not be spared. Cut off his head before he remounts his chariot."

Arjuna then took out an arrow fitted with an *anjalika* head, shaped like folded palms. Placing that gold shafted arrow on his bow he invested it with the power of Indra's Vajra weapon. As he drew it back to his ear and took careful aim an eerie silence enveloped the battlefield. All the warriors froze. The sky seemed to shake and the rishis watching from the heavens cried out, "All peace! All peace!"

Arjuna held the arrow for a moment and muttered, "If I have ever practiced penance, and respected my elders then let this arrow slay Karna." He then let it go and it streaked toward Karna shining like the sun. It caught him on his broad and powerful neck. His head was instantly severed and thrown to the earth, where it lay with its gold earrings gleaming. His trunk collapsed to the ground, gushing blood. To everyone's amazement a brilliant light left his body and went up into the sun.

The Pandavas were overwhelmed with joy. Dancing on the battlefield, they blew their conches and gazed in wonder at the fallen Karna, who resembled a mountain struck down by a bolt from heaven. Krishna praised Arjuna and Yudhisthira came up to his side, warmly congratulating him over and over. Yudhisthira wept tears of happiness and relief. His greatest fear was gone. The war was now all but over. Surely the Kauravas' end was very near.

Duryodhana fell from his chariot. He beat his chest and rolled about in grief with tears flowing down his face. The other Kauravas surrounded Karna and cried out in sorrow. They walked round his body in respect and were joined by the Pandavas. As the day ended the sun-god went in grief to the western hills, shedding his last rays on his fallen son's body.

* * *

As the eighteenth day dawned the Kauravas were almost totally despairing. Duryodhana had been up most of the night, inconsolable. He sat alone in his tent, gazing at Karna's empty seat. When the sun rose, he slowly dragged himself up to perform his morning ablutions. Distracted with sorrow he made his way out of his tent to consult with his remaining ministers. As he thought about the way that Karna had been slain his grief gave way to anger. His friend had been ruthlessly murdered as he stood deprived of his chariot. It had to be avenged. He strode toward his own chariot, tightly grasping the long sword by his side.

Kripa tried advising Duryodhana that it was time to make peace with the Pandavas and accede to their demands. They now possessed a superior force and before long the Kaurava army would be rooted out, but Duryodhana was resolute. "Everything is on fire. I have created an enmity with the Pandavas that will be ended only with either theirs or my death."

Installing Shalya as his commander, Duryodhana gave the order to march out once more. The remants of his army cheered and headed out to fight, a glorious death now staring them in the face. Swarming out over the field the two armies collided with roars and the clash of weapons.

On Krishna's advice, Yudhisthira headed straight for Shalya, intent on sending him to the heavens. Sahadeva, rememembering his vow at the dice game, sought out Shakuni. Arjuna engaged with Ashvatthama and Kripa. With frightful shouts Bhima rushed at the last of Dhritarastra's sons. At the same time both armies continued to grind each other down. Once again, the battlefield became a quagmire, thick with blood and entrails.

The fight between Yudhisthira and Shalya resembled that between two tigers fighting in the forest over a carcass. The circled and feinted with speed and grace. Each wounded the other with swift arrows. For a long time Shalya displayed remarkable prowess. He withstood Yudhisthira's attack and simultaneously slew thousands of Pandava troops. Gradually though, Yudhisthira began to overpower him. He shattered Shalya's armour and broke down his standard. Killing his charioteer and horses he stopped him in his tracks.

Shalya took up a polished steel sword and rushed at Yudhisthira. Seeing his foe charging at him with ferocious yells, Yudhisthira raised a glowing golden dart. Shouting, "You are killed," he hurled it with all his power. The dart flew at Shalya like a meteor dropping from the sky. It struck him on the chest and passed clean through his body. Blood shot from Shalya's mouth, nose and ears and he dropped to the earth. Like a dear wife rising to embrace her beloved spouse, the earth seemed to rise up to meet Shalya. After enjoying her for so long, the Madras monarch finally fell into her embrace and died.

Duryodhana knew the war was over. Bhima had slaughtered all his brothers. After a fierce fight Sahadeva had killed Shakuni and all his Gandhara warriors, and Arjuna was wiping out the last of the Kaurava forces. Gripped by utter despair, the Kaurava prince turned and fled from the battlefield. His mind was a maelstrom of mixed feelings. Regret for having neglected the advice of his elders fought with boiling anger against the Pandavas. It had been a miscalculation to confront them in the first place—an inconceivable cosmic power was obviously aiding them—but now they had slaughtered everyone he had held dear. Karna's death particularly rankled. His killing had been highly unrighteous. So too had been Drona's, but it was too late to do anything now. Everything was lost.

Racing away from the field Duryodhana came across a great lake. He dived in and swam to the bottom. By yogic power he solidified the water and remained underneath. He needed time to rest and recover. After that he could decide what action to take.

Unknown to Duryodhana there were still three Kaurava warriors surviving—Kripa, Ashvatthama and Kritavarman—but when they saw that Duryodhana had fled they too ran from the battlefield. On their way they encountered Vyasadeva and the rishi told them where to find Duryodhana. They went to the lake and called out to their leader. Ashvatthama exhorted him to come back to the fight. "We are still ready to confront your enemies, O king. Rise up. We shall certainly slay them today. Indeed, I will not remove my armour till I see the Pandavas and all their troops killed. My father's death will be avenged."

Duryodhana had lost all heart for battle. He shouted back, "Hear me, mighty-armed ones, it is fortunate that you still live. I too am fortunate to have such devoted followers. When morning comes, I will join you. Let me rest for now."

Some hunters were in the forest nearby. When they heard the discussion between Duryodhana and Ashvatthama they realised that the prince was hiding in the lake. Knowing that Yudhisthira would likely reward them for that information, they went quickly to tell him.

The Pandavas had returned to their camp after unsuccessfully searching for Duryodhana. Learning from the hunters where he had gone, they set off at once to find him. The war would not be over till he had either surrendered or been slain.

As the Pandavas approached Duryodhana's hiding place, accompanied by their remaining forces, the other three Kauravas heard them from a distance and they ran into hiding. Reaching the lake Yudhisthira looked with wonder at the solidified water and said to Krishna, "Just see how the deceitful Duryodhana hides in fear. However, he will not escape me now."

Yudhisthira shouted out to Duryodhana to come out and fight. "Why are you trying to save yourself after millions have died for you? Coward! Face the consequences of your acts. Death is better than such dishonour. Fight with us. Either govern the world after winning victory, or, slain by us, embrace the cold earth."

The Pandavas surveyed the scene. Waterfowl walked across the solid surface of the lake, mystified by its sudden change. A breeze rustled through the surrounding trees, which were covered with bright blossoms. After the heat and dust of the battlefield the brothers felt soothed simply by seeing that picturesque region.

After some moments Duryodhana shouted back from the lake bottom. He asked Yudhisthira to wait some time while he rested but Yudhisthira was insistent. "You shall not be spared today. Rise out of this lake or we shall drag you out. Finish what you have started. Killed by us you will ascend to the heavens."

Angered and with his pride wounded, Duryodhana decided to fight. The lake water swirled and and bubbled, and the prince suddenly emerged. With his great mace on his shoulder, he looked like a mountain rising from the ocean. He looked around at the Pandavas and their forces and laughed. "Here I am, ready to send you all to Death's abode, but how can I, one man, fight so many at once?"

Bhima grasped hold of his mace and started forward. He was ready to smash Duryodhana's head at once, but Yudhisthira raised a hand to check him.

Yudhisthira smiled. "The time has come for you to pay for your crimes, wretched minded one. We should kill you now as you killed Abhimanyu, but I will give you a chance. Select any one of us and fight with the weapon of your choice. If you win you may keep the kingdom. Otherwise, proceed to heaven."

Yudhisthira was convinced that Krishna would protect him and his brothers. Krishna glanced at him in surprise. It was a rash offer. Duryodhana was peerless with his mace. Even Bhima would be hard pressed to beat him.

Duryodhana laughed again. "I care not which of you fights with me. Take up a mace any one of you. I will kill you at once and then all of your brothers, one by one."

Bhima looked achingly at Yudhisthira. "Permit me to slay this wretch, lord," he begged. "I shall end this war. Your victory is assured."

Yudhisthira placed a hand on Bhima's massive shoulder. "Be it so. Go forward and deal him the punishment he so richly deserves. Fulfill your vow—but be careful. He is no mean opponent."

Bhima and Duryodhana glared at one another. It was always going to come to this. Anticipating this day, Duryodhana had spent many hours in Hastinapura practicing with his mace on an iron image of Bhima. The two men whirled their maces above their heads and marched back toward the battlefield. Like a lion and an elephant meeting in the forest, they stood to face each other. "Recall now all your depraved and sinful acts, O worst of men," Bhima spat out to his sneering enemy. "The final reckoning has come. All your brothers are dead and now you too will follow the path taken by them. Your pride and your hope for the kingdom will today be crushed by me."

Duryodhana raised his mace and smiled. "What use are these words? How can you defeat me? See here my mace, like the summit of Himavat. I have already obliged you to become a cook in Virata, and Arjuna to become a eunuch. Today I shall today pound you both to death."

The two enraged fighters slowly circled one another. Every muscle in their bodies was tensed. Their eyes resembled glowing embers. Clenching and unclenching their hands around their maces, they watched for an opportunity to strike. Suddenly they both leapt forward. Their maces collided with a deafening crash. Showers of sparks flew upward. Like two furious bulls fighting for a female they roared and grappled together. Both exhibited graceful moves, spinning, feinting and leaping high. As the celestials looked on the two mighty warriors contended to the limit of their power.

For some time neither could land a blow on the other, but gradually they began to penetrate each other's defenses. Blows landed with terrific thuds. Both men were sent reeling, but they quickly recovered and resumed their positions. They knew every move and displayed the full range of their skills. The onlookers gasped and cheered.

Bhima's mace resembled Yamaraja's death-dealing staff. It sounded like the rushing wind as it fell upon Duryodhana. The Kaurava moved with blinding speed and dexterity. His own mace swung with such speed that it sent forth tongues of fire.

Unknown to Bhima, Duryodhana had been blessed with a special strength by his mother. Gandhari had known that her son would eventually meet Bhima in a mace fight. She had thus summoned him to come naked before her. The Kuru queen knew that by her glance, imbued with all her ascetic power, she could render Duryodhana's body invincible, but the prince had been unable to appear naked before his mother. He had worn a loin cloth and thus his upper thighs had not been strengthened. The rest of his body, however, was impervious to Bhima's strikes. The Pandava stared in amazement as Duryodhana remained standing even after receiving his most powerful blows.

Gradually Duryodhana gained the upper hand. He repeatedly smashed Bhima, laughing all the while. Bhima grew wild with anger. Rocked by Duryodhana's powerful blows he perspired and breathed like a snake.

Krishna could see that Bhima was avoiding striking his foe below the belt. Although he had made a vow to break his thighs, it appeared that Bhima first wanted to defeat Duryodhana in a fair fight. Krishna knew about Gandhari's blessing. Bhima's only chance was to smash

Duryodhana's thighs, he caught the Pandava's eye and then slapped his own thigh.

Bhima understood Krishna's sign. It was clear that Duryodhana would not be defeated in any other way. The Kaurava was taking his best shots and coming back for more. Remembering his vow, Bhima circled his foe. After another furious exchange of blows, Bhima suddenly stepped back and swung his mace round by its long sling. As he expected Duryodhana leapt up to avoid the blow. Bhima quickly pulled back his mace as the prince somersaulted in the air. The Pandava then stepped forward and again swung his mace in a great arc, his huge biceps glistening with sweat as they were fully exerted. As Duryodhana dropped back to the ground he was caught across the thighs by Bhima's onrushing mace. The iron mace, which could only be lifted by three strong men, smashed Duryodhana's thighs like a thunderbolt smashing a pair of trees. The Kaurava fell flat on the earth, screaming in pain.

The fight was over. Duryodhana was mortally wounded by Bhima's tremendous blow. He could hardly move, and blood bubbled from his mouth. The Pandavas sent up a great cheer. Krishna clapped his hands and applauded Bhima. Still seething, Bhima looked down at his fallen enemy and lifted a foot to place it on his head. Yudhisthira called out, "No Bhima! Desist. Do not insult our cousin in this way." He went over to Duryodhana and knelt by his side. "O child, the hostilities are over. Due to your pride, avarice and folly you have suffered this calamity. Millions of heroes lie dead for your sake. Now you shall follow them. It is we who should be pitied, not you. Surely you will reach the heavens, while we shall have to remain here in this world of suffering, surrounded by grieving widows."

Tears flowed from Yudhisthira's eyes as he thought of the war's terrible toll. He stood up and was comforted by Krishna. Duryodhana said nothing. He writhed in pain, both from his wounds and from the thought of how he had been defeated. Yudhisthira's gently spoken words did not make him feel any better. He looked over at Krishna and angrily said, "I saw your sign to Bhima. You are deceitful and sinful. It is only thanks to your cunning that the Pandavas have won this war."

Grimacing in pain, the Kaurava fell back, his face covered in perspiration. Krishna retorted, "Fool, have you forgotten how it was me who came to Hastinapura, trying to save you from the war in the first place? Do not rail uselessly. You are receiving the consequences of your own deeds and nothing else. Your wicked acts against the Pandavas, against their wife, and against Abhimanyu, have come back to you today."

Duryodhana was unable to make any reply. He lay gasping, his mace by his side. As the sun set Krishna suggested to the Pandavas that they return to their camp. Bidding farewell to Duryodhana, they then departed, leaving the Kaurava prince to await his death.

CHAPTER TWENTY-EIGHT

POWERFUL EMOTIONS

O f the two great armies all that remained were less than a thousand Pandava troops. Filled with joy at having finally attained victory against the mighty Kurus, they wearily returned to camp. As the eighteenth night fell, they lay down their weapons and rested. Krishna had suggested to Yudhisthira and his brothers that that they spend the night in the Kauravas' camp, in accord with tradition. As the victors it was now their prerogative to take possession of the Kauravas' property. They also needed to provide leadership and protection to the Kauravas' many servants and women who were at the camp. Along with Krishna the five brothers entered Duryodhana's great tent and rested there for the night.

Out in the forest Kripa, Ashvatthama and Kritavarman were resting beneath a large banyan tree. After finding the fallen Duryodhana they had been infuriated when he told them how he had been defeated. The prince encouraged them to continue the fight the next day. Completely fatigued they then collapsed beneath the tree, but Ashvatthama could not sleep. He still burned with a desire for vengeance. As he gazed up at the tree branches, he saw a great owl suddenly swoop down from the sky. There were many crows asleep in the branches and the owl began killing them as they slept. Watching those slain birds dropping from the tree Ashvatthama began to reflect. Perhaps this was a sign from destiny. There was little chance that he and his two companions could defeat the Pandavas, but now they would be buried in slumber. Of course, killing sleeping men was generally forbidden, but these were sinful enemies. They had to be punished by any means possible.

Drona's son sat up. He woke the other two men. When they heard his plan they sat in silence, too shamed to reply. After some moments, Kripa said, "O hero, we have tried our best to defeat the Pandavas, but destiny decreed that it be otherwise. Duryodhana has met with calamity due to his own foolishness. As his followers we too have been sunk in sorrow. I cannot see the point in any further fighting, especially by such a sinful means. Let us now return to Hastinapura."

Ashvatthama was resolute. His mind was set upon slaying his enemies and he was not interested in any arguments. He made that clear to Kripa. Again, the old Kuru tried to dissuade him. "If you must fight then do so in fair combat. Wait till the morning. We will then join with you."

Ashvatthama stood up and reached for his weapons, his silver armour glinting in the moonlight. "No. We cannot possibly win in an open encounter. I am going now to their camp. Catching them unawares I will slay them like animals. That is all they deserve."

Kripa and Kritavarman watched in dismay as Drona's son mounted his chariot. Kripa tried hard to dissuade him from his dark plan, but Ashvatthama was unmoved. He headed off into the night. When he reached the Pandavas' camp he encountered a strange looking being at the gates. Tall and frightful, he was draped in a bloodsoaked tiger skin and had a black snake around his neck. In his awful face there were a hundred eyes and his huge mouth seemed to be ablaze.

Fearful for his life Ashvatthama immediately attacked him. He launched all his most powerful weapons at the terrible-looking creature, but they had no effect. Drona's son saw that his arrows were all consumed and the being stood unmoved.

Ashvatthama lowered his bow. This was almost surely the great god Shiva, whom he had long worshipped. He got down from his chariot and prostrated himself on the ground. The being then spoke in a thunderous voice. "O child, I am Shiva. I have protected Pandu's sons throughout this war. Out of love for Krishna I am always inclined to his worshippers but now the Pandava warriors are being assailed by time. They have carried out the plan of Providence, relieving the earth's burden, and now their own destined end has arrived."

Shiva held up a huge sword. "Son of Drona, take this weapon. It is ordained that you shall be the instrument of their destruction. Empowered by me you will kill them all."

Ashvatthama stood up and took the brilliant sword, which had a handle set with gems. Shiva then vanished from the spot. Feeling himself infused with enormous strength, Ashvatthama smiled and raised the sword. He silently entered the Pandavas' camp and at once began to slay the sleeping warriors. Taken by surprise they jumped from their beds and fumbled for their weapons. Ashvatthama slew them without any mercy. In one tent he found five warriors sleeping together. Believing them to be the Pandavas he joyfully crept up to their beds. With a great blow from his sword he killed them one by one. He then ran on, laughing hideously and swinging his bloodied sword. In less than an hour he had killed everyone in the camp. He then severed the heads from the five men he believed were the Pandavas. They would make excellent trophies to show to Duryodhana. The Kaurava would at least die knowing that his enemies were also slain.

After placing the heads in his chariot, Ashvatthama rode quickly to where Duryodhana lay. The sun was rising, and he saw the prince looking pale, obviously close to death. Carnivorous beasts circled him and Ashvatthama scared them away. He placed the heads near the prince and said, "My lord, your enemies are killed. Here are their heads."

Duryodhana lifted his head slightly and smiled. He replied with difficulty. "Well done, friend. You have accomplished what even Bhishma, Karna and your own father could not. Well done."

Duryodhana reached out and took hold of one of the grim-looking heads, its face a mask of shock from having been so brutally slain while sleeping. The prince found it hard to believe that the Pandavas were dead. It was difficult to tell their identities from the appearance of the heads, but there was one way he could know. Exerting the last of his strength, Duryodhana pressed the head and it immediately collapsed. He did the same with the other four. In disappointment he said, "This is not the Pandavas. The brothers have heads like iron. Even my hardest mace blow could not smash Bhima's skull. It seems you have killed their five young sons. Alas, this was a heinous act. Who now will continue the Kuru line?"

Repeatedly gasping "Alas, alas," Duryodhana slumped back. His head fell to the side and he gave up his life. Ashvatthama was filled with dismay and sorrow. With the sunrise he had felt Shiva's power leave him. There was no question of confronting the Pandavas now. They would soon be looking for him. He remounted his chariot and headed into the forest, unsure which way to run.

* * *

Soon after sunrise the next day the Pandavas saw Dhristyadyumna's charioteer run panic-stricken into the Kuru camp. Somehow, he had escaped the massacre. The brothers listened in horror as he told them what had happened during the night. They cried out in grief. Yudhisthira was particularly afflicted. The soft hearted Pandava felt personally responsible for the killing. The whole war was due to him. It had happened just so he could become king. Well now he was king—but what a poisoned chalice. All his beloved elders, his friends, cousins and now even his sons were dead. He dropped to his knees and spoke in an agonized voice. "An already bitter victory has become even more bitter. What happiness will we enjoy with all our friends and kinsmen dead? What will become of Draupadi? How will she live when she hears that her five sons are slain?"

Draupadi rolled about beating her chest in grief when she heard the news. Taking their distraught wife, the five brothers went quickly to their camp. They were met by gruesome scenes. Mutilated bodies were strewn everywhere. When Draupadi saw her beheaded sons, she fell senseless to the ground. Coming around again, she wept uncontrollably. Her body shook violently. Looking toward Arjuna and Bhima, who had Krishna by their side, she said, "I will not move from this spot until Ashvatthama is punished. Slay him like a beast. If he does not pay for this crime, I will give up my own life."

Krishna agreed. "Ashvatthama must certainly be caught. He is wrathful, wicked and cruel. Let us leave at once."

Krishna and Arjuna set off from the camp in Krishna's personal chariot. They sped off into the forest, looking for signs left by Ashvatthama. Finding his trail, they gave chase and soon caught up to him. When Ashvatthama saw them approaching he was terrified. He immediately invoked the Brahmastra and released it with all his power. A circle of brilliant white light began to emanate from his chariot. Krishna spoke urgently to Arjuna. "In his blind panic the wretched fool has indiscriminately fired the Brahmastra. This missile can destroy the whole world. Counter it with your own weapon and then withdraw both."

Arjuna quickly followed Krishna's instruction. He released another Brahmastra and it joined with Ashvatthama's missile. The weapons came together like two suns in the heavens. A brilliant light filled the sky.

Seeing even his Brahmastra confounded, Ashvatthama realised his end was near. He thought of wreaking one last violent act against the Pandavas. Knowing that Abhimanyu's wife Uttara was pregnant, Ashvatthama decided he would try to slay her unborn child. By mantras he could redirect the Brahma missile toward her womb. Her child was the Pandavas' hope for the future. It would break their hearts if he was killed. Concentrating his mind Drona's son sent his missile toward Uttara.

Not realising what Ashvatthama had done, Arjuna recited the mantras to withdraw his own weapon and the brilliant light subsided. In the Pandavas' camp Uttara suddenly felt herself in great danger. Her limbs trembled and she fell to the ground. She immediately began praying to Krishna. "O all-powerful Lord of the universe, please protect me. In this fearful world of death, you are the only shelter."

Hearing her prayer even as he stood on Arjuna's chariot, Krishna, who had understood Ashvatthama's intentions, at once expanded himself by his supreme power. In a mystical form he entered Uttara's womb. As the Brahmastra approached he deflected it and neutralised its power. Uttara saw a glowing light approach her and then shoot harmlessly up into the sky.

After he had withdrawn the Brahmastra, Arjuna fired another weapon which bound Ashvatthama with strong cords. He then jumped down and dragged him by his hair onto Krishna's chariot. Although longing to kill him, Arjuna was reluctant to slay his teacher's son. Drona's death had already given Arjuna great pain and killing his only son was difficult. He turned to Krishna, who was urging him to kill Ashvatthama at once. "I feel unable to slay this wretch, O Krishna. Let me take him before Yudhisthira and he can decide what to do."

Krishna agreed and Arjuna dragged the bound Ashvatthama onto his chariot. Arriving back at the camp he threw him at Yudhisthira's feet. "Here is the killer of our sons. What should be done with him?"

When Draupadi saw the miserable looking Ashvatthama she felt compassion. Her desire for vengeance dissipated and she said, "Release him, Arjuna. He is a brahmin and your guru's son. Do not make Drona's wife weep like I am weeping. Show him mercy."

Yudhisthira applauded his wife's words, but Bhima argued that Ashvatthama should be killed at once. "He has mercilessly slain sleeping boys. What kind of brahmin is that? Why should he be spared?"

Krishna looked at Arjuna, who was standing over Ashvatthama. "You must find some way to satisfy both your wife and your brother."

Arjuna drew his sword and raised it, taking hold of Ashvatthama's hair with his other hand. Draupadi gasped as he brought the razor-edged sword down in a sweeping arc, but Arjuna only severed Ashvatthama's top-knot with its shining jewel-encrusted clasp. Presenting the jewel to Draupadi he said, "Beautiful lady, this one is now as good as dead. Cutting off a warrior's hair is equal to killing him, and this jewel was the repository of all Ashvatthama's power."

Ashvatthama seemed to shrivel as his hair was cut. He collapsed to the ground and Krishna said to him, "Cruel son of Drona, you shall be known as a coward and a wretch. For three thousand years you will wander this earth, afflicted with disease and reviled by men everywhere. After thereby receiving the consequences of your acts you will finally rise to higher regions. Now go."

Ashvatthama got up and slunk away, his head hanging down. Krishna then consoled the Pandavas and Draupadi, instructing them with eternal spiritual truths. After this Yudhisthira arranged for the funerals of all the slain warriors, and he and his brothers went to the Ganges to make offerings for the departed souls.

* * *

Hearing of the war's conclusion and Duryodhana's destruction, Dhritarastra and Gandhari sat mutely in their palace, seized with unbearable grief. Every one of their sons was dead. The Kuru house was destroyed. Bhishma, their greatest well-wisher and esteemed elder, still lay dying out on the battlefield.

Sanjaya tried to console the grieving king and queen. He explained how Vyasadeva had told him that everything had been ordained by the

Supreme. "Duryodhana was an incarnated expansion of Kali, the evil spirit of the dark age. By divine arrangement he marshalled the demonic elements who were burdening the earth, and then led them to destruction."

Gandhari's breast heaved as she loudly sobbed. The Kuru queen accepted Sanjaya's words. She had always known her son was evil-minded. He should have been abandoned at birth but somehow the gods had a different plan. Now it was complete. More than six million warriors were dead, among them hundreds of kings.

Along with all of Hastinapura's citizens, Dhritarastra and his wife made their sorrowful way to the Ganges to offer oblations for the dead. When they arrived at the river, they saw the Pandavas nearby. Seeing their elderly uncle and aunt, the five brothers went before them and bowed down to the ground. Dhritarastra wept as he heard them announce their names. He embraced each of them with difficulty. When he heard Bhima's name he was overcome by anger. Krishna saw this and he pushed Bhima aside as the blind king was about to embrace him. By his mystic power Krishna at once brought the iron statue of Bhima from Duryodhana's palace. He had it appear in front of Dhritarastra and the king seized it in a furious embrace. Before everyone's astonished eyes he crushed the metal image into tiny fragments. Choking and vomiting blood, he slumped to the ground.

Sanjaya knelt by the king's side and gently raised him. "Do not act in this way," he chided.

Having vented his wrath and feeling sure he had killed Bhima, Dhritarastra cried out, "Alas! What have I done?"

Krishna told him not to grieve. "You have only smashed Bhima's image, king. Give up your spite and be peaceful. How will killing Bhima bring back your sons?"

Dhritarastra hung his head in shame. Helped by his servants he walked down to the river and silently took bath. There was nothing he could say. He had been advised by everyone to reject Duryodhana and his foolish schemes. Now he was reaping the sure result of that omission.

Gandhari was also struggling with her anger. When the Pandavas came to offer her their respects, she said to Bhima, "Could you not have spared even one of my sons? How will I and my blind husband survive in this world without any support?"

The Kuru queen then thought of Krishna. She felt her anger rise even more. So many times she had heard the rishis describe how he was the all powerful supreme person who was kindly disposed to all living beings. Why then had he allowed so many men to be slaughtered? When Krishna greeted her, she said to him, "The Kuru dynasty has been rooted out, Keshava, even before your eyes. Why did you permit it? For this neglect I curse you that your own dynasty will die in the same way, slain in a fratricidal war."

The Pandavas were shocked. What was Gandhari thinking? How could anyone curse Krishna?

Krishna smilingly said, "O chaste lady, your words will not prove false. None can kill the Yadus. Therefore, when the time comes for their departure they will kill each other. I thank you for this curse."

The Pandavas faces fell. The thought of Krishna's departure was unbearable—and another fratricidal war? It was too much to contemplate. Surely though there was some divine plan. Thinking about Krishna's words, the brothers then left Gandhari and met with their mother. Kunti trembled with emotion as she embraced her sons. She praised Krishna again and again for saving them. As the brothers made their way to the river to offer oblations, she walked behind. Thinking of Karna, she wept silently. She looked up at her other sons. It was time to tell them the truth. Taking a deep breath, Kunti said, "O heroes, offer an oblation for Karna. That great hero was Surya's son, born of me. He was your eldest brother."

The five brothers stopped in their tracks. They turned and looked at their mother, their mouths falling open. Yudhisthira shook his head in amazement. He recalled how on several occasions he had seen a marked similarity between Karna's feet and those of Kunti. He had wondered but never dared think that Karna might be his brother. Now it was confirmed beyond doubt. He threw up his arms and cried out. "Oh, how were we never told? How did he become your son? Noble lady, tell us everything. Hearing this news my grief rises like the ocean at the full moon."

Kunti told her astonished sons the whole story. When she had finished, she fell sobbing to the ground. Yudhisthira gently raised his mother and stroked her forehead. "Dear mother, you must have suffered so much."

The brothers then entered the Ganges to make their offerings. Krishna came to the griefstricken Yudhisthira and said, "Karna knew his true identity. I tried once to convince him to take your side, but he would not be moved. Even his father Surya tried and so did your mother but Karna was unshakeable in his determination to support Duryodhana."

Yudhisthira still felt that he should have been informed. His mother should have trusted him. So much bloodshed might have been avoided. As he came out of the river Yudhisthira said, "I do not blame you for your silence, dear mother. Surely you were moved by supreme destiny. Still, I feel you should have confided in me. I therefore say that from this day on no woman will be able to keep a secret."

When all the rituals had been completed Yudhisthira sat with his brothers and Krishna. It was time for him to again assume rulership of the earth, but he felt unable. The enormity of the war burned into his heart. There were now millions of bereaved women and children. Yudhisthira felt directly to blame. He sat gazing vacantly at the earth. Was his sovereignty so necessary? For all his faults Duryodhana had been an efficient enough administrator, even maintaining the brahmins with abundant wealth. Now he, his brothers, the Kuru elders, and countless other kings were dead. Yudhisthira wept. Perhaps it would have been better to have stayed in the forest.

Heaving a deep sigh, Yudhisthira said, "Like dogs fighting over a piece of meat we have waged war for the kingdom. Now we longer desire that meat. I will throw it aside. The whole endeavour was useless. I do not want to take the burnt remnants of the war, won at the cost of so many lives. Let me retire to the forest. Let Bhima or Arjuna become king."

Yudhisthira's brothers gazed at him in dismay. They had fought hard to win back his kingdom. What comparison was there between him and Duryodhana? Under Yudhisthira's rule the people would not only be materially well situated, but much more importantly they would be spiritually guided. The faithless Duryodhana could never have directed them in such a way.

One after another, Yudhisthira's brothers argued that he should not hesitate to become king, but he remained unmoved. During the discussions many rishis came to join them. Finally, Vyasadeva spoke. He also argued at length how it was Yudhisthira's duty to become king. Hearing the immortal sage speak, Yudhisthira at last began to accept that he should ascend the throne. Especially as the sage again made it clear that the war had been directly arranged by the Lord. Yudhisthira understood that no sin had accrued to him as a result of the war, but he still had doubts about kingly duties themselves—were such duties not fraught with sin? Being a king entailed possessing and enjoying wealth, attacking and subduing other kings, as well as various other seemingly violent and selfish acts. He looked toward Vyasadeva. "Great sage, it is said that a king is even culpable for the sins committed by men in his kingdom. What should I do? I have no wish to be covered by sin, thus incurring the Lord's displeasure."

Yudhisthira glanced over at Krishna, who had sat silently listening to the discussion. Vyasadeva also turned toward Krishna, inviting him to speak, but Krishna only smiled and raised a hand for the sage to continue. Vyasadeva then said, "O king, if you wish to hear of morality and the duties of kings then you should approach Bhishma. He is still living and there are none in this world who understand morality better than him. He will clear all your misgivings."

Tears again sprang to Yudhisthira's eyes. "How can I go before my grandfather now? Bent on my own ends I slew him deceitfully."

Krishna placed a hand on Yudhisthira's shoulder to reassure him. "You should do as the sage has suggested. Bhishma will surely be pleased to see you, and he will certainly dispel your doubts. After that you should become king."

Krishna's words convinced Yudhisthira. "So be it. I shall get myself duly consecrated by the brahmins and then go to the Kuru grandfather."

For the good of the world the Pandava then stood up and prepared to go to Hastinapura. His brothers cheered and together they set off for the city.

CHAPTER TWENTY-NINE

DELIVERANCE

After the installation ceremony was completed Yudhisthira left to see Bhishma. He went out of Hastinapura accompanied by his brothers, Krishna, Dhritarastra, Gandhari and thousands of other citizens. All of them longed to see the old Kuru hero one last time. Reaching Kurukshetra they were met by dire scenes of destruction. The field was littered with wreckage. Skulls lay everywhere, like brilliant white conches. There were countless skeletons, picked clean by the buzzards and jackals, but as the party approached Bhishma they saw that the whole area where he lay was aglow with effulgence. He was surrounded by rishis and his body appeared like the setting sun.

The Pandavas and Krishna dismounted from their chariots and went on foot to see the fallen Kuru. They offered him prostrate obeisance and then sat around him. Krishna, with tears running down his face, said, "O hero, I trust that your mind and understanding are as clear as ever. It is indeed wonderful that you can remain alive in this condition. Who else in all the worlds could do this? Your devotion to truth, penance, charity and virtue is without equal."

Krishna then told the Pandavas that Bhishma was an incarnation of Dyau, the leader of the powerful celestials known as the Vasus. He explained how it came to pass that Dyau had taken a human birth, and when he had finished, he turned again to Bhishma and said, "O great one, kindly destroy Yudhisthira's grief and doubts. He is overcome with anguish due to the death of his kinsmen and elders. The gentle king is reluctant to take his rightful position as the world's ruler. Please reassure him. Explain to him everything about duty and morality, for you are the best of all speakers."

Bhishma, who still lay on the bed of arrows protruding from his body, raised his head slightly and looked at Krishna. "Obeisance to you, divine Krishna. You are the supreme cause of everything. I am now aware of your all pervasive universal form. Lord, be merciful to me. Pray tell me what is best for me now. I only desire to reach your eternal abode."

Krishna reassured Bhishma that he would surely rise to the highest regions of spiritual bliss. He asked him again to speak to Yudhisthira. "Tell him all you know. When you leave this world, your great knowledge will leave with you."

Bhishma looked doubtful. "How can anyone speak on religion in your presence, Lord? What is more, I am in too much pain. My mind is clouded, and I can hardly discern anything. I think you should speak."

Bhishma was shaded from the hot sun by a large umbrella. The brahmins surrounding him softly chanted Vedic mantras and a servant stood by his head, fanning him with a whisk. Although feeling great discomfort, Bhishma wept tears of joy as he gazed at Krishna. He felt unlimitedly fortunate. The Supreme Lord had personally come to see him as he lay dying.

Krishna again reassured Bhishma. "By my grace you will feel no more pain. Your memory and intelligence will be perfect. All your knowledge will appear before you like fishes seen in a crystal clear pond."

As Krishna spoke a shower of flowers fell from the sky. Celestial instruments were heard, and a cool, fragrant breeze began to blow. Everything became peaceful. Even the animals and birds were silent.

Bhishma then started to speak. He began by explaining how Yudhisthira and his brothers, as faithful and devoted souls, were always protected by God. Therefore, they emerged successful from all kinds of tribulation. The Kuru grandfather assured Yudhisthira that everything was happening according to God's inscrutable will. No one should lament for such inevitabilities. He looked up at Krishna. "Vasudeva's son Krishna is the supreme controller. He is all knowing but unknowable. Accepting everything as his inconceivable plan you should do your duty, firmly adhering to virtue."

Bhishma spent some time speaking about Krishna. He described how Krishna acted only for the good of all beings, making no discrimination in terms of bodily designation. He had no material purpose to fulfill. All his acts were transcendental. As he spoke Bhishma was absorbed in ecstatic feelings of love and tears flowed from his eyes. "Krishna is equally disposed to all, and yet he has come before me now because I am his unflinching servitor."

When the sun set everyone went to their encampment. They lived there for more than fifty days as Bhishma delivered his instructions to Yudhisthira. He answered all the Pandava's questions to his full satisfaction. Yudhisthira felt his doubts and fears being removed. Gradually the sun moved toward its northern declination and when at last it reached it, Bhishma had finished. He then thought of departing. Gazing at Krishna, who stood before him manifesting a four armed form and dressed in glittering yellow garments, he prayed, "Let me now invest my full consciousness in you, Lord. May my mind remain fixed on the memory of you running toward me with chariot wheel held high, your face smouldering with anger and your silk garments flowing in the wind."

Bhishma went on praying to Krishna as the sun reached the meridian. He then said his final farewells to the Pandavas and closed his eyes. His breathing stopped and he entered a trance. Suddenly his life air shot out from the crown of his head and went into the sky like a blazing comet. The rishis saw him leave his body in a shining spiritual form and enter Krishna's eternal abode. Yudhisthira and his brothers sat in silent respect, shedding tears. After some minutes conchshells were blown and drums beaten. Demonstrations of honour and respect were made by all present and the gods showered flowers from the sky.

The Pandavas sadly performed the last rites for their grandfather. After wrapping his body in silken cloth and smearing it with scents and sandalwood pulp, they placed it on the funeral pyre. Everyone cried out as the body burned. Finally, his ashes were consigned to the Ganges, from where he had first taken birth. The river goddess was seen to rise from her waters to receive her son's remains. Yudhisthira and his brothers then returned to Hastinapura to begin the task of ruling over the kingdom.

* * *

Krishna stayed with the Pandavas for some months, continuing to reassure and console the still grieving Yudhisthira. Eventually he took Yudhisthira's permission and returned to Dwaraka. The Pandava king shed tears of sorrow, but having been encouraged by Bhishma's words he applied himself to his duty with full determination. Yudhisthira was the embodiment of justice and virtue. Due to his piety and expert leadership his people wanted for nothing. The gods co-operated with him and thus there were not even natural calamities. Rain fell in season and crops grew abundantly. The people were not afflicted by disease, anxiety or even excessive heat and cold. They enjoyed long lives and, following their king's example, practiced virtue. At the end of their lives they went directly to higher regions.

In time Uttara gave birth to a son who was named Pariksit. As Dhaumya performed the name-giving ceremony, he said, "This child was saved by Krishna even while still in the womb. He will therefore be known as Vishnurata, 'one who is always protected by Vishnu'. Growing to be an irresistible hero, he will rule the people exactly like Rama in ancient times. He will expand the fame of your family like Bharata himself."

Filled with joy to hear these and other such descriptions, the Pandavas felt assured that a worthy heir to the throne had been born, and their grief at losing their own sons was assuaged. Yudhisthira then thought of consolidating his position as emperor. There would be some kings, relatives of those who had sided with Duryodhana, who would be inimical. Yudhisthira did not want anyone to cause another great war. He decided to perform a sacrifice similar to the Rajasuya which would re-establish him as the world's ruler. A challenge horse was sent out to roam the earth, and Arjuna followed it with a large force of men. Anyone who would not accept Yudhisthira's position was soon subjugated by Arjuna. Within a few years the entire earth was again under the Pandavas' sway.

The years passed without incident. Feeling compassion for Dhritarastra, and still respecting him as his elder, Yudhisthira treated him as a superior. His opinion was sought on all matters of state. He and his wife were honoured by everyone in the royal household—except Bhima. Unable to forget the many ills that the Kauravas had given to him and his brothers, Bhima only reluctantly offered Dhritarastra respect. Inwardly he resented the royal treatment that Yudhisthira accorded him. Bhima would look for opportunities to give pain to the old Kuru leader. Sometimes he would stand within earshot of

Dhritarastra and slapping his arms would loudly say, "With these two mace-like arms I have crushed all of the blind king's sons."

Dhritarastra silently tolerated these utterances, not wanting to disturb Yudhisthira. His wife also said nothing. She accepted Bhima's painful words and behavior as the inevitable reactions to hers and her husband's past acts.

More than thirty years elapsed after the war. Vidura, who had gone on an extended pilgrimage when the war had started, came back to Hastinapura and was received with great affection by the Pandavas. Vidura told them about his travels and the many spiritual instructions he had heard from the rishis at the holy places. He stayed in the palace for some time. Seeing the condition of his blind brother, he felt pity for him. He could see that Bhima was often giving him pain, and that Dhritarastra still felt remorse for having failed to check his foolish sons.

Finding an opportunity to speak alone with his brother, Vidura said, "O king, it is well past time that you retired. You are living now on the charity of your former enemies. Your family are all dead and death fast approaches you. Leave at once. Come with me to the forest and spend your final days in penance and meditation."

In strong words Vidura exhorted the blind king to give up his material attachments. Dhritarastra was convinced by his arguments. On the next full moon night he and Gandhari left with Vidura and went to the forest. Kunti also went with them. For many years she had already been spending her days in prayer, fasting often and living very simply. The party left secretly, telling no one. It was always the accepted custom to retire to the forest without announcement at the end of life, for death itself never made announcements when it arrived.

When the palace residents saw that their elders had left, they cried out in sorrow. Yudhisthira felt especially saddened. "Alas, where is our beloved mother? Where too is my esteemed uncle? Surely the old king has gone away in grief. Although he accepted us when we were fatherless children, I repaid him by killing all his sons."

At that time Narada came to the palace. He told the Pandavas how Dhritarastra and the two ladies had gone with Vidura. They would soon leave their bodies and ascend to higher regions. "O king, do not lament for anyone, for everyone is under God's control. Ultimately it is he who brings men together and disperses them. We are all helplessly moved by his infallible laws. His will is supreme, therefore all men should simply worship him and accept his shelter. This is always in their best interest."

Narada went on instructing the Pandavas. He described how affection for other living beings based upon their bodies was illusory. "No one is anyone's father, son, uncle or anything else. We are all eternal parts of the Lord, living only temporarily in different bodies."

When Narada had finished instructing the brothers he took their leave and then rose into the sky and vanished. They felt consoled but realised that their own retirement was also drawing close. As predicted by Dhaumya, Pariksit had grown into a powerful and competent prince. Yudhisthira installed him as the heir apparent and, some time after Dhritarastra's departure, he began thinking of leaving for the forest himself. Before he left, he wanted to hear news of Krishna's plans. He knew that Gandhari's curse, accepted by Krishna, would have to take effect. Soon the Yadu dynasty would be gone, along with Krishna. Yudhisthira therefore sent Arjuna to Dwaraka to see Krishna one last time. Perhaps Krishna might even be persuaded by his dear friend to make a final visit to Hastinapura.

As the months passed after Arjuna's departure, Yudhisthira grew increasingly anxious. He began noticing inauspicious omens. The seasons appeared out of order, and men were abandoning their duties. Constant disputes arose between the citizens. They seemed to be overcome by pride, anger and greed.

Yudhisthira spoke with Bhima. He could understand the omens. "I fear that Krishna's departure is near, dear brother. Just see how the jackals howl at the rising sun. The air is filled with the shrieks of owls and crows. In the temples the deities seem to perspire and tremble. It looks as if they are about to leave at any moment. The earth was fortunate to be marked with Krishna's footprints. These signs indicate that this will no longer be."

Not long after Yudhisthira's discussion with Bhima, Arjuna returned. He appeared dejected and tears flowed from his eyes. His face was pale and he could hardly look at anyone. Yudhisthira felt almost afraid to ask him what he had discovered in Dwaraka. He placed an arm around Arjuna's shoulder to comfort him. "Dear brother, how are our friends and relatives in Dwaraka? Are they well?"

Yudhisthira asked after many members of the Yadu family and then about the welfare of Arjuna himself. He was hoping that somehow his worst fear would not be confirmed. When he finished speaking Arjuna made no reply. His limbs trembled and he buried his face in his hands and wept. Managing at last to compose himself, he said, "O king, I have just lost him whose separation for even a moment would render all the universes void and lifeless. The Supreme Personality, Lord Krishna, has left this world."

Absorbed in thoughts of his friend, Arjuna recounted at length the many incidents when Krishna had protected him and his brothers. He recalled the initimate moments that he had spent with Krishna. "We would eat, sleep and loiter together. Joking and sporting, I would sometimes laughingly reproach him when he spoke of his prowess. He would never take offense, even though the greatest of the gods cannot approach the smallest fraction of his power."

Arjuna broke off, unable to continue. He covered his face again. His brothers sat stupefied with grief. There was complete silence, broken only by Arjuna's stifled sobs. After some time Yudhisthira asked him to relate how Krishna had left. Arjuna again composed himself and described what had happened. He explained how all the Yadus had gone for a pilgrimage to Prabhasa, a holy place on the coast. After performing sacrifice and worshipping the gods they had partaken of the wine which had been offered in sacrifice. Influenced by destiny they became intoxicated and began brawling among themselves. The fight became heated and they lost all compunction and restraint. Father slew son, and brother his brother.

By Krishna's will, and in accord with Gandhari's curse, all of them were soon killed. "Only Krishna and Balarama survived that terrible fight. Then they too, by their own mystical powers, left this world. I am utterly undone. Distracted with grief I somehow made my way back here, a wanderer with a vacant heart."

The brothers sat looking downward. All they could think of was Krishna. Without him their lives were meaningless. After a long silence Yudhisthira said, "We should now retire. In the morning I will formally hand over the kingdom to Pariksit. Then we shall leave for the Himalayas."

When Draupadi heard the news about Krishna she too was overcome with grief. She made up her mind to follow her husbands. As they walked out of the city, clad in ascetic garb and surrounded by grieving citizens, she went behind them. They walked northward, travelling for many days. Finally reaching the great Himavat mountain they began to ascend its steep paths. As they climbed upward, their bodies emaciated with fasting and worn out from their journey, they began to fall one by one and give up their lives. None of them stopped or looked back. Their minds were fixed on attaining ultimate liberation. Knowing that the self was different from the perishable body, they cast off all material attachment and lamentation.

At last only Yudhisthira survived. As he rose higher up the mountain, he saw that a dog had begun to follow him. It stayed at his heels for some time as he continued to climb. Suddenly he saw Indra's blazing chariot ahead of him. With a great sound it descended on to the mountain. Indra approached Yudhisthira and said, "Climb aboard, O Bharata hero. I will take you to heaven."

Dazzled by the god's brilliance, Yudhisthira folded his palms and replied, "I have no desire for heaven, my lord. Nor can I leave my brothers and chaste wife who have fallen on this mountain."

"You will soon see them all in their self-same bodies. Come with me."

Yudhisthira pointed to the dog that had sat down by his side. "This creature has taken shelter of me. How can I abandon it now?"

Indra laughed. "There is no place in heaven for dogs. Leave it here and we shall go."

"No, I cannot. I have vowed never to abandon one who seeks my shelter."

Despite Indra's entreaties Yudhisthira made it clear that he would sooner forsake heaven than leave the dog. Then, before Yudhisthira's eyes, the dog transformed into Dharma. Seeing his father standing before him, Yudhisthira lay on the ground in obeisance. Dharma raised him up and said, "Your virtue is without compare. I examined you at Dwaitavana and you answered every one of my questions. Today you have shown the perfect example of morality. O king, go with Indra. Regions of bliss await you."

Yudhisthira mounted the chariot which then rose into the sky. He saw many celestial beings surrounding him and praising both him and

Indra. The chariot entered Amaravati, Indra's heavenly abode, and descended into a shining mansion. Hosts of beautiful Apsaras danced to the exquisite music of the Gandharvas. Every type of celestial food and drink lay on many gold tables. Pious souls, with glowing bodies of great beauty, enjoyed themselves everywhere.

Yudhisthira was not attracted to any of the sights or sounds. Even on earth he had always controlled his senses, seeking instead the transcendental happiness of spiritual realization. The Pandava knew that sensual pleasure, even in heaven, was temporary and followed inevitably by suffering. Not seeing his brothers anywhere, he asked Indra where they had gone. The god then commanded some of his servants to take Yudhisthira to them. The servants led him onto a path which went away from heaven. As they walked Yudhisthira found himself enveloped in darkness. A fetid smell wafted on the air and swarms of wasps, gnats and mosquitoes flew about. Through the gloom Yudhisthira saw a wasteland covered with rotting corpses. Crows and vultures with iron beaks picked at those bodies, while many kinds of evil spirits with grotesque forms moved around, wailing hideously.

Yudhisthira was astonished. He turned to his guides. "Where are we? Why have you brought me here?"

Indra's servants replied that they were taking him to his brothers. He then heard voices around him. "O king, we are pleased to see you. Simply by your presence we feel uplifted and our suffering is dispelled."

"Who are you?" Yudhisthira called out.

From all sides the voices called back, "I am Bhima. I am Arjuna. I am Nakula. I am Sahadeva."

Yudhisthira was shocked. How had this happened? What had his brothers ever done to deserve such a hell? Wondering if he was dreaming, or had perhaps become insane, Yudhisthira told his guides to leave him. "If my brothers are here then I shall not leave them."

The celestials went away and Yudhisthira stood alone. He thought of Krishna. Was this some other part of the Lord's plan? As the Pandava stood in thought the whole region suddenly grew bright. He again saw Indra coming toward him, accompanied by the other principal gods. The terrible sights of hell vanished and were replaced with heavenly landscapes. To his amazement Yudhisthira saw that he was now in a beautiful garden of celestial flowers and blossoming trees.

293

Indra smiled. "O best of men, be peaceful. Neither you nor your brothers are in hell. It was an act of deception that made you see that dark region. No man can ever perform good deeds alone. Those whose piety is great will first receive the fruit of their sins and then they will enjoy very great happiness."

Indra explained that the sin of lying to Drona had obliged Yudhisthira and his brothers to see hell. Now they were freed of that slight stain they could remain in heaven for vast amounts of time. Yudhisthira's performance of the Rajasuya entitled him to enjoy Indra's celestial opulences for as long as Indra himself.

"Bathe here in the Mandakini and you will attain a celestial form, O king." Indra pointed to the clear waters of the nearby river. Yudhisthira entered the water and when he emerged, he felt his grief and anxiety gone. In a resplendent form he followed Indra into his palace. To his great joy he saw Krishna seated on a fine golden throne, manifesting a beautiful four-armed form. Arjuna was worshipping him and his other brothers were surrounding him. Close to Indra sat Pandu in dazzling splendour. Draupadi was also present, in a brilliant form resembling the Goddess of Fortune. Numerous Siddhas, Charanas and other celestial beings were praising the Lord, along with thousands of rishis. Yudhisthira saw Narada among them and he asked the sage, "How long will I and my brothers remain here?"

Narada replied that by their practice of virtue they had earned an almost endless stay in heaven. "However, king, you and your brothers are eternal associates of Krishna. You will go with him wherever he goes."

Explaining that Krishna is forever appearing in one material world after another, Narada said, "Krishna always manifests his activities with pure souls like you, thus attracting all men back to him. No one can fully understand his pastimes. Although seeming to become involved in human affairs, he is always aloof, acting only to save all souls from their suffering. In illusion men do not recognise him, being too attached to material enjoyment."

Yudhisthira felt an overwhelming joy. He was certainly not attached to material things. All he wanted to do was be with Krishna. Nothing else seemed to matter. Heaven and its pleasures were nothing by comparison—indeed it would be hell without Krishna. Yudhisthira knew his brothers and Draupadi all felt the same. Gazing at Krishna's face he wondered where they would go next.

END

GLOSSARY

Acharya	Teacher
Anjalika	An arrow with a head shaped like folded palms.
Apsara	Heavenly nymph of great beauty.
Arghya	A drink offering made to respectable persons consisting of honey, milk, and ghee.
Ashram	Dwelling where one practices spiritual life and asceticism.
Astra	Celestial weapon.
Asura	Celestial demon.
Atiratha	A warrior able to fight with sixty thousand warriors simultaneously.
Avatara	An incarnation of God who descends to the material world.
Balarama	Krishna's elder brother, accepted by the Vedas as a manifestation of God.
Bharata	A powerful king after whom the earth was named. Later kings in his line, the "Bharata dynasty", are sometimes referred to by the same name. (It is also a name often

	used, even currently, to refer to the Indian subcontinent)
Brahma	The creator of the universe (in the *Bhagavat Purana* there is description of how he was born from a cosmic lotus flower). The term "brahma" is also used to refer to spirit.
Brahman	The supreme spiritual energy.
Chakra	Circular weapon with a razor sharp edge.
Champaka	Tree bearing a beautiful yellow blossom.
Charana	A class of celestial noted for their singing ability.
Dakshine	The charity given to a priest at the end of a sacrifice.
Daityas	Celestial demons and enemies of the gods.
Danava	Class of powerful celestial demon.
Datura	Poisonous plant.
Destroyer	Time personified is also known as the Destroyer.
Dharma	Religious duty. Also the name of the god of religion.
Gandharva	A class of celestial.
Kali	The last of the four Vedic ages, an age of hypocrisy and quarrel. Also, one of the four dice throws in the Vedic

game (the other three being, Krita, Treta and Dwapara—the names of the other three ages)

Karma Work performed with a selfish desire for the result; also the actual results of work.

Kaurava Descendant of Kuru—but a name particularly applied to Dhritarastra's sons and their followers.

Kshatriya The warrior and ruling class.

Kumbhaka Yogic technique for stopping breathing.

Kuru A powerful king of ancient times who founded the Kuru dynasty.

Maharatha A warrior capable of contending with ten thousand other warriors.

Maya The illusory potency of God, personified as a female deity who is also known variously as Durga, Bhadrakali, etc. Also, the name of the architect among the Asuras.

Mridanga A two-headed drum.

Pandava Son of Pandu.

Prapti A mystic power which allows one to fetch objects from distant places.

Pratikamin	Chief servant.
Pratismriti	A mystical power enabling one to perform supernatural deeds.
Rakshasa	Powerful man-eating demon.
Rajasuya	The greatest of all sacrifices which establishes its performer as emperor.
Rasa	A celestial drink.
Ratha	Chariot fighter who can contend with a hundred others.
Rishi	A powerful ascetic.
Sabha	An assembly hall.
Siddha	A class of celestial; literally, 'perfected being'.
Suta	A class of men generally employed as charioteers.
Swayamvara	A ceremony in which a woman selects her own husband from a number of suitors.
Tirtha	Place of pilgrimage.
Vasu	A class of celestial.
Yadu or Yadava	A member of the Yadu dynasty founded by the king of the same name.

Author's Note

I originally began writing Mahabharata with the intention of sharing its wonderful stories and wisdom with as wide a class of reader as possible. However, it is a large work (the original Sanskrit text by the sage Vyasadeva is 100,000 verses of four line poetry) and thus my first effort became a book of some 900 pages, even after it had been considerably abridged. Realising that this would likely make the book a little daunting for some readers, I decided to write it again, abridging it even further, and that became the version you are now reading.

The basic narrative of the main Mahabharata story is all here, simply trimmed down. In the larger version you will find more details and more stories which are corrollary to the narrative. In this smaller book I have mentioned only some of those stories. I thus hope I have produced a book which can be read by anyone who wishes to dip into the Mahabharata and get a taste of its immortal nectar. I hope that by so doing you will be drawn into the magnificent epic and go on to read the larger version.

I thank the writers of the two translations which I used as source material, namely Sri Manmatha Dutt and Sri Kishari Mohan Ganguli, two fine scholars. This book is thus based upon what is known as the Calcutta edition of the northern manuscript. Readers may therefore find some details different from what they have read in other versions. I pray that this may not give offense, but I think it should be understandable that after five thousand years there will be some variations here and there between different manuscripts. However, the essential story of the Pandavas, as presented here, is common to all versions.

I have also referenced the works of His Divine Grace A.C.Bhaktivedanta Swami (Srila) Prabhupada such as *Bhagavad-gita As It Is*, for their spiritual teachings. I offer that esteemed spiritual master my most respectful obeisance.

I very much hope you have enjoyed reading the book. I must point out that this is not intended to be a scholarly version and you may have found some details slightly at variance with the original text. This was done in order to make for a smoother narrative. If you have any comments or questions then do feel free to write to me. I can be reached via my website www.krishnadharma.com where you will also find information about my other works.

Om Tat Sat

Krishna Dharma

Printed in Great Britain
by Amazon